Introducing
Microsoft®
Exchange

Bill Kilcullen

PUBLISHED BY
Microsoft Press
A Division of Microsoft Corporation
One Microsoft Way
Redmond, Washington 98052-6399

Library of Congress Cataloging-in-Publication Data
Kilcullen, Bill, 1953–
    Introducing Microsoft Exchange / Bill Kilcullen.
        p.   cm.
    Includes index.
    ISBN 1-55615-941-2
    1. Microsoft Exchange.   2. Client/server computing.   3. Electronic
mail systems.   I. Title.
QA76.9.C55K52   1996
651.8'53--dc20   95-26476
                                                           CIP

Printed and bound in the United States of America.

1 2 3 4 5 6 7 8 9   QMQM   1 0 9 8 7 6

Distributed to the book trade in Canada by Macmillan of Canada, a division of Canada Publishing Corporation.

A CIP catalogue record for this book is available from the British Library.

Microsoft Press books are available through booksellers and distributors worldwide. For further information about international editions, contact your local Microsoft Corporation office. Or contact Microsoft Press International directly at fax (206) 936-7329.

AT&T is a registered trademark of American Telephone and Telegraph Company. Apple, AppleTalk, and Macintosh are registered trademarks of Apple Computer, Inc. Banyan is a registered trademark of Banyan Systems, Inc. cc:Mail is a trademark of cc:Mail, Inc., a wholly owned subsidiary of Lotus Development Corporation. Compaq and ProLiant are registered trademarks of Compaq Computer Corporation. CompuServe is a registered trademark of CompuServe, Inc. Arcada is a registered trademark of Conner Peripherals. All-In-1 and DEC are trademarks of Digital Equipment Corporation. Dun & Bradstreet is a registered trademark of The Dun & Bradstreet Corporation. Hewlett-Packard is a registered trademark of Hewlett-Packard Company. Intel and Pentium are registered trademarks of Intel Corporation. IBM, OfficeVision, OS/2, and PROFS are registered trademarks of International Business Machines Corporation. Verimation is a registered trademark of K. J. Law Engineers, Inc. Lotus is a registered trademark of Lotus Development Corporation. MCI is a registered trademark of MCI Communications Corporation. Microsoft, MS-DOS, PowerPoint, Visual Basic, Visual C++, and Windows are registered trademarks and Windows NT is a trademark of Microsoft Corporation. NetWare and Novell are registered trademarks of Novell, Inc. Shiva is a registered trademark of Shiva Microsystems Corporation. Sprint is a registered trademark of Sprint Communications Company L.P. Telex is a registered trademark of The Telex Corporation. Timex is a registered trademark of Timex Corporation. UNIX is a registered trademark in the United States and other countries, licensed exclusively through X/Open Company, Ltd.

Acquisitions Editor: Casey D. Doyle
Project Editor: Brenda L. Matteson

This book is dedicated to:

My wife, Janet, and my children, Erinn, Robert, and Daniel.
You are my life, my hope, and my joy.

Contents at a Glance

Contents

Acknowledgments

In any project as large and complex as Microsoft Exchange, there are a great many people whose contributions add up to make the product a success. The same is true of this book. To acknowledge each person individually would take the entire page count allotted to the book. But there are some very special people and groups of people whose assistance to me personally during this project deserves mention.

First is Aaron Con. Without his tireless support of this project, it would not have come to fruition. Several members of the Microsoft Exchange team, Elaine Sharp, Paul and Tracey Waszkiewic, and Steve Masters for always being there, no matter what the venue. To Eric Lockard, for taking Microsoft Exchange from Spitfire to the end of the tunnel. To the entire Canadian contingent—you know who you are—without whom there would be no mail. The Messaging Specialists for being there first and the SEs and Consultants who go where mere mortals fear to tread. To Marc Seinfeld, the student becomes the master. To Mike Riddle, Rusty Pitman, Steve Thues for believing. To, Brian Rolfe, the quiet, get-it-done guy.

No acknowledge would be complete without Jim Brown, Casey Doyle, Brenda Matteson and the Microsoft Press crew, whose support and encouragement helped immeasurably. Special thanks go to Dennis Lone, writer, editor, scheduler, project manager and fun person to work with. Andrew Adams of designLab, designer, artist, co-conspirator and true professional. To Ellen Loney, editor, wrestler (of computers) and tireless corrector of errors. To Ron Douglas, Alexis Bor, Paul Gough, Nina Burns, Sara Radicati, Dwight Davis and Steve Swartz for agreeing to contribute, ridiculous deadline and all.

Finally, most importantly, to Brian "Drill Sargeant" Valentine, Terry "Elvis" Williams, and the entire Microsoft Exchange team of managers, developers, testers (totally unsung heroes: Angel, Phil, Laurent, so many others) and the brave hearts, for tirelessly, endlessly running naked along the information highway for so long to bring us the wonders of Microsoft Exchange. Thank you one and all.

best regards,
Bill Kilcullen
"Some Fear! Cause if you've never been scared, you haven't been going fast enough!"

Foreword

Having spent the last 32 months living on the frontier of the Microsoft Exchange world as the project manager for corporate migration to Microsoft Exchange, I'm happy to have the opportunity to recommend this book to you who are just setting off on your journey through this land.

After four years in internal technical support at Microsoft, during which I became the "e-mail guru," I wanted to play a larger role in the company's evolution to new messaging technology. I lobbied my manager for a position researching and managing the migration to the often talked about new messaging technology, then known simply as EMS. Within a few weeks, the job was mine, and my career took a turn that I could never have dreamed of.

I started with the Corporate Exchange Migration Project as the Research Lead for the Messaging Research and Implementation team. A year later, I became the Project Manager for corporate migration. Our job was to move a major corporation, where electronic mail is of the very essence of our corporate culture, smoothly to a new messaging platform—and to do that in parallel with the development of the product.

At Microsoft, we believe in "eating our own dogfood"—using our products in real, production situations before we turn them loose on the world. When this implementation project began in 1993, I knew we were betting the company's ability to do its day-to-day work on the beta version of a new product.

We did have one thing in our favor: We had the luxury of being a substantially homogenous environment, so we didn't have the burden of dealing with a myriad of messaging systems and gateways. We also had a highly centralized administrative model.

Introducing a new messaging system posed challenges from both a systems management standpoint and the end-user support perspective. New features and capabilities demanded the rethinking of many long-established conventions. Furthermore, we had to appreciate the pace at which end-users could successfully adapt to a new system.

The first priority in our research was to analyze and document message volumes on the legacy messaging system. The message volume data proved to be invaluable in the development of the project. Not only did it enable us to predict the growth of the system, but it also proved to us that we had a unique user base. The Microsoft community was producing a little over half a million messages a day with an average message size of 7.2K. With only 14,000+ employees, that put us at an astounding average of 38 messages per user. That's almost 4 GB of data per day. Today, our messaging system delivers just over one million messages per day for 22,000 users—more than 5 GB of data on a daily basis.

It was vitally important to begin with a thorough understanding of the existing enterprise network and systems management structure. Identifying the locations in which the company has offices, what type of connectivity exists between the offices, and where our administration resources exists was also important.

Other objectives of the project focused on providing a thorough review of the system specifications, performing modeling on the first test releases, providing feedback to modify the product so that it scaled to globally distributed enterprise environments, and committing to system platform choices. In addition, the analysis of the existing network and messaging topologies were necessary in order to design the new environment.

Because we are a centrally administered company, the Microsoft Exchange site topology was configured to reflect the connectivity between regions and sites as well as the distribution of support responsibilities at Microsoft. When determining the Windows NT® domain and Microsoft Exchange site strategies, we considered the underlying network, bandwidth, protocols, network costs, and traffic patterns.

The Microsoft Exchange Migration Project presented the opportunity to fulfill a long-term company goal to provide access to multiple, disparate message types through a common interface. We began working with third parties to extend the capabilities of the system to provide for access to voice, fax and video through the new Microsoft Exchange Client as well as to provide for "richer" retrieval options when out of the office. These options could be accessed via things like "fax back" of any object in the inbox or voice retrieval of not only voice but e-mail and fax as well.

Based on our plans of usage and the end-user analysis, our server configurations needed to be high-end. We provided for up to 50 MB of central store space per user. We adopted three standard configurations to ease troubleshooting and ensure a high level of operational capability. All configurations were Pentium-based ranging from 32 MB to 128 MB of RAM and 10-GB to 24-GB hard disk arrays.

Over the months, as we worked on implementing and supporting Microsoft Exchange, we also worked closely with the developers. We were, in effect, a test bed for the product (along with many other organizations that took part in the Early Adopter program). As a result, I believe Microsoft Exchange is built on a substantial foundation of real-world experience.

My work on the migration project has given me a unique opportunity to view a product from two sides at once—the development side and the implementation side. Believe me—it's been a real E-ticket ride.

In the process of implementing and working with Microsoft Exchange, we've learned a lot. Bill Kilcullen has condensed much of this learning into this book, so that you can have the benefit of the knowledge without the long days (and nights) and furrowed brows that went into gathering it.

Ronald Douglas
Exchange Corporate Migration Project Manager
Microsoft Corporation, 1996

Part One

An Introduction to
Microsoft Exchange

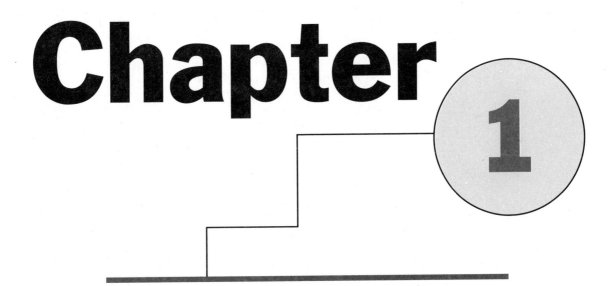

Chapter 1

The Corporate Communication Conundrum

"Time is money." "Information is power." We've spent billions of dollars developing ways to compute, communicate, travel, and produce faster. We can find, gather, and move thousands of pages of information with a few button clicks.

Has the result been more money and more power? Not as much as we might have expected.

Today, we're in an interesting (read: frustrating) paradox: Our electronic communication systems can get a message from one point to another in a fraction of a second. But our communication systems have grown up independently, with little or no thought to integration with one another or with the processes of business. As a result, the systems are working against each other, clogging their own gears and preventing us from achieving the benefits we were expecting.

A Brief History of Messaging—and the Mess It's Gotten Us Into

We'll start by tracing the development of business communication. I want to make two very important points:

1. As each new means of communication is developed to overcome the shortcomings of the ones before, we become more demanding of communication, so that soon we need yet another means that's still better. But, instead of leading us to the ultimate communication solution, this "communication feeding frenzy" has led us, so far, to a communication mess.

2. Each new communication means is developed and used in parallel with those that came before. This fact, and its importance, will become clearer as we go along.

6¢ for Airmail

What we're talking about is "messaging"—the business of getting some information from point a to point b. A message can be many things—a phone call, a letter, a fax, a computer file, the beep of a pager, or two people talking face to face. A message can be meant for one person or a whole multitude of people.

"Messaging" is a pretty broad topic, so we need to narrow it down a bit. To begin with, we'll limit ourselves to business messages, so we'll eliminate things like radio, television, and movies. A little later on, we'll limit our discussion some more to include all kinds of electronic messages.

Messaging probably started with smoke signals or drums or just people shouting at each other: "Honey, pick up a loaf of bread on your way home from the tyrannosaurus hunt." But we're interested in somewhat more modern business communication, so we don't have to go back that far. For our purpose, let's start with mail—regular, slap-on-a-stamp-and-drop-it-in-the-box mail.

Here's a drawing that will help you visualize the communication process:

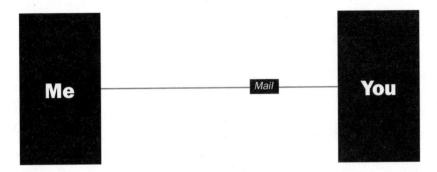

Mail has been the communication channel for business for hundreds of years. In the beginning, a messenger carried a message directly from the sender to the recipient. In those days, the speed of communication—and the pace of business in general—was determined by how far a horse could go in a day.

Later on, the postal system was invented. Then businesses didn't have to employ messengers. The sender could put an "address" ("Hon. Js. Fairbody, Thebes Hotel, Marmot") on the message and turn it over to the post office, which, for a fee, would deliver it—usually. The postal system didn't necessarily move mail any faster; it still depended on people afoot and on horseback to carry the letters. But it was cheaper to send a message through the postal system than to hire a messenger, so communication became available to more people. Business people began sending more mail. Of course, they also began receiving more mail.

Over the years, technology has been applied to make the postal system more efficient and faster. Horses and stage coaches gave way to trains, trucks, and airplanes. Numbering systems were devised for businesses and houses, and addressing rules were standardized. The Zone Improvement Plan divided the entire country into small delivery areas and gave us the ubiquitous ZIP Code®. Computerized, high-speed machines were developed to speed up the sorting and routing of mail. Special fast-delivery services were added. The process of physically moving a piece of paper from one location to another has been highly refined—perhaps to the point that there are no more significant improvements to be made. And even though we may be at the zenith of postal capability, it can still take an agonizingly long time to get a letter across town.

"Watson, get that, would you?"

The next major development in communication was the telephone. From Mr. Bell's original idea, the telephone system has grown into a marvel of efficiency and speed. But along the way, we had to string wires all over the land and sea, and we had to give every telephone a number so people could call it, and we had to devise routing schemes and build switching centers to get the calls from here to there. Now, with satellites, fiber-optic cable, and cellular telephones, the system is capable of connecting people nearly anywhere on earth.

With the advent of the telephone, our communication drawing became twice as complicated:

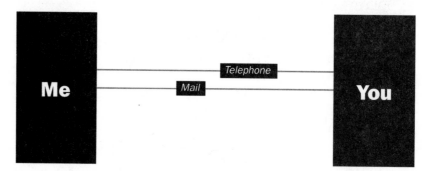

Of course, the most technically advanced system still can't guarantee that the person we're calling will be there, so some enterprising person invented the answering machine. And from that simple device has developed voice mail (along with the ever-popular game, phone tag). With the capability to screen, forward, reply, and broadcast as well as save messages, voice mail has turned into its own distinct communication medium. Add another line and more complexity to the communication drawing.

Nobody Calls It "Facsimile"

The telephone is fast, but it can't transmit a printed document. Mail is great for printed documents, but it's slow as all get out. So how do you kill two shortcomings with one technological stone? You invent the fax machine.

From its humble beginning as a clunky machine with a spinning drum that slowly—oh, so slowly—transmitted a crude image to another machine, the fax machine has become a major tool for business communication. With the right computer hardware and software, you don't even need a fax machine to send faxes.

Of course, to send a fax, you have to know the recipient's fax number, and if their machine doesn't get along with your machine just right, it may take some effort and a voice call or two to get it all to work.

Now we've added another communication medium—and some more complexity—to our communication drawing:

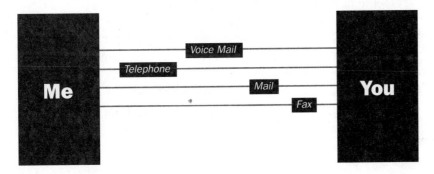

Next Came Telex®

If something isn't working the way we want, we make it better. We're good at that. And in fact, we've been doing that with our communication channels for years.

Take e-mail, for example. E-mail is a direct descendent of Samuel Morse's telegraph by way of something called Telex. Telex subscribers used teleprinter (also called teletype) machines to send messages to one another. The operator of the machine typed the message at a typewriter-like keyboard, and the message was encoded on punched paper tape. The tape was fed into a reader and the message was transmitted (at speeds up to a blistering 300 baud) to the recipient teleprinter machine, which printed it on paper.

Telex messages were text-only, and fairly crude text at that. The process of preparing and sending messages was complex and lengthy enough that most companies had specially trained operators to handle Telex traffic. Still, the Telex system met a need, and 10 years after it was introduced, it had more than 25,000 business subscribers.

The introduction of the microprocessor brought rapid change to the Telex market. With the new processing power available to them, manufacturers reduced the size of the hardware and added cathode-ray-tube (CRT) displays. The ubiquitous "glass teletype" was born.

The fierce competition among Telex suppliers during this period spawned rapid development of newer, faster, more powerful Telex systems. These systems began to resemble miniature computers and, in fact, were much more computer systems than we realized at the time. It wasn't long before one of the newer systems was able to replace as many as 8 or 12 of the older single-function machines.

New communication protocols were added almost daily. Soon, one computerized Telex machine could connect the Telex world to the mainframe world through use of the 2780/3780 batch communication protocols and software routines. The first gateway machines were born. But the proprietary nature of the newer Telex systems, coupled with the specialized communication hardware they required, made them expensive and complicated to install and operate.

In 1984, the breakup of AT&T® and the deregulation of the telecommunication world started a stampede of new companies eager to carve out a piece of the communication pie. The easing of restrictions on who could provide long distance service and on what type of equipment could be connected to the telephone network set the stage for the demise of Telex.

And Then There Was E-Mail

The early adopters of personal computer technology found that modems and off-the-shelf software packages could turn the desktop device into a communication tool. Common carriers recognized the opportunity and began to develop their own forms of electronic mail systems that used the desktop PC as originator and recipient of the information and the network as provider of mailbox, storage, and transfer services. These systems were the forerunners of the electronic mail that we all know, and some of us love, today.

(Around this time, IBM® introduced its Professional Office System, (PROFS®), which introduced the first widely accepted workplace e-mail system. PROFS® included an integrated user interface, single-point administration, network management tools, security, scheduling, and custom programming—many of the features that are just now appearing in personal computer-based e-mail systems. The only problem with PROFS was that you needed a mainframe to use it.)

Because the government had deregulated the only company large enough to impose a standard, each carrier developed its own unique electronic mail system. These systems were designed by people from the Telex world, so their early efforts did little more than emulate Telex style of operation.

In a typical session, the user started the computer, started the communication software in the appropriate terminal-emulation mode, dialed the provider's access number, spent several minutes logging into the mail system, and then spent more time reading mail, generating mail, and performing mailbox maintenance functions.

Modems capable of speeds beyond 1200 bits per second were still rare and quite expensive, and phone company switching equipment was still struggling with using voice-grade circuits for data transmission, so these early systems were slow, expensive, and not very productive. A more important limitation was the fact that, because there were no standards, competing systems didn't talk to each other. If you wanted to make sure you had the broadest possible coverage (and the broadest availability to those who wanted to send you messages), you had to have more than one service.

Within organizations, the development of the local area network (LAN) allowed users to share information rapidly and inexpensively. A group of users could share files by placing them on a network disk drive everyone had access to. It didn't take long for some bright person to come up with the idea for the shared-file mail system.

Basically, a shared-file mail system is nothing more than a network disk drive to which all users have read/write access plus software for their computers that automates the process of saving and retrieving files and letting users know when there's something new for them to look at. That scheme works okay within a workgroup or a small organization where all users can be on one local area network. It works less well in large organizations and in organizations where change is common.

This type of e-mail system has three main shortcomings:

1 It's difficult to make the system bigger to serve growing numbers of users.

As the number of users increases, so does the number of repositories for information. Each of these repositories, generically called a post office, requires a number of resources for management and maintenance. Each time another post office is added to the system, all the other post offices have to be updated, one at a time, to let them know how to find the new one.

2 It's difficult to rearrange the system when the organization changes.

In a shared-file system, each post office has to have a directory to tell it where to find each user. Moving a user from one location on the system to another means that each post office's directory has to be updated with the user's new location.

3 It's difficult to administer the dispersed elements of the system.

With a shared-file mail system, administration is done one post office at a time. To make a change on a post office, the administrator has to establish a direct link to the post office over the network, using that post office's unique address and password. In a system with a hundred or more post offices, that can take a lot of time. Also, there's no way for the administrator to "see" the entire system at one time, so it's difficult to monitor overall activity.

The Impact of Personal Computers

In spite of the difficulties, e-mail is growing apace. Today, the annual growth in individual electronic mailboxes is well over 200 percent, and the installed base is expected to exceed 100 million mailboxes worldwide by 1996. Four key computing trends have led to this growth:

Growth in personal computer usage. More than 100 million personal computers have been shipped. Today, the combination of performance increases and price decreases is driving the entry of computers into huge new markets such as the home. The result is an increased number of computers that can run e-mail programs, as well as an increased amount of information that needs to move between them in an efficient way.

Adoption of the graphical user client (GUI). The intuitive, icon-based graphical user client made personal computing easier and more accessible for a wider range of users. E-mail has directly benefited from this trend because GUI-based e-mail applications are easier to use and can create more sophisticated messages than predecessor DOS- and host-based systems.

Integration of messaging in the operating system. As messaging functionality has become part of the operating system, applications have become "mail-enabled," so users can distribute documents and data from within applications. Messaging functionality in the operating system also provides a platform for critical new business applications, such as forms routing and electronic collaboration.

Client-server computing. Client-server computing offers the flexibility of LAN-based systems together with the power of mainframe host-based systems.

In addition to the growth in mailboxes, these advances have also led to the development of a broad range of products that build on this messaging infrastructure. Shared discussion databases, scheduling, forms, project management and work-flow automation applications are a few examples.

And So On, and So On

You can see where this is leading. Each development in communication technology fills the egregious shortcomings of the methods that came before, but then exposes its own failings, which give rise to still more communication technologies.

Now that's the way things ought to work. An outmoded or less capable method should give way to a better idea, which itself should yield to the next better idea. That's called progress. In the area of communication, however, there's one big problem: The outmoded communication methods refuse to go away. When we come up with something better, we still hang onto the something-not-as-good. But it's a big world out there, and we can't expect everyone to adopt the same standards, so to ensure that we can communicate with everyone, we need to accommodate every method of communication.

If we put in all the methods of communication that are commonly found in business today, our communication drawing looks like this:

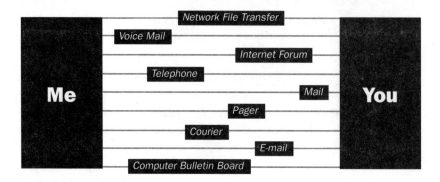

Rules, Rules, and More Rules

Now think of this: Each one of these communication channels has its own set of rules: different numbers, different addresses, different passwords, different interfaces, different procedures to remember. "Let's see—555-1357—is that Marge's voice-mail number, or her pager number, or her cellular number, or her fax number?" "To send a fax, do I click on 'Printer' or do I open my mailbox?" "To transfer that file over the Internet, I have to use UUENCODE, or I can send it in Microsoft Word format as an e-mail attachment—or is it the other way around?"

And how do you keep straight the information you're receiving over these channels? When you have a pile of faxes, a string of voice-mail messages, a list of unread e-mail, and a handful of files downloaded from the Internet, it's up to you to sort them out—to figure out which ones refer to the same subject, which ones are more recent, which ones are more important.

Now, suppose you've gone to all the trouble to learn all the rules and all the interfaces. Just when you're beginning to think you've got it all under control, you have to take a trip. If you thought communicating was complicated in your office, just try doing it from a hotel room across the country. "Let's see, to connect to remote mail, I set the baud rate to 9600 and dial the phone number for the remote-access service and...." "Harry said he left his voice-mail message at 5:30 P.M., but was that his time or my time?" "Shirley, you'll have to fax the quote to the hotel desk in the morning, and be sure to mark it 'confidential.'"

Technology to the Rescue?

Technology has improved every other form of business communication just as it did the Telex. Telephone systems are smarter and more versatile. Fax equipment is much better, smaller, faster, and less expensive. Public computer networks and information services are ubiquitous and cheap.

Each communication channel ends in an open spigot that's deluging you with information. Each of them has gotten better over the years, but that only means that the flood of information from each one has grown. It's up to you to integrate, sort, and prioritize the information flowing from these sources. It's up to you to master the arcana of operating them.

Overall, the system isn't getting better. The reason is that all of these communication methods work in parallel, largely independent of one another. What we need isn't better channels (although each has room for improvement), but a way to bring them together, to integrate them and the information flowing from them. We need a way to offload the integration and processing workload from the human user so the human can get on with more important things.

What We Really Need

We know what the problem looks like: information chaos being compounded—made worse, not better—by the very technology that was supposed to be our salvation. It's a tricky problem. Simply laying on more, bigger, faster technology doesn't seem to be the solution.

How do you know what to look for in a solution? Let's start by looking at the problems that face those who use messaging systems. Here are four categories of people who have some interest in the organization's messaging system:

1. Users
2. Team or workgroup members
3. Communication system administrators and managers
4. Top management of the organization

Users

A user is anyone who needs to send or receive information to someone else inside or outside of your organization. (Yes, in this increasingly interconnected world, that includes people outside your organization—people such as customers and suppliers. Although you're probably not going to supply these people with messaging software, your system should facilitate their communicating with you.)

Here are some of the problems these people face:

✗ **Having many** communication channels with many different interfaces and operating rules lowers efficiency.

✗ **Incoming information** isn't organized, prioritized, or screened. The user's workload increases, and communication isn't reliable.

✗ **Users can't find** the information they need when they need it, so their effectiveness decreases.

✗ **Incompatible communication** channels create dispersion instead of coherence in communication.

✗ **Users who travel** or work at home often are cut off from most or all of their business communication channels.

✗ **Information resources** are draining productive time rather than increasing it.

Team or Workgroup Members

These folks are users, of course, but their membership in teams or workgroups brings some additional problems with communication:

✗ **Changes** to the messaging system often lag behind when teams are formed, delaying their effectiveness.

✗ **Team members** who are geographically dispersed have difficulty communicating across time zones and accessing information on different network segments.

✗ **Different hardware** and software platforms used by various team members make communication and information sharing difficult or impossible.

✗ **Multicompany teams** face barriers at organizational boundaries.

✗ **The heterogeneous,** inter-disciplinary nature of teams places extra demand on the facilities for sharing information.

✗ **Members who** serve on more than one team at a time face extra challenges in keeping information organized.

Administrators and Managers

Administrators and managers have to keep the whole thing working and make sure the users are happy. Their work usually goes unnoticed—until something goes wrong.

✗ **Messaging systems** are increasingly mission-critical. Downtime is expensive and often not acceptable. This places extra stress on the administrator to ensure that the downtime is minimal.

✗ **Organizations change** shape and size quickly and repeatedly. Messaging systems that are difficult to scale and reconfigure inhibit the company's ability to move quickly, or they result in lost effectiveness while users wait for them to catch up.

✗ **Non-integrated,** dispersed messaging systems require redundant physical facilities and support staffs.

✗ **Support costs** eat up a large share of scarce capital.

✗ **Management tools** don't span disparate communication channels, leading to administrative inefficiency.

Top Management

Top management sees the effect of the communication system on the total organization. They are primarily concerned with enhancing the organization's ability to compete and its profitability.

✗ **As communication** technology advances, users' expectations grow, raising the stakes for failure.

✗ **With its growing** dependence on information flow, inefficient messaging tools put the organization in a tenuous position.

✗ **Inadequate messaging** systems make it difficult for information systems departments to develop and deploy strategically important applications.

✗ **The high cost** of ownership of traditional messaging systems, mainly for support, pulls down the company's profitability.

What a Solution Would Look Like

If you could design the ideal messaging system, what would it look like? What key features would it have? See if these make sense to you.

Integrated Interface

There are three kinds of interface integration that can help users be more productive.

First, they should need only one interface for all of the messaging channels they use—e-mail, fax, file transfer, Internet traffic, and so on.

Second, a messaging interface should be consistent across hardware platforms and operating system, so users wouldn't have to relearn the procedures for using their messaging systems when they move from one platform to another.

Third, messaging should be integrated with the appellations people work with routinely.

Intelligent Messaging

The messaging system should "bring something to the party" beyond the simple ability to deliver messages. It should be smart enough to help the user filter, sort, store, and reply to messages and other information.

Group Computing

The messaging system should help team and workgroup members—both on-site and remote—work together more efficiently and effectively. There are several examples of good collaborative computing:

✗ **Make it easy** to share information.

✗ **Provide tools** for automating group processes.

✗ **Help users** keep track of schedules for people and resources.

✗ **Help organize** and track tasks.

Standards-Based and Global

The messaging system should be able to cross organizational, geographic, political, logical, physical, language, and time boundaries. It should be able to use common standards for communication, and it should present a standard programming interface for use by others.

Secure

The messaging system must be secure from unauthorized access, and it must offer security for information as it travels over networks. At the same time, the security features must be easy to use and unobtrusive so they don't impede users.

Manageable

The messaging system should be as friendly behind the scenes as it is to the user. That is, it should be designed for easy, efficient administration and support. It should be easy to add, move, and delete users.

Lower Cost of Ownership

This is really the sum of all of the features I've listed, but it shouldn't go unstated. The cost of the messaging hardware and software is important, but even more important is the larger cost of support and administration. Balanced against these costs are the benefits of greater efficiency and greater capability. It may be impossible to reduce all of these factors to monetary terms, but the net effect should be greater productivity.

Chapter

2

The Microsoft Exchange
Server Solution

Think about the last time you bought a car. You entered the dealer's showroom and there on display was the latest model, all shiny and sleek. You checked it out from all angles. Then you got in. You sunk into the plush upholstery, looked over the placement of the gauges, checked the visibility out all windows, tried to imagine what it would be like to own and drive this car. And then you made your first decision—this could be the car for you, if all the details check out and the price is right. You decided to take the next step in evaluating the car.

This chapter is like the dealer's showroom. I want to show you enough of the car for you to make that decision to go to the next step in evaluating it. Remember, this is just the first look. I'll have more details for you in later chapters.

Microsoft Exchange Server

Microsoft Exchange Server is a client-server, corporate messaging system that incorporates e-mail, scheduling, electronic forms, document sharing, and custom applications in a single, unified product.

Microsoft Exchange consists of *client* components (the software that runs on each user's desktop computer) and *server* components (the software that runs on each of the Microsoft Exchange Server computers). These client and server components work together across networks to accomplish tasks. The client makes requests of the server, such as sending a mail message or obtaining a mailbox address, and the server carries out those requests or provides the requested information.

Microsoft Exchange Server has five functional components:

1. **Client:** The messaging software that runs on the user's desktop computer.

2. **Server:** The messaging software that runs on the server computer.

3. **Scheduling:** The scheduling software that runs on the user's machine.

4. **Systems Administrator:** Administration software that runs on the server computer.

5. **Forms Designer:** Application development software.

Microsoft Exchange Server provides five main functions:

1. **Messaging services:** Compose and send mail and fax messages; receive all kinds of electronic messages.

2. **Scheduling:** Manage personal time, track personal and group tasks, and schedule personnel and resources for meetings.

3. **Group information sharing:** Post information on a bulletin board, track customer accounts from a shared database, and access product information from a reference library.

4 **Information management:** Use forms, filters, rules, and views to manage the flow of information.

5 **Custom applications:** Develop applications—with or without programming—that automate tasks and processes for yourself, your workgroup, or your organization.

After you have planned and set up your system, the people in your organization will be able to do the following:

✗ **Send information** to users in other sites, organizations, and systems—even across the Internet—and receive information back from them.

✗ **Store and organize** all types of information.

✗ **Share information** using public folders and forms to participate in discussions, post information in a bulletin board, track customer accounts from a shared database, or access product information from a reference library.

✗ **Develop** personal, workgroup, and organization-wide applications with little or no programming.

✗ **Schedule** appointments and group meetings, as well as track tasks.

✗ **Protect their privacy** by using digital signatures and encryption (scrambling data), two security features of Microsoft Exchange Server.

Microsoft Exchange Server runs on a Windows NT Server computer. It is tightly integrated with the Windows NT Server network operating system and can make full use of its features, such as:

✗ **Centralized** management of services.

✗ **Integrated** security.

✗ **High-performance** network connectivity.

✗ **Interoperability** with a variety of networking and messaging systems.

Most important, you can centrally manage your organization, including sites, servers, and clients, through an easy-to-use graphical interface.

Features of Microsoft Exchange Server

Scalability

The Microsoft Exchange Server messaging system can be scaled to virtually any level of performance, from the requirements of a small, growing office to those of a global organization. This is because Microsoft Exchange Server is built on the scalable Windows NT Server architecture that will support the full array of Intel® and RISC-based servers. A small office of 20 employees can benefit from Microsoft Exchange Server running on a server with a single processor, single drive, and 32 MB of RAM, while larger companies can host several hundred users on a single computer with multiple processors, multiple striped drives, and additional memory. What's more, as companies grow, Microsoft Exchange Server makes it easy to add to existing sites. Routing and directory replication happen automatically between the existing and new servers in the site.

Industry Messaging Standards

As the world becomes increasingly interconnected, businesses need to communicate outside the boundaries of their own messaging systems. Microsoft Exchange Server acknowledges this need by providing interoperability with a variety of different messaging systems through support for all key industry messaging standards. This support includes a 1984 and 1988 certified X.400 Message Transfer Agent (MTA) and an Internet Mail Connector that supports RFC 821, RFC 822 (SMTP), and RFC 1521 (MIME) for Internet connectivity. Microsoft Exchange Server also offers interoperability with MAPI-compliant third-party client applications and third-party gateways.

Reliability

E-mail is a mission-critical application, and Microsoft Exchange Server is designed to deliver mission-critical reliability. Microsoft Exchange includes:

- ✗ **Intelligent routing:** Multiple connections can be configured between Microsoft Exchange Server sites. If one goes down, Microsoft Exchange Server will automatically and intelligently route messages through another connection. It can even do load balancing over the remaining routes.

✗ **Fault-tolerant directory management:** Directories are synchronized throughout the Microsoft Exchange Server organization and directory information can be recovered from even catastrophic failures.

✗ **Monitoring:** Monitors built into Microsoft Exchange Server continually observe system status and automatically notify administrators if certain conditions occur. They can restart suspended services and server computers.

✗ **Integration with Windows NT tools:** Windows NT Server includes several tools that make it easier to obtain complete system statistics and information. The Performance Monitor, for example, can display statistics on more than 300 system performance elements, including many that maintain real-time information on the network, quickly diagnose traffic patterns, and eliminate potential bottlenecks.

Windows NT also offers a logging facility for recording application, security, and system events. Microsoft Exchange Server uses Event Viewer to report information on system status, providing an easy review of system performance which helps plan further optimization of resources.

Security

Microsoft Exchange Server inherits all of the security features of Microsoft Windows NT Server, and then adds a few of its own. Security features include:

✗ **Public and private key** encryption of messages to ensure confidentiality.

✗ **Digital signatures** to help ensure end-to-end authentication and message integrity.

✗ **Detailed security** for public folders, mailboxes, and distribution lists.

Microsoft Windows NT Server provides security at many different levels, including:

✗ **Secure logon:** Users must identify themselves by entering a unique logon ID and a password before they are allowed access to the system.

✗ **Discretionary access control:** An owner of a resource, such as a public folder or a service, can determine who can access that resource and what they can do with it.

✗ **Auditing:** Attempts to create, access, or delete system resources, as well as other important security events, can be detected and recorded along with the logon ID of the user or process that performed the action.

✗ **Security ID:** Security descriptors are attached to every object in the system, including files, services, public folders, and applications, providing a high degree of access control for every system resource.

Client and Server Communication

Microsoft Exchange Server is based on the client-server architecture. The client sends requests to the server, and the server obtains the information that the client requests, using remote procedure calls (RPC). RPC is an industry-standard protocol for client-server communication. With RPC, clients and servers can communicate with one another efficiently and independently of the network type.

Client and server components communicate through the Messaging Application Programming Interface (MAPI). Messaging applications and information services that comply with MAPI can be "plugged" into Microsoft Exchange Server and Microsoft Exchange Client to provide additional functionality.

Integrated Interface

The Microsoft Exchange Client interface provides three levels of integration:

1 Microsoft Exchange's universal inbox is a single interface to multiple types of information coming from different sources. A mail message, a fax message, a voice-mail message, or the output of an application can all be stored together in the inbox. Even a link to a World Wide Web page can be part of a message stored in the inbox.

2 Functions for viewing, organizing, and preparing mail are the same in each of the following desktop environments:

✗ **Microsoft® Windows® 3.1**

✗ **Microsoft® Windows® for Workgroups**

✗ **Apple® Macintosh® System 7**

✗ **MS-DOS®**

✗ **Microsoft® Windows NT®**

✗ **Microsoft® Windows® 95**

3 The Microsoft Exchange messaging capabilities can be easily integrated with other desktop applications, especially desktop productivity applications in the Windows world. With Windows® 95, mail can be created and viewed using Microsoft® Word as the editor. Application-specific information, such as a Microsoft® Excel chart, can be embedded and edited right inside a mail message. This integration is made possible by OLE, which also allows importing application properties, such as author or date created, as columns in the view.

Intelligent Messaging

Microsoft Exchange Server has a variety of aids to help the user manage messages and other information. Here are just a few examples of what Microsoft Exchange can do for the user:

✗ **Automatically reply** to mail with a message that the recipient is away from their office.

✗ **Sort incoming mail** by subject or sender and store messages in appropriate folders.

✗ **Show the contents** of a folder in a variety of views.

✗ **Allow the user** to name a delegate to screen and answer mail on their behalf.

These intelligent "assistants" run on the server, not the client, which results in faster processing and eliminates the need to download messages before acting upon them. They are always active, even when the user is not logged on.

Group Computing

Microsoft Exchange Server helps users work together in many ways. The key workgroup features are:

- ✗ **Public folders** where users share information and participate in group discussions. Public folders also serve as convenient distribution points for information such as policies, best practices, and help-desk tips.

- ✗ **Microsoft® Schedule+ 7.0** software for arranging meetings and for planning and tracking group tasks.

- ✗ **Forms Designer** for quickly and easily producing workgroup applications. Many common applications, such as help desk, contact tracking, and discussion and response are built into the product and are ready for immediate use.

- ✗ **Messaging Application Programming Interface** (MAPI) to enable other applications to work with Microsoft Exchange Server.

- ✗ **Object Linking and Embedding** technology for efficient information sharing.

Standards-Based and Global

Microsoft Exchange and Windows NT Server were built to operate in a global work space. Here are the key standards Microsoft Exchange supports:

- ✗ **1988/1992 X.400 Message Transfer Agent**

- ✗ **SMTP/MIME Internet Mail Connector**

- ✗ **Multiple transport/network protocol support**

- ✗ **OSI: TP4/CLNP, TP0/X.25**

- ✗ **Internet: TCP/IP, RFC1006**

- ✗ **LAN: IPX/SPX, NetBEUI**

Multiple language support is inherent in Microsoft Exchange and Windows NT Server and both are available in an ever-increasing number of native languages around the world.

Microsoft Schedule+ and Microsoft Exchange operate accurately across time zones.

Microsoft Exchange is based on Microsoft's MAPI, and it makes extensive use of the industry-standard OLE technology. These features make it easy for other software developers to produce products that work with Microsoft Exchange.

Microsoft Exchange Server has built-in connectivity to Microsoft® Mail 3.x for PC Networks and Mail 3.x to AppleTalk® Networks, and connectors to other mail systems can easily be developed.

Remote access is integral to the product, not an afterthought. Remote access gives users complete access to mail, public folders, and Microsoft Exchange-based applications.

Secure

Microsoft Exchange offers several levels of security:

✗ **Account administration**

✗ **Account authentication**

✗ **File security**

✗ **Message security**

Microsoft Exchange makes use of the security features built into Windows NT Server. That provides a high level of security while it cuts down the number of steps required to use the messaging system. (Once a user has logged on to Windows NT Server, they're automatically logged into Microsoft Exchange Server and Schedule+.)

In addition, Microsoft Exchange provides a public key encryption and digital signature mechanism for additional message security.

Manageable

Manageability was designed into Microsoft Exchange Server. The main management feature is a single-seat view of all the servers in the organization, regardless of their location (as long they are connected by a LAN or a WAN). This feature allows the administrator to monitor and manage the infrastructure from one desktop.

In addition, the Administrator program provides comprehensive administration functions. The monitoring facility monitors Microsoft

Exchange services remotely. Actions can be taken automatically when services are missing. This feature ensures that the administrator is the first to know about problems, not the user.

Because of the integration with Windows NT services, there is less to administer. For example, when a new user is added to the Windows NT domain, a Microsoft Exchange mailbox can be automatically created. Mailboxes can also be automatically created from Windows NT and NetWare directories.

Microsoft Exchange Server has been designed to work with what you have. For example, it can be deployed in a Novell® NetWare® environment without any additional burden on the NetWare client. It can also coexist with a number of LAN- and host-based messaging systems because of its integrated connectivity.

Microsoft Exchange offers fault-tolerant and least-cost routing methods that ensure message delivery even when a particular route goes down. At the same time, the cost of routing is reduced.

Microsoft Exchange and Windows NT are designed to be highly scalable, which reduces the burden of reconfiguring the system every time the organization changes or grows.

Lower Cost of Ownership

Cost of ownership equals the capital outlay required to own and maintain the product minus the incremental improvement in productivity that results from having it.

The cost of administration and support is by far the biggest element in this cost equation. It is estimated that more than 72 percent of the cost of implementing client-server architecture comes from keeping the system running smoothly. The overhead of administration has wiped out some of the gains in other areas of a messaging implementation.

Microsoft Exchange lowers the cost of ownership in two ways: First, by designing the product to be easy to manage and support, Microsoft has attacked the largest segment of monetary outlay. Second, by building in extensive messaging and application development capabilities, Microsoft has increased the potential for productivity improvement.

Microsoft Exchange greatly enhances the productivity and effectiveness of information system departments. Depending on the degree of complexity of the application, the development can be done by users, power users, Microsoft® Visual Basic® or Visual C++® programmers. Sample applications that come with the product and applications that start out at the workgroup level can be extended and modified for use by the entire organization.

Internet Integration

Microsoft Exchange Server is designed to let users take advantage of the Internet in several ways:

✗ **Send and receive Internet e-mail** directly from the Microsoft Exchange inbox. Users can simply type an address directly in the form XXX@YYY.ZZZ, and it will be recognized as a valid Internet mail (SMTP) address, and sent. Messages received from a foreign Internet system are indistinguishable from messages received from within the organization. Messages can include MIME and UUENCODE attachments.

✗ **Connect to your Microsoft Exchange Server** over the Internet from the Microsoft Exchange Client. Users will no longer have to rely on a dial-up, dedicated Remote Access Service (RAS) connection to reach a Microsoft Exchange Server.

✗ **Use the Internet to replicate** groupware applications and data to other servers or to a client laptop. With Microsoft Exchange Server, deploying workgroup applications in distributed organizations no longer requires that an organization maintain its own WAN. The Internet Mail Connector can also connect two (or more) Microsoft Exchange Server sites through the Internet or another system that uses SMTP for message exchange.

✗ **Make newsgroup data available** to Microsoft Exchange Server users. Microsoft Exchange Server and the Microsoft Exchange Internet News Connector make the complete set of newsgroups easily available to users through public folders.

✗ **Access public folder data** by using the Microsoft Internet Explorer or other World Wide Web browsers. Organizations will gain an easy way to make information available to internal or external Web users without storing information in redundant locations or manually reformatting information into HTML format.

When you type a URL address in the body of a Microsoft Exchange message, it is automatically recognized by the client software and converted into a Web hotlink, which is designated by blue and underlined text. When the user clicks on this hotlink, if there is a Web browser on the same computer, that browser is launched and the Web page in the URL address is displayed.

The diagram below highlights how all of the Microsoft Exchange Server components fit together to help users and organizations connect to and use the Internet.

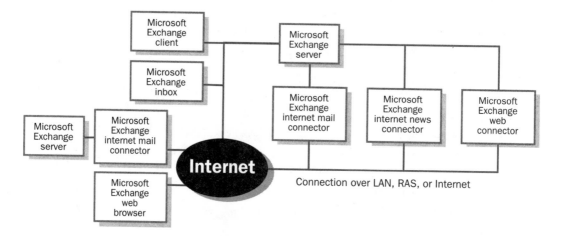

Internet Mail Connector

This Microsoft Exchange Server component provides native, built-in support for Internet and SMTP/MIME mail. It's designed to provide secure, high-volume delivery of messages between an organization and the most popular public network. Since all Microsoft Exchange Server users are automatically assigned an SMTP mail address in the Internet Mail namespace, they can send and receive mail on the Internet as though they were connected directly, but only the machine hosting the Internet Mail Connector actually needs to be connected to the Internet.

Administrators can configure security options such as which TCP/IP addresses to reject and which users and groups within the Microsoft Exchange organization are allowed to send mail to the Internet. They can also control the MIME attachment type mappings and configure the default format that messages will be sent in. This can be done on a per-domain basis. For example, mail can be sent in rich text format to any address at "microsoft.com" but as plain-text mail to all other domains on the Internet.

System Administration

Single-Seat Administration

The Microsoft Exchange Administrator program displays the organization's messaging system in a hierarchical structure that makes it easy for the administrator to navigate and manage the elements of each level. Using this program, the administrator can, from a single computer, touch every instance of every object on all servers throughout the organization.

A single Microsoft Exchange Server consists of a number of objects. Some of these objects, such as mailboxes and distribution lists, belong to the user. Others, such as public folders and connectors, facilitate connectivity, communication, and team collaboration.

This central management brings to LAN-based messaging all the benefits previously associated only with host-based messaging without sacrificing the functionality of the desktop computer.

However, centralized management is optional. If it fits your organization better, you can operate a decentralized environment. The choice is yours.

Administrator Program

The Administrator program is a graphical interface that you use to configure and maintain the organization, its sites, and its servers from a single location. The Administrator program can run on a Windows NT Server or Windows NT Workstation computer.

Directory hierarchy shows
objects in the organization.

This window shows the contents
of the currently selected
container (Recipients).

Choosing an object opens it.

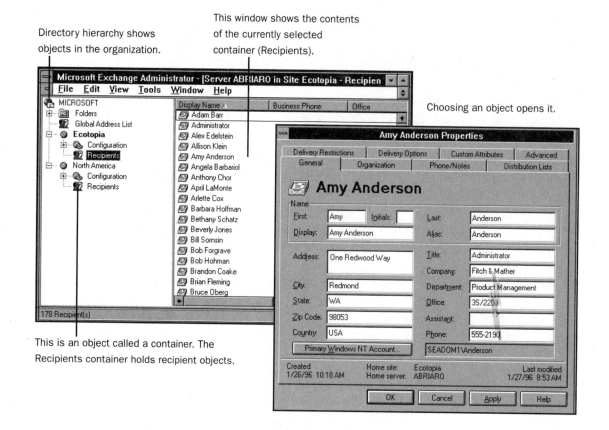

This is an object called a container. The
Recipients container holds recipient objects.

Data Protection Using Backup

Microsoft Exchange Server includes an enhanced version of the Windows NT Backup application. This version includes all the standard file and directory backup functionality as well as the ability to backup and restore Microsoft Exchange Server directories and information stores. Full, differential, incremental, and copy backups can be performed.

The backups are performed while the server is online, so no downtime is necessary. Administrators only need to specify which server(s) and which components should be backed up.

System Availability and Monitoring

In a distributed environment, if one or more servers is down or performing poorly, it can adversely affect the productivity of a large number of users. Microsoft Exchange Server includes several monitoring tools that enable administrators to stay aware of the overall health of the system. That helps eliminate trouble spots before they turn into problems, and it saves time in finding the source of a problem when it does occur.

Microsoft Exchange provides a complete monitoring system with all of these capabilities:

- ✗ **Queue monitoring**
- ✗ **Server monitoring**
- ✗ **Connection monitoring**
- ✗ **Performance monitoring**
- ✗ **Alerts**
- ✗ **Logging**

Organization of the Microsoft Exchange System

The Microsoft Exchange system is organized in a simple hierarchy. From the top down, the levels are:

- ✗ **Organization:** An organization is a collection of sites.

- ✗ **Site:** A site is a collection of servers that share the same directory information and can communicate over high-bandwidth, permanent, and synchronous remote procedure call (RPC) connections. All directory changes in a site are updated and replicated automatically.

- ✗ **Server:** A server is a collection of users.

- ✗ **User:** A user is the person who sends and receives mail.

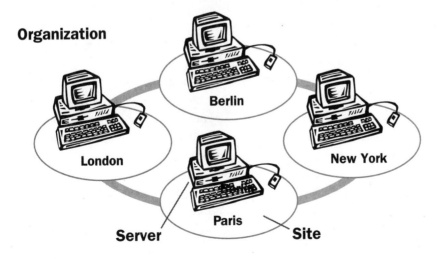

The Server

Microsoft Exchange Server is a comprehensive system with everything needed to manage organization-wide communications. The server components of Microsoft Exchange include a directory service, information store, MTA, connectors, and system attendant. The Microsoft Exchange Server components run as Microsoft Windows NT Server services and work together to:

✗ **Store and maintain** all information about the organization and each of its sites in the Microsoft Exchange Server directory.

✗ **Control** who can access information from the directory and how the information can be used.

✗ **Provide** a structured repository of information that enables users to submit, retrieve, and manage information, such as electronic messages and documents.

✗ **Receive, deliver, transfer, and route** messages throughout and beyond the organization.

✗ **Monitor** the state of the servers and their connections.

✗ **Ensure** that all the servers within and across sites have the same directory information.

✗ **Manage** replication schedules and replication conflicts.

The server components process requests from the client components, such as looking up names, sending messages, and storing information in personal and public folders.

Each server has core and optional components. The core components are installed during setup. They must all reside on the same Windows NT Server computer and must be running at all times. The core components provide the main messaging services: message transfer, delivery, and storage, as well as directory services.

The optional components provide connectivity and directory exchange with other systems, as well as advanced security. All server components are implemented as Windows NT Server services. The following illustration shows the server components.

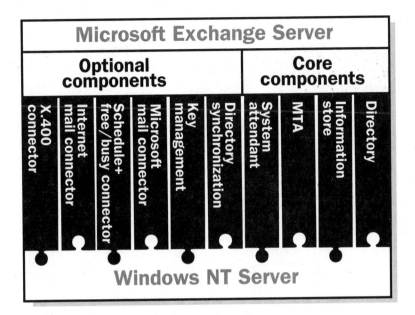

Directory

The directory is like a telephone book: It contains information about an organization's users and resources such as mailboxes, public folders, distribution lists, and servers. Other components use the directory to map addresses and route messages.

Information Store

The information store provides server-based storage, which holds users' mailboxes and public folders, and enforces security. The information store also replicates public folders, enforces storage limits, and delivers messages to users on the same server. It maintains information in two databases: the public and private information stores. The public information store maintains information stored in public folders. The private information store maintains all messages in users' mailboxes.

Message Transfer Agent

The message transfer agent submits, routes, and delivers messages to other Microsoft Exchange Server MTAs, information stores, connectors, and third-party gateways. It also maps addresses, routes messages and converts message formats. The X.400 Connector is integrated with the MTA.

System Attendant

The System Attendant is a maintenance service that must be running in order for Microsoft Exchange services to run. It performs the following tasks:

- ✗ **Assists** in running monitoring tools by gathering information about the services running on each server in a site.

- ✗ **Verifies** messaging links between servers within a site, in different sites, and in different systems.

- ✗ **Checks** directory-replication information and corrects inconsistencies.

- ✗ **Logs** information about messages sent during message tracking.

- ✗ **Builds** routing tables in a site.

- ✗ **Generates** mail addresses for new recipients.

- ✗ **Helps** enable and disable digital signatures and encryption for mailboxes.

Directory Synchronization Component

The directory synchronization component exchanges directory information between systems that use the Microsoft® Mail 3.x directory synchronization protocol. The directory synchronization component maintains information in its own database and enforces security on the information.

Key-Management Component

The key-management component manages security information used for digitally signing and encrypting messages sent between users within a Microsoft Exchange Server organization.

Connectors

Connectors connect Microsoft Exchange Server with other systems such as Microsoft Mail, the Internet, X.400 systems, FAX, PROFS, and SNADS. The Microsoft Mail Connector provides connectivity to Microsoft Mail for PC Networks and Microsoft Mail for AppleTalk Networks. The Internet Mail Connector enables users on Microsoft Exchange to exchange messages with Internet users.

The Client

There are three components that run on the user's computer: the client itself, Schedule+, and the Forms Designer.

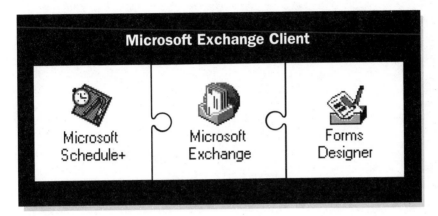

The Viewer

The Microsoft Exchange Client interface is called the Viewer, from which users can access, organize, and exchange information such as mail, documents, graphs, voice mail, faxes, spreadsheets, meeting requests, expense reports, sales orders, and so on. The Viewer toolbar makes performing tasks such as printing, creating a new message, deleting an item, or viewing the Address Book only a point and click away.

The Viewer displays information in a tree-like hierarchy. The mailbox and personal and public folders contain all types of information—including schedules, mail, documents, and even other folders—regardless of their origin. Objects in folders, such as mail messages, can be copied or moved to other folders by dragging and dropping. Icons indicate the object's type and priority and whether a file is attached to the object. The location of these folders is transparent to users; they don't need to know where the information is stored.

All incoming mail and other electronic messages are delivered into the user's mailbox. Information in a user's mailbox is stored on the user's home server.

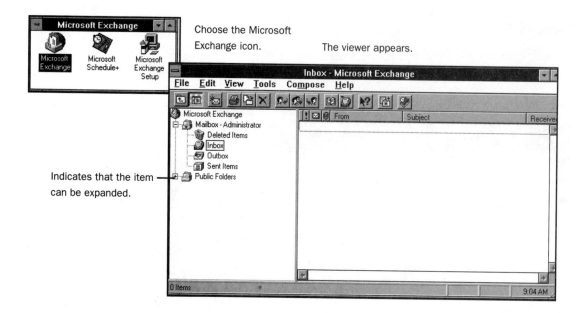

Choose the Microsoft Exchange icon.

The viewer appears.

Indicates that the item can be expanded.

Folders

Information can be organized in folders. Objects in folders, such as mail messages and files, can be copied or moved to other folders by dragging and dropping.

Microsoft Exchange has two types of information folders: personal and public. In the Microsoft Exchange Viewer, personal and public folders are part of a larger hierarchy that is presented as a logical tree.

All items are presented to the user within a single hierarchy of folders, regardless of their physical location. That means information can be on one or several servers anywhere in the organization. Users can readily access information without ever knowing the name of the server on which it is stored. Microsoft Exchange Client makes the connections to information in mailboxes and folders so the users themselves don't need to connect to servers.

Although they have the same capabilities, personal and public folders serve different purposes.

Personal Folders

Personal folders are used to store items such as documents and mail messages that the user may not want to share with other members of the organization. Personal folders may reside on the Microsoft Exchange Server, on a local hard drive, or on any file server. An electronic mail inbox is an example of a personal folder.

Personal folders can also be designated as the delivery location for mail if a user wants to store mail messages locally. Mail delivered to a personal folder is still funneled through a user's mailbox on the Microsoft Exchange Server computer, but is stored on the user's hard disk.

Public Folders

Information that is shared by a group of users is found in public folders. These folders can contain information such as text documents, spreadsheets, graphics, mail messages, and anything else that is to be available to more than one person. Users who have permission can access public folders from anywhere in an organization without needing to know the name of the server on which the public folders are located.

A public folder can be an application, such as a bulletin board service, a sales tracking application, an electronic help desk, or a document library. I'll tell you more about that a little later.

Views and Sorting

Users can create custom views for specific folders. A view specifies which of the property fields of the message, attachment, or custom form (author, date, subject, and so on) appears in the Viewer's columns. For example, a user may want a view that shows customer and document type for a customer sales tracking application.

When messages and forms are received in the folder, the specified fields are displayed in the appropriate columns, and the items are sorted automatically. Users can also apply a filter to a folder so that only items meeting certain requirements are shown in the Viewer.

Auto Assistants

Auto Assistants are intelligent agents that run on the server, even when the user is not logged on to the network. They can be configured by users at all levels without writing macros or scripts. It's all done with simple dialog boxes that let users specify the "rules" the assistant should follow.

The Inbox Assistant can automatically sort and process incoming messages, file them in appropriate folders, and even respond immediately with a specified action such as forwarding them to another person, calling them to the user's attention, or generating a reply automatically. The Out of Office Assistant can handle mail while users are away.

Searching

Users can quickly search through items stored in any folder, looking for wide range of search criteria can be used, such as messages addressed to the user or an alias the user belongs to, documents related to a certain topic, or messages received after or on a specified date. Searches can be left on, making them persistent and dynamic and allowing users to find specific types of messages in a single location.

Sharing Information

There are two fundamental ways in which users exchange information with each other: sending and sharing. With Microsoft Exchange, users can send information with mail. They can also share information using public folders. With public folders, users can retrieve information they need when they need it, rather than relying on someone to send it. For example, someone can create a report and post it in a central location where others can access it. Information-sharing applications, such as bulletin boards, customer tracking applications, and reference libraries, can be created to meet specific needs of an organization. Custom forms designed for specific types of information can also be included in the public folder for posting information.

Sending Mail

With the Microsoft Exchange Client, users can:

- ✗ **Compose messages** with rich-text formats.

- ✗ **Send messages** with attached files, objects, or other messages.

- ✗ **Assign a priority** (high, normal, or low) to a message and request automatic delivery or read notification.

Formatting

The Microsoft Exchange Client supports rich-text formatting and extensive editing features to help users easily compose messages that communicate with impact and clarity. The environment for creating messages is identical across platforms, and rich-text formatting is preserved across graphical platforms. If a message is sent to an e-mail application that does not understand rich-text formatting, the message is converted to regular text.

Formatting features, most of which are accessible through the customizable toolbar, include the following:

- ✗ **Fonts:** Any font installed and supported by the underlying operating system, in any supported font size.

- ✗ **Paragraph alignment:** Left-aligned, right-aligned, and centered.

- ✗ **Paragraph indent:** Move paragraphs to the right.

- ✗ **Bullets:** Automatically inserts bullet characters and gives the paragraph a hanging indent.

- ✗ **Character formatting:** Bold, italic, underline, and color.

- ✗ **AutoSignature:** Create a standard signature line, even with graphics, that can be automatically added to every message or just to those you choose.

Editing tools include:

- ✗ **Spelling checker:** Ensures professional communication.

- ✗ **Drag-and-drop editing:** Move spreadsheets and graphics into your mail message, then edit them in place. (You can even drag a mail message into another mail message.)

Attachments

To add files or attachments created by any application to your mail message, simply drag and drop them onto the message, or use the appropriate insert command. Icons, complete with file names, represent each attachment and can be positioned anywhere in the body of the message. Because the Microsoft Exchange message body supports object linking and embedding, recipients can edit the attached and embedded files they receive.

Addressing

The global Address Book can include everyone in your company as well as external recipients who aren't even using Microsoft Exchange. The address book lists individuals by friendly, familiar names, not cryptic e-mail aliases. It can even function as a corporate directory, listing an employee's department, phone number, office number, or other relevant information. Names can be added by importing them from personal address books or by typing them directly. Users can also create a personal address book that contains frequently used addresses.

Message Options

Users can set several options when they send a message:

✗ **Set** high priority to indicate to the recipient that they should read the message immediately.

✗ **Request** to be notified automatically when the message is delivered or when the recipient reads it.

✗ **Indicate** that the message is personal, private, or confidential.

Microsoft Schedule+

Microsoft Schedule+ provides personal calendar, group scheduling, and personal information management (PIM) tools. These tools allow users to manage their time and tasks, maintain information about personal contacts, and coordinate with others through scheduled meetings.

With Schedule+, users can:

✗ **Manage personal time** by tracking their appointments and tasks and viewing their schedules on a daily, weekly, monthly, or yearly basis. Schedule+ can also remind them of appointments.

✗ **Prioritize and organize** tasks by prioritizing and organizing them in different ways. Tasks can be grouped by project and sorted by start date, end date, priority, billing code, and so on.

✗ **Manage projects** by assigning and tracking group tasks.

✗ **Coordinate schedules** with others by requesting meetings, sending meeting notifications, viewing other users' free and busy times, and booking business resources such as conference rooms and audiovisual equipment.

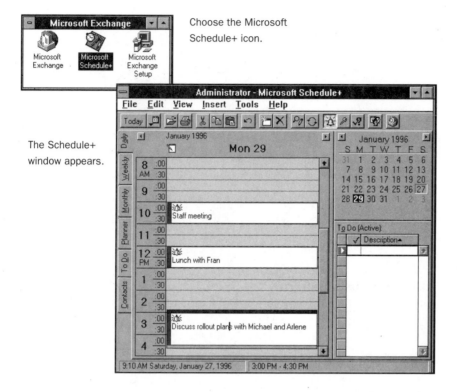

Choose the Microsoft Schedule+ icon.

The Schedule+ window appears.

Personal Scheduling

Schedule+ displays each day's commitments in a graphical representation of a paper day planner, making it easy for users to keep an up-to-date schedule. The user can create a new appointment simply by typing a description into the selected time slot. Recurring appointments can be also created.

Group Scheduling

Schedule+ facilitates setting up meetings. Users can view the availability of all potential attendees on their computers and quickly determine a suitable meeting time.

To further simplify the process of arranging meetings, Schedule+ includes a unique Meeting Wizard. The Meeting Wizard asks a few questions about the meeting you want to arrange, then suggests a time when all meeting participants and resources are available. It even creates a preaddressed meeting request that can be e-mailed to the attendees.

Views

Schedule+ lets users see their schedule information in a variety of ways.

- ✗ **Daily View:** The default view displays a single day's appointments as well as the day's To Do list.

- ✗ **Weekly View:** Users can display from one to seven days. Reschedule an appointment by dragging it to another day or time.

- ✗ **Monthly View:** Show a full month's appointments. Zoom in on any day and scroll through that day's appointments.

- ✗ **Other Views:** Microsoft Schedule+ includes several other standard views, including Meeting Planner, Yearly Planner, Personal Planner, and Task views. Views can be tailored to suit individual needs.

Contact Management

Schedule+ allows users to access the names, phone numbers, and other information about the people and organizations they deal with day to day.

The Contact view has fields for name, business address and phone number, home address and phone number, fax number, birthday and anniversary dates, and international phone numbers. A notes field can keep track of conversations and action items.

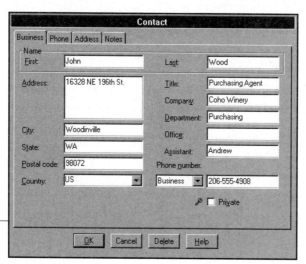

Contact information can be imported from other applications, and it can be used to create custom lists for printing or for mail merge with a word processing program.

Task and Project Management

Tasks are entered and displayed on the To Do list, which is visible from any of the calendar views. Users can group tasks by project, date due, or priority. For tasks that stretch over long periods, Schedule+ lets users set a start date and a duration for the work, and enables them to record their progress with the "% Complete" field.

Recurring tasks can be entered as easily as recurring appointments. Reminders can be set for any task, and tasks can be marked as private. If an item is not completed by its due date, it is automatically carried forward to the next day and highlighted in red to indicate that it is overdue.

Schedule+ also offers a variety of tools for organizing To Do lists:

✗ **Outlining:** Users can create multi-level outlines of tasks. For example, a To Do list can be outlined by project. Each of the projects can be expanded to reveal the underlying tasks.

✗ **Sorting:** Up to three columns at a time can be selected for sorting in either ascending or descending order.

✗ **Filtering:** Filters can limit the range of tasks that are displayed.

✗ **Shared To Do Lists:** Tasks can be shared with other users.

Microsoft Project Integration

Schedule+ for Microsoft Exchange offers more advanced project planning and task delegation through integration with Microsoft Project. By using Microsoft Project with Schedule+, project managers can send out three additional types of e-forms:

✗ **Send Task Request:** Sends initial project tasks to team members for their confirmation.

✗ **Send Task Updates:** Sends project tasks that have changed.

✗ **Request Task Updates:** Sends a "request for status" on all tasks the team member is responsible for. The user can record progress on each task using the Schedule+ Estimated Effort, Actual Effort, and Percent Complete fields, and the project manager can update the Microsoft Project file with the information from the e-form.

Forms Designer

Using the Forms Designer, you can design custom forms that make your workgroups more productive. These electronic forms, used in place of paper forms, automate and streamline processes. A form may be a "send" form, such as a purchase requisition or expense report, or a "post" form used for posting information in a folder. Although you don't need programming experience to design forms, familiarity with Microsoft® Visual Basic® 4.0 is helpful.

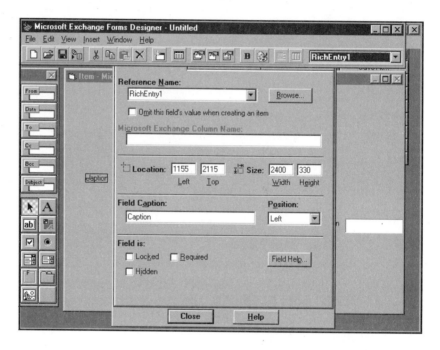

Building applications on Microsoft Exchange goes beyond sending rich-text notes with attachments. Using Forms Designer, you can create applications such as these:

✗ **Discussion Applications:** Also known as "bulletin board" applications. Allow users to post messages to public folders for leisure browsing and searching.

✗ **Routing Applications:** Person-to-person routing forms such as expense reports.

✗ **Reference Applications:** Central repositories where users can find information. For example, an employee handbook could be published in a public folder and replicated throughout the organization as needed.

✗ **Tracking Applications:** Allow users to track various activities. An example could be a customer-support application that tracks customer calls and question resolution.

What Is a Microsoft Exchange Application?

Instead of an executable program with supporting files, a Microsoft Exchange application usually has two main parts:

✗ **Folders** that serve as containers for information and associated forms. They can also be used to control who has access to specific information.

✗ **Forms** that serve as the means to enter and view information. Just as the standard message form is used to display message information, forms can be tailored to display specific other kinds of information in a structured manner.

Along with folders and forms, there are also categories of applications. The two categories of applications are:

✗ **Stand-alone applications** are used to send structured information from one user to another. A stand-alone application uses "stand-alone forms," which are addressed from one user to another and are not associated with a particular folder.

✗ **Folder applications** receive and distribute information using customized public folders. The forms used in this type of application are called "folder forms" because of their association with a public folder.

For example, you could develop a customer tracking folder. A salesperson could use this folder to open a call report form, type in a brief report of the call, and then save the report. The call report would be stored with a unique icon in a public folder. Other users could then see which customers have been contacted and when, eliminating duplication of efforts.

An application such as this can be built without programming. Users simply select options from dialog boxes to describe the type of information that should be displayed in the folder and how it should be organized. Then the relevant documents can be dragged into the newly created public folder.

Creating a Microsoft Exchange Application

The application design environment in the Microsoft Exchange Client consists of several tools that make it easy to create applications. Additionally, sample applications are shipped with Microsoft Exchange Server that can be used as a starting point for designing custom applications.

The Forms Designer is a visual design tool that enables users to define the appearance and behavior of forms, form windows, and fields without programming. The functionality of the forms built with the Forms Designer can be extended with the Microsoft Visual Basic programming system.

Creating Folders

Folders for an application are created the same way you create folders that contain mail messages, by using the Microsoft Exchange Client. The only difference between creating a personal folder and a folder for use in an application is that an application's folder is usually saved in the Microsoft Exchange public folders.

Creating Forms

Forms created with Forms Designer are based on Visual Basic; however, the graphical design environment requires no programming skills or specific knowledge of Visual Basic.

Microsoft Exchange Sample Applications

Several sample applications are shipped with Microsoft Exchange. These applications are designed to be used right out of the box or as a starting point for custom applications. Several of the applications were developed entirely using the Microsoft Exchange application design environment. Others were created using the Forms Designer and then modified using Microsoft Visual Basic or Visual C++.

Part Two

Microsoft Exchange Operations

Chapter 3

The Microsoft Exchange Client

At one time, "messaging" meant e-mail. Now, functions such as group scheduling, discussion/conferencing, and document sharing, and the ability to create customized business applications have all come to be accepted as core requirements for a modern messaging system.

In keeping with the evolution of messaging, Microsoft Exchange Server has been designed to provide advanced, yet easy-to-use support for all of these key application categories right out of the box.

E-Mail and Beyond

I'm going to do my best in this chapter to help you see how Microsoft Exchange can make everyday tasks easier, more enjoyable, and more productive. But I know I can never be completely successful. You can't really appreciate Microsoft Exchange just by reading about it, any more than you could skiing or hang gliding. The best I can hope to do is to whet your appetite enough that you'll want to get your hands on the Microsoft Exchange Client and take it for a spin yourself.

If you've been paying attention through the first two chapters, you know by now that Microsoft Exchange is much more than just e-mail with a new face. It is truly the messaging foundation for the organization. Much of the functionality of that foundation is found on the Microsoft Exchange Server, which is described in the next chapter.

In any workplace, there are two ways to exchange information with others—sending and sharing.

✗ **Sending:** Information such as memos, documents, and other data is sent to specific people or groups. Electronic mail has revolutionized this process, saving time and effort previously spent at the photocopier or in inter-office mail.

✗ **Sharing:** People share information with everyone from their workgroup to the entire organization. For instance, someone may create a report and want to make it available to anyone who is interested in reading it. Or, while creating a report, the individual may need to gather other reports and data that have already been compiled. In these instances, users typically confront a number of obstacles: Where is the information they need? Will they have access to it when you find it? Who owns the needed information? Who else may have information to add? How can they let people know their report is available?

Just as electronic mail revolutionized the first process of sending various types of information to specific parties, Microsoft Exchange is revolutionizing the way people find, access, and share specific information with others.

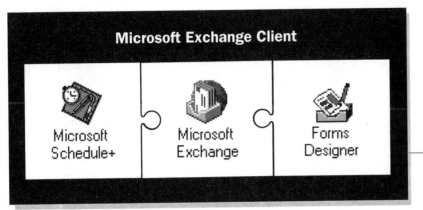

Microsoft Exchange Client

Microsoft Schedule+

Microsoft Exchange

Forms Designer

The client components of Microsoft Exchange Server are Microsoft Schedule+, the Microsoft Exchange Client, and Microsoft Exchange Forms Designer.

E-Mail Done Right

Messaging means a lot more than just e-mail, but e-mail is still by far the most important and the most widely used messaging function, so it had better be done right.

In Microsoft Exchange Server, the mail mavens have advanced the state of the e-mail art in two key areas:

1 It is easier to use, richer, and more integrated with the rest of the user's desktop.

2 It provides a centrally manageable, no-compromises messaging system capable of being scaled from small business servers to the organization backbone.

The Forms Designer and custom applications are described fully in Chapter 8. In this chapter, we'll concentrate on the client and Schedule+.

A Universal Inbox for Information

The Microsoft Exchange Client has been designed to work with a wide variety of different mail services—both LAN-based systems and on-line information services. It is written as a Messaging Application Programming Interface (MAPI) 1.0 application. MAPI provides a way for the same application to work with different types of servers through the use of different "drivers," which are called *MAPI service providers* or simply *services*.

In the universal inbox, users can receive, access, organize, and exchange information of all kinds: mail, word processing documents, graphs, voice mail, faxes, spreadsheets, presentation graphics, meeting requests, customer contact reports, expense reports, sales orders, and so on.

```
┌─────────────────────────────────────────────────────────┐
│ ─            Inbox - Microsoft Exchange          ▼ ▲    │
│ File  Edit  View  Tools  Compose  Help                  │
├─────────────────────────────────────────────────────────┤
│ Microsoft Exchange          ! ⊠ 0 From    Subject  Received│
│ └ Mailbox - Administrator                               │
│    ── Deleted Items                                     │
│    ── Inbox                                             │
│    ── Outbox                                            │
│    ── Sent Items                                        │
│ ⊞ Public Folders                                       │
│                                                         │
│ 0 Items                                        11:49 AM │
└─────────────────────────────────────────────────────────┘
```

What that means is that anyone who wants to produce an application that sends information to Microsoft Exchange can do so simply by writing their application to use MAPI commands. If your microwave oven were programmed to use MAPI commands, it could send a message to Microsoft Exchange to let you know your hot dog was ready.

You can think of MAPI as the messaging equivalent of a printer driver, where Microsoft Exchange is the "printer." When someone writes an application that needs to be able to print, they don't need to worry about including code to run every printer made. As long as they write their program to work with the printer drivers built into the operating system, they can be sure their application will be able to use whatever printer is hooked up. In the same way, MAPI enables other applications to work with Microsoft Exchange.

There are two pieces to MAPI: the client piece and the server piece. The client piece takes care of sending the right procedure calls when the application wants to send a message. The server piece recognizes those standard calls and translates them into something that the server can take action on.

For example, when I am working on a Microsoft Word document and I need to send it to you for review, I just choose the Send command from the File menu. The MAPI code in Microsoft Word calls the MAPI provider and says, "send this document." The MAPI code on the server checks to see if the messaging subsystem is running (and starts it if it is not), logs me in, opens the Address Book so I can select the recipient, and then submits the message to the server. Except for selecting the address, I don't have to know anything about the process of sending the document. Neither, for that matter, does Microsoft Word.

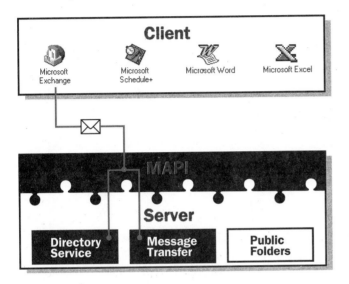

Microsoft has written service providers for different messaging systems, including Microsoft® Mail 3.2, Internet Mail, Microsoft® Fax, the Microsoft Network®, and of course, Microsoft Exchange Server. A wide variety of other companies, including Novell®, Lotus®, Apple®, Banyan®, DEC™, and Hewlett-Packard®, have also announced they are developing MAPI service providers for their mail systems.

Several service providers can be installed on the client, so different clients can communicate directly with different systems. Or, you can install just one service provider (Microsoft Exchange Server provider) on each client and install service providers for other systems on the Microsoft Exchange server. With this approach, the server handles the communication with multiple systems, consolidating incoming and outgoing messages. Microsoft Exchange Server excels at this task, because of its built-in support for Internet mail and X.400 mail. Also, with this approach, you can update and add service providers without having to deal with each client.

Rich Text for More Expressive E-Mail

Most e-mail today is pretty boring: nothing but text in one size of a monospaced font with no emphasis. If you want to send something more interesting and effective, you have to send it as an attachment— to a boring e-mail message. That's like wrapping the Mona Lisa in a plain, brown grocery bag.

But now there's Microsoft Exchange.

The Microsoft Exchange Client provides rich-text editing and display without sacrificing compatibility with older, plain-text e-mail systems.

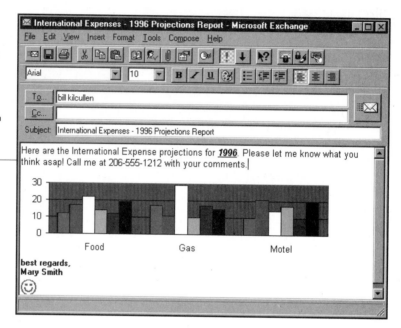

The Microsoft Exchange message editor supports multiple fonts, sizes, and colors of text. You can control paragraph alignment and create bulleted lists. You can use drag-and-drop editing to move text within a message or between messages, and you can drag and drop text directly from Microsoft Word documents into a mail message. You can also use Microsoft Word as the editor for mail messages if you like the idea of working in a single interface. The environment for creating messages is identical across platforms, and rich formatting is preserved across graphical platforms.

Rich-text messages can even be sent over the Internet or other traditionally plain-text backbones. If the recipient has a Microsoft Exchange Client or another MAPI rich-text compatible mail client, they will receive the full rich text. If not, they will receive a faithful plain-text rendering of the message.

Formatting features, most accessible through the customizable toolbar, include:

- ✗ **Font**

- ✗ **Font Style:** regular, italic, bold, bold italic

- ✗ **Size:** the sizes available depend on the selected font. If the size you type is not available, the Microsoft Exchange Client chooses the closest available size.

- ✗ **Effects:** strikeout and underline

- ✗ **Color:** one of the 16 predefined colors. To display color, you must have a color monitor. To print color, you must have a color printer. To display selected text in the Window Text color that you set in the Windows Control Panel, select Auto.

- ✗ **Paragraph alignment:** left, center, right

- ✗ **Paragraph bullet**

The built-in spelling checker saves you from those embarrassing misspellings, and the *Auto Signature* feature lets you insert a "signature block" automatically at the end of every outgoing message or to selected messages with a single keystroke.

Intelligent Attachments

The Microsoft Exchange Client can handle multiple files or attachments created by any application. The attachments are "intelligent": Icons representing each attachment, complete with file names, can be positioned in the body of the message as an integrated part of the message text. Because the Microsoft Exchange message body supports OLE 2.0, you can edit the attached and embedded files you receive, and you can drag and drop objects—such as graphs or spreadsheets—into a message. Have you ever wished that you could drag a message onto a message? You can do that easily with Microsoft Exchange.

You can insert attachments or objects *anywhere* within the body of a message. You're not limited to a special "attachment envelope" at the beginning or end of the message.

Addressing and Directory Services

Corporate messaging systems have outgrown the days when a simple address book on each server was sufficient for e-mail. A true organization-wide directory service containing users, mailboxes, distribution lists, and other objects is now a must.

When you open the Microsoft Exchange *Global Address List,* you're looking at a complete corporate directory that contains all of the mailboxes and distribution lists for the entire organization. The Address Book lists individuals by friendly, familiar names, not cryptic e-mail aliases. You can select a name from the list, or you can search just by typing in the name you're looking for. As you type the letters of the name, the address list scrolls to match the letters you type.

The directory contains a wealth of attributes for mailbox objects—including users' phone numbers, office location, even the corporate organization chart. Administrators can create links between users based on company reporting structures, or they can simply import data from their human resources database, and users can view who the manager is and who the "direct reports" are for anyone in the directory.

The directory is also extensible. System administrators can add up to 10 custom attributes to mailboxes in their directory. This is useful for information such as employee number, resource type, or shoe size (if your company manufactures shoes). At many companies, for example, updates are entered from the human relations database and not the mail directory, so it's important to include this type of information.

Delegate Access

It's common for a manager to have an administrative assistant manage their mailbox on their behalf. With most mail systems today, unfortunately, the manager has to give their logon ID and password to the assistant so the assistant can log in to the system as the manager. This makes for a potential security problem; at the very least, it compromises the privacy of the manager.

Microsoft Exchange Server allows users to grant access to their mailbox directly to others. In Microsoft Exchange, users always log onto the Windows NT Server domain as themselves—never as someone else. When they do, their own Microsoft Exchange mailbox opens. If the user has permission to open other mailboxes, they can open them as well. An assistant can keep both their own personal mailbox and their manager's mailbox open at the same time, reading and replying to mail in either one.

This facility can also be used when a mailbox doesn't correspond to a specific person but to a title or a role, such as, "fund drive chair person." This mailbox may be used by several different people or by different people at different times. Regardless, whoever is the current fund drive chair person logs on to the network as themselves and opens both their own personal mailbox and the "fund drive chair person" mailbox. They will be able to reply to mail either as themselves or as the fund drive chair person.

Users can grant multiple levels of access to each of their mailbox folders. A manager might grant their assistant read access to all of their folders except for the personal folder. Additionally, users can decide if they want to let others send e-mail on their behalf. Finally, the system administrator (not users) can go one level further and grant full Send As permission. In this case, the recipient would not be able to tell that someone other than the sender named in the message really sent the message (although the administrator could still tell from their server logs).

For example, if Joseph sends mail "on behalf of" Diane, the recipient will see a message in their inbox that appears to be from Diane. When they open the message, they will discover it was really sent by Joseph "on behalf of" Diane.

A Consistent, Cross-Platform Client

Microsoft Exchange provides a single, consistent client across different platforms, including:

✗ **Microsoft Windows 3.1**

✗ **Windows® for Workgroups**

✗ **MS-DOS**

✗ **Microsoft Windows NT**

✗ **Microsoft Windows 95**

✗ **Apple Macintosh System 7**

This cross-platform approach ensures that users can effectively share information regardless of their preferred desktop platform. Of course, each version also takes specific advantage of its native operating system's user-interface conventions and facilities.

Information Management

Most of the work done in organizations today is shared across teams, departments, and even companies. As a result, these groups need to share something else—information, ranging from simple text memos, voice mail, e-mail, and faxes to reports, spreadsheets, presentations, to highly structured information such as customer contact reports, expense reports, and sales orders.

Alas, people aren't as orderly as computers. We tend to create something here, modify it over there, pass along a slightly different version to our friend in accounting "just to see what they think," and stash a copy on that server no one else uses "just for safe-keeping."

Information winds up hidden away on a multitude of file servers and desktops because there is no central location to post things and no logical scheme for what should be put where. The information exists, but it's as good as lost.

And things don't always get better once you find the information. For one thing, you can never be sure it's the latest version. For another thing, the information you want is often mixed in with a lot of other stuff you have to sort before you can find those pearls of wisdom.

Microsoft Exchange has a better way: Combine a single interface for accessing information with powerful information management and organization capabilities that allow users to find the information they need, when they need it.

Solving Information Chaos with Folders

The Microsoft Exchange Client uses *information folders* to store all types of information, including documents, files, electronic mail messages, phone messages, forms, and meeting requests. Finding, sorting, arranging, and outlining information is much simpler when it's all in one place.

The Microsoft Exchange Client has four types of folders: the mailbox, personal folders, public folders, and offline folders.

- ✗ **The mailbox:** The delivery location for all incoming mail messages for a designated owner. Information in a user's mailbox is stored in the private information store on the client's home Microsoft Exchange Server computer.

- ✗ **Personal folders:** Contains private information. Personal folders may reside on the Microsoft Exchange Server, a network file server, or a local hard drive.

Personal folders can also be designated as the delivery location for mail if a user wants to store mail messages locally. Mail delivered to a personal folder is still funneled through the mailbox on the server but is stored on the user's hard disk. This is a good way to work offline or remotely.

✗ **Public folders:** Located on Microsoft Exchange Server computers, public folders are used to store information that is intended to be shared by a group of users. Designated users throughout— or even outside—an organization can access the information.

✗ **Offline folders:** Copies of public folders that are stored on your local hard drive. Microsoft Exchange automatically synchronizes the contents of the server and local copies.

A public folder can be an application such as a bulletin board, a sales-tracking application, an electronic help desk, or a document library. These types of applications can be built without programming, using only the capabilities built into the Microsoft Exchange Client. Users simply select options from dialog boxes to describe the type of information that is to be displayed in the folder and how it is to be organized. Then the relevant documents can be dragged and dropped into the newly created public folder.

The mailbox and personal and public folders contain all types of information regardless of its origin, including scheduling, mail, and files of any kind. They can also contain other folders. Objects in folders can be copied to other folders or moved by dragging or dropping. Icons indicate the object's type and priority and whether a file is attached to it.

A user's inbox is a network resource that can be shared with other users to help distribute the workload, share information, and organize workgroup activity.

As an example, users in the sales department can share the mailbox called SALES, and the sales department as a whole may be addressed as sales@company.com. This address can be given in company literature and advertisements and published in directories. Mail sent to the sales department will automatically be captured here, where it can be viewed by any member of the sales team.

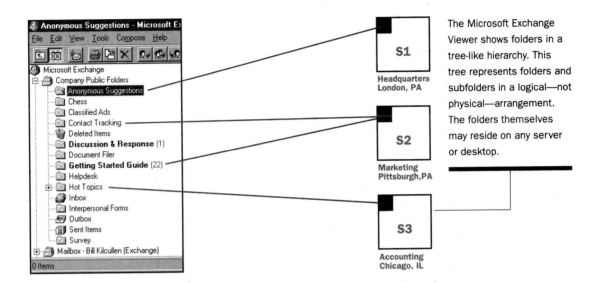

The Microsoft Exchange Viewer shows folders in a tree-like hierarchy. This tree represents folders and subfolders in a logical—not physical—arrangement. The folders themselves may reside on any server or desktop.

Users view information independent of the data's physical location. There is never a need to know the name of a server on which a document or application is located. Instead, all items are presented to the user within a single hierarchy of folders, regardless of where they are located.

Finding and Organizing Information

Microsoft Exchange gives you tools to find, organize, and manage information.

The Finder

With the Finder, you can search through items stored in any folder. You can select a wide range of search criteria. For example, you can find a mail message to or from a specific person, topics related to a subject, or meeting requests received after a specified date.

The Finder uses programs that run in the background, searching for items that meet the specified requirements. The Finder stays on your desktop and looks just like a client window; it can be minimized, maximized, and moved. Changing, deleting, or moving an item in a Finder window changes, deletes, or moves the actual item.

Rules

You can set up rules to inspect incoming mail and take a variety of actions, such as moving mail to a particular folder, forwarding it to another user, or deleting certain types of information. AutoAssistants can be used to sort items even when the user is not logged on. There are two types of AutoAssistants: the Inbox Assistant, which sorts incoming items, and the Out of Office Assistant, which handles a user's mail while the user is away from the office.

Views

With views, users can organize and view information in different ways. There are two types of views: folder views and common views. Folder views apply only to a particular folder and are automatically saved each time the view is modified. Common views can be applied to any folder. Users can select predefined views from the Folder Views and Common Views commands or they can define their own custom views.

With predefined views, users can sort the contents of a folder based on author, date, keywords, and other properties. With custom views, users can sort folder contents by properties defined in custom form fields. For example, if a user frequently receives a custom form with Customer and Order Number fields, the user can create custom views to group items based on one of these fields.

You can customize folders, creating views that specify fields that should appear in the window. For example, you may want a view that is sorted by customer and document type for a customer-tracking application.

A view can sort the contents of a folder based on author, date, key words, or even type of content. You can create different views in a variety of ways. Items can be sorted simply by clicking the column heading. New columns can be created easily from fields defined on custom forms, such as customer, order number, and case number. When these forms are received in an inbox or public folder, they're grouped automatically and the specified fields of the form are displayed in the appropriate columns.

Filters

You can apply a filter to a folder so that only items meeting certain requirements will be shown in a view. In Chapter 8, I will show you how this simple feature in Microsoft Exchange is integrated with the other Microsoft applications through the magic of OLE to give the developer a distinct advantage for building advanced business solutions.

Stay in Control with AutoAssistants

Anyone who uses electronic mail needs to be able to separate important mail from "junk" mail, so time isn't taken away from important tasks just sorting through mail. The Microsoft Exchange Server has an Inbox Assistant that can be configured to automatically sort and process incoming messages, file them in appropriate folders, or even respond immediately with a specified action such as forwarding it to another person, calling it to your attention, or generating a reply.

There is even a special Out of Office Assistant to handle mail while you're away.

These advanced AutoAssistants are intelligent agents that run on the server, even when you're not logged on to the network. They can be configured by users at all levels without writing macros or scripts—it's all done with simple, understandable dialog boxes that let you specify the "rules" the AutoAssistant should follow.

Information Sharing

Microsoft Exchange makes it easy to share information. With public folders, users can post information for others, and they can retrieve information they need when they need it. For example, someone can create a report and post it in a central location where others can access it.

Information-sharing applications, such as bulletin boards, customer tracking applications, and reference libraries, can be created to meet specific needs in your organization. And custom forms designed for specific types of information can be included in the public folder for posting information.

Public folders in Microsoft Exchange Server provide secure, replicated storage for many types of objects—not just messages. Public folders can also store files and documents. In particular, the public folders are excellent for storing OLE 2.0-compatible documents (such as those created by Microsoft Office applications).

You can drag any file or document from your file system (File Manager in Windows 3.1 and Windows NT Server, Explorer in Windows 95) and drop it directly into a public folder. A copy of the document is stored in the public folder information store on the Microsoft Exchange Server. Users can then simply double-click on the document to open it.

If the document is an OLE compound document, then the Microsoft Exchange Server will automatically extract any OLE document properties it contains. This includes both the standard summary OLE properties, such as author, title, keywords, and comment, and custom OLE properties that were defined by the author of the document. These document properties can be included in views on the folders. Note that Microsoft® Office for Windows® 95 applications are capable of creating these custom OLE properties.

Documents stored in a public folder are replicated just like any other folder contents. If simultaneous edits occur on two servers, then the changed documents are marked as being in conflict, and users will be able to select between multiple versions.

Advanced Features

Offline Folders

The offline folders function, sometimes called "local replication" in other products, is the two-way synchronization of a folder on a server and a copy of that folder on a local machine. For example, a sales executive can use a customer-tracking application on a business trip, update it based on customer calls during the trip, then use the offline folders function to synchronize both the server and local versions of the folder when they return. The offline folders function is better than merely copying a file onto a local computer because the offline folder that contains the application understands its relationship to the server folder and performs the synchronization automatically.

With Microsoft Exchange Server, the user can synchronize the information by connecting to the network upon returning to the office after a trip or by dialing up the server via modem from the road. Users benefit from shorter and less expensive phone calls, the ability to work when not connected to the server, and local processing that offers better performance.

The offline folders function extends both the built-in support in Microsoft Exchange Server for remote mail as well as the ability of Schedule+ to synchronize meetings, tasks and group resources.

Built-In Mobile Support

Increasingly, workers won't stay put. We flit about, working in the office, working at home, working in airplanes and hotel rooms, working at customers' offices. But we still need to stay in touch—to keep up with e-mail, to update information stored at the office, to find information on the home network.

To address these issues, the Microsoft Exchange Client is designed to let users work equally well whether they're in the office on the LAN, dialing in over a phone line, or completely disconnected. Unlike many systems that make mobile features an extra-cost option, Microsoft Exchange Clients provide remote connectivity right out of the box.

Most roving users have a portable computer or laptop and connect to the network over a slow link, such as a voice-grade telephone line. The Microsoft Exchange solution for mobile user support is to establish a remote network connection to the Microsoft Exchange Server computer.

Two basic modes of operation are available for remote use of Microsoft Exchange Server: a batch connection and a continuous connection. In a batch connection, the client connects with the network, performs operations the user has directed (such as retrieving mail headers), and disconnects. Continuous connections allow users to perform any operation, including accessing public folders, just as if they were connected to the LAN in the office.

Optimized for Slow Links

The Microsoft Exchange Client provides a number of ways to help you be more efficient when you have to work with a slow link, including the ability to work offline. Users of the Microsoft Windows 95 operating system can also take advantage of location settings such as dialing prefixes and time zones, that ease the process of connecting remotely.

Microsoft Exchange Client supports a personal information store—a local file that can be used for downloading mail or storing documents and messages for use while offline. Users can read their downloaded mail and compose responses without being connected to the server, turning downtime on an airplane or train into work time. When users reconnect to their server, mail is synchronized automatically: New mail is downloaded and outgoing messages are sent to their destinations.

The Microsoft Exchange Client includes support for remote networking connections, which allows a remote client to function exactly as it would on the LAN. Through the use of point-to-point protocol (PPP), Microsoft Exchange Clients running on Windows® and DOS operating systems can remotely connect over all popular network protocols, including Novell® IPX/SPX, TCP/IP, and NetBEUI.

A wide variety of media are supported, from 2400-baud modems to high-speed X.25 and ISDN lines to the latest in wireless communications. A number of wireless network providers will ensure integration with Microsoft Exchange Server.

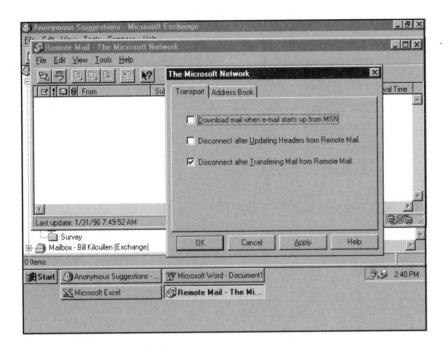

Clients can dial into a variety of back-end remote network access services, including the Microsoft® Remote Access Service (RAS) built into the Windows NT Server. Third-party servers that support the PPP protocol, such as the Shiva® LanRover, can also be used. You can choose from devices that support from 1 to 256 or more simultaneous modem connections. Remote network access servers allow other applications— not just Microsoft Exchange—to utilize the remote connection as well.

The versions of the Microsoft Exchange Client for Windows and Macintosh also support a unique feature called Remote Mail, which helps users make the most of their time while away from the office.

Here's how it works:

✗ **The user connects** by way of modem to their Microsoft Exchange Server. This can be done manually or automatically at selected times.

✗ **The user can** set up a filter that will download only mail that meets the criteria they specify, such as mail from the boss.

✗ **As an alternative,** the user can very quickly download headers for messages waiting to be delivered to them. The user can see the sender, subject, size, and estimated download time of all new mail waiting for them. The connection can be dropped at this point to save connect cost.

✗ **The user marks** the items they'd like to download, skipping less important messages or large documents if they're in a hurry.

✗ **The user reconnects** to the server. Selected messages are downloaded to the user's machine, and mail they've composed is automatically sent.

The user can have the client connect automatically to send and retrieve mail at scheduled times, such as at night, when telephone rates are cheaper.

Addressed for Success

Addressing mail while offline is a challenge if you don't have access to the corporate directory service. Microsoft Exchange Server solves this problem by allowing you to download the entire corporate Address Book (or whatever subset the administrator chooses) to your machine for offline use. The offline version of the corporate Address Book contains only the main properties and is compressed for efficient downloading.

In addition to the corporate address book, you also have a personal Address Book (PAB) where you can enter addresses of friends and business associates, regardless of what type of address—Internet, X.400, MCI®, CompuServe®, and so on. You can add addresses from incoming mail to your PAB with the click of a mouse button for future reference.

You can also just type e-mail addresses directly, without having to enter them in an address book first. If you type XXX@YYY.ZZZ, the address will be recognized automatically as a valid Internet mail (SMTP) address. You can also choose from a set of addressing templates in case you are unsure of the syntax of the address. The template gives you a form to fill in with the appropriate information, and Microsoft Exchange builds a valid address for you.

Group Discussions (Bulletin Boards)

There are many categories of so-called "groupware" applications, but none is more widely used than discussion forums, sometimes also called bulletin boards (BBS) or conferencing. A discussion forum is a distinctly different experience from e-mail. While e-mail distribution lists can be used to carry on discussions among those on the list, the volume of mail can quickly become burdensome. Worse, people just joining a particular distribution list have no easy way to get up to date on the history of the discussion because none of it is stored in a central location; it's all stored in individuals' mailboxes. The discussion itself could be a valuable record of the organizational memory. It could be used to share best practices, facilitate group decision-making, and keep people from re-inventing the wheel.

Microsoft Exchange Server lets you set up organization-wide discussion forums right out of the box, with no programming or development required whatsoever. The server provides the infrastructure needed for creating and managing the discussion forums, including automatically threading all discussions, so new readers can catch up on the discussion. The Microsoft Exchange Client provides a simple user interface with built-in support for sharing information in discussion forums.

Public Folders

The key facility in Microsoft Exchange Server for supporting discussions is public folders. To the user, public folders look just like any other folder in the Microsoft Exchange Viewer. The owner of the folder can give access permission to individuals or to groups of people (distribution lists).

Replication

Microsoft Exchange Server supports true bidirectional, multimaster replication of public folders. This allows users on many servers across a large organization to participate in the same discussion group as if they were all on the same server. Changes made on any replica are automatically sent to all other replicas and merged. This can happen immediately and continuously, whenever changes occur, or it can be scheduled by the administrator to happen on a regular basis. Replication is a very efficient means of keeping multiple copies of folders in sync, because only the changes—not the entire database—are sent between servers.

Server administrators can choose to place replicas of public folders on as many of their servers as they need for local access speed and load balancing.

All of this is completely transparent to the user. The server has the intelligence to automatically connect users to the nearest replica of any given public folder. In fact, users don't need to know the physical location of public folders at all.

Conflict Resolution

In any system that allows true multimaster replication, the possibility of conflicts arises: People might make simultaneous changes on two different servers. Microsoft Exchange Server automatically detects such conflicts and flags all "conflicted" documents. Whenever a user opens such a document, they are alerted to the fact that there are now multiple versions of the document and are prompted to pick the version they'd like to work with. Users with sufficient permissions in the public folder can also resolve the conflict either by picking a "winner" from the conflicting versions or by choosing to save the versions into separate documents.

"Posting" vs. "Sending"

Traditional e-mail uses the paradigm of "sending" information from one user to another. A slightly different paradigm is used for discussion and information sharing: Items are "posted" to a public folder, which is analogous to saving a record in a database. The Microsoft Exchange Client supports both paradigms equally well, with built-in forms for "sending" (standard e-mail note), and "posting" ("Post in this Folder" form). Custom forms can also support both types of behavior.

Conversation Threading

In an ongoing discussion, it's useful to be able to see who said what, and to whom. Items posted to a public folder in Microsoft Exchange Server are tracked in conversation threads. All folders have a built-in view called Group by Conversation, which displays the contents of the folder organized hierarchically. Each separate conversation topic is a thread that can be expanded or collapsed.

Custom Information-Sharing Applications

For an information-sharing application to be truly integral to the operation of a business, it must be customizable to the specific needs of that business.

A custom Microsoft Exchange application normally revolves around a public folder with specialized forms that enable users to input and read information in a structured way. Forms allow organizations to efficiently handle almost any type of information-gathering and workflow needs, such as customer contact reports, help desk requests, claims processing, even expense reports.

A good example of this capability is a customer tracking folder. A salesperson could use this type of folder to open a Call Report form, type in a brief report of the call, and then save the report. The call report would then be stored with a unique icon in a public folder. Other users could see which customers have been contacted and when, eliminating duplication of efforts. Using the Microsoft Exchange solution design environment, custom forms can be designed and integrated into a Microsoft Exchange application with no programming.

Here's a brief view of what you can do with Microsoft Exchange; I'll tell you more in Chapter 8.

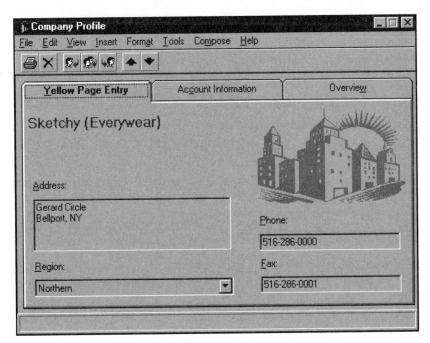

Security with Flexibility

Security and privacy are very important issues in any organization. There are a variety of security mechanisms in Microsoft Exchange, and we will visit them in greater detail in subsequent chapters. For now, we'll introduce the basics.

Compared to existing messaging systems, Microsoft Exchange provides both enhanced security and a great deal of flexibility. Users can log on from anywhere on the network to send and receive mail, but password verification across the network prevents unauthorized users from accessing mail. Users can also create password-protected, encrypted personal folders on local hard drives, ensuring security even if someone else has access to the machine. Messages and information stored on the Microsoft Exchange Server are protected by the user's network identity and password. However, all these security features come with the option of unified logon: Logging on to the network can log users on to their mail without forcing them to remember several different passwords.

Access to items stored in public folders can be controlled easily through a simple dialog. In most cases, users are assigned to the default group, which gives them the ability to create and read information but not to edit or delete data that was created by another user. Typically, every public folder has one or more users who are given additional privileges, such as deleting messages, so they can act as folder administrators. This allows folders to be kept manageable and up-to-date while eliminating problems of data being incorrectly changed or deleted. In addition, using more advanced security, messages can be digitally signed and sealed for a completely secure messaging system. More on that later.

Integrated Management for Time, Tasks, and Contacts

The most popular "workgroup" application, after e-mail, is scheduling. Microsoft was a pioneer in the field when it introduced the personal calendar/reminder program called Microsoft Schedule in Microsoft Mail for AppleTalk Networks. From that humble beginning, the application has grown into Microsoft Schedule+, a full-featured schedule, contact, and task management application integrated with Microsoft Exchange and Microsoft® Office applications.

Schedule+ requires no special setup or administration. It even uses the same user account information and Address Book as the rest of Microsoft Exchange. So once you've created a user account for Microsoft Exchange, you've created it for Schedule+, too. Fully extensible Schedule+ can act as a foundation for business-specific activity management applications.

Schedule+ excels in the three main scheduling tasks:

1 Helping you manage your own time and contacts.

2 Helping you manage meetings.

3 Helping you manage projects.

Manage Your Time and Contacts

The Schedule+ graphic user interface uses a day-planner metaphor that most people find familiar and easy to use. Here's what the Daily view (the default view) looks like:

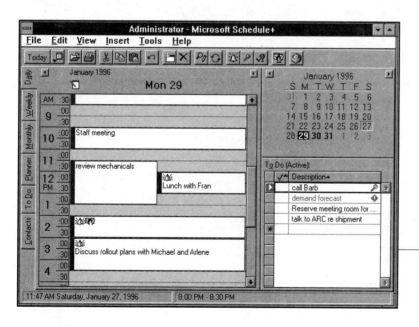

The day's schedule and To Do list are clearly visible, along with the full-month calendar. Tabs at the left allow you to choose Weekly and Monthly views of your schedule as well as the Planner, To Do, and Contacts views. (You can even add, delete, and rename the tabs.)

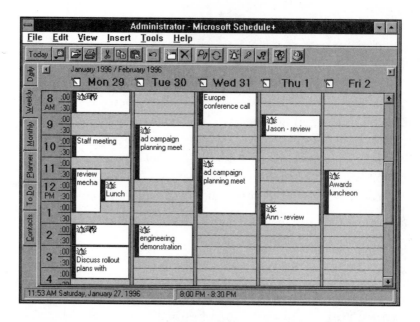

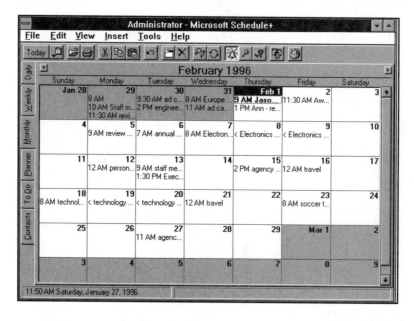

Creating a new appointment is as easy as typing a description into the selected time slot. An appointment can be moved simply by dragging it to a new time or day on the schedule. Overlapping or simultaneous appointments are displayed side by side, allowing users to track many activities at once and spot conflicting appointments. Recurring appointments, such as weekly or monthly staff meetings, can be created in seconds.

Delegating Calendar Access

You can give someone else permission to view, create, or modify appointments on your calendar and even send and receive meeting requests on your behalf.

You decide who has which type of access to your calendar. You can allow another person to view only certain parts of your calendar, such as appointments or the To Do list. You can also designate any appointment as private, so even people with access to your calendar won't be able to see the details of the appointment.

Keeping Track of Contacts

The contact management features in Schedule+ allow you to easily store and find the names, phone numbers, and other information for the people and companies you deal with day in and day out. Schedule+ can keep track of:

✗ **Name**

✗ **Title**

✗ **Company**

✗ **Department**

✗ **Office location**

✗ **Assistant's name**

✗ **Phone numbers (business (2), home (2), fax, mobile, pager, and assistant)**

✗ **Business and home addresses**

✗ **Spouse's name**

✗ **Birthday and anniversary dates**

✗ **Notes**

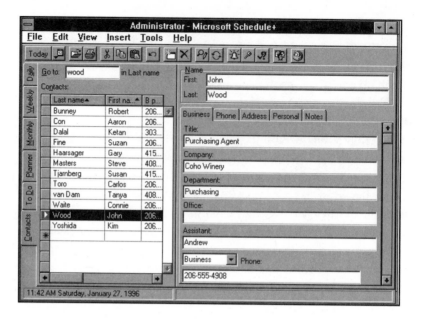

And if that's not enough, there are four user-defined fields where you can keep track of anything you want.

Schedule+ can import contact information from applications such as Microsoft Excel, Microsoft® Access, and other database applications. Once information has been entered in Schedule+, the program's grouping and sorting capabilities can be used to create custom lists for printing or for merging with a word processing program such as Microsoft Word.

Sophisticated Printing

Users can take daily, weekly, monthly, monthly tri-fold, and other printed versions of their schedules and To Do lists with them. Multiple overlapping appointments are displayed in the printed version, and any overlapping appointments that don't fit are printed to overflow areas so users always have all of their appointments noted. Simple dialog boxes guide users through the process of selecting the appropriate print format. A Print Preview option lets users make sure their work looks the way they want it to before they print it.

Organize Meetings with Ease

Maybe the only thing worse than going to meetings is trying to organize them. Now, instead of spending hours playing telephone tag or running up and down the hall checking people's schedules, you can let the Schedule+ meeting wizard do the checking, coordinating, inviting, and tracking.

Just tell the meeting wizard who needs to attend the meeting, where you want to hold it, and how long it will last. You can also tell it if you have special requirements such as audio-visual equipment.

Schedule+ overlays all the attendees' busy times on a single calendar display and finds the first available time period (if there is one) when everyone can attend. It even provides a pre-addressed meeting request that can be mailed to the attendees.

You can also use the Meeting Planner to organize meetings. The Meeting Planner performs the same functions as the meeting wizard, but it gives you more options for finding an acceptable meeting time and place. Objects in Schedule+ can be designated as resources. Conference rooms, the cafeteria, and the company volleyball court can all be treated differently from a user account.

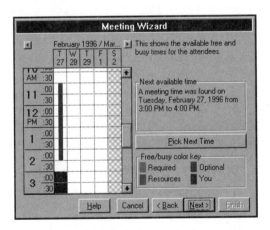

Just as you do with the meeting wizard, you select the attendees, putting those who must attend in one group and those whose attendance is optional in another. You also select a meeting room and other resources such as computers or projection equipment.

The Meeting Planner then shows the availability of all attendees and resources on a single calendar, with each group indicated by a different color. If you can't find a time that works for all attendees and resources, you can include and exclude people and resources individually or in groups to see how their schedules affect the available meeting times.

For example, suppose you want to schedule a meeting in the main conference room so you can use its built-in video projector. When you check the Meeting Planner, you find that there is no time that works for everyone. You click the conference room resource to remove it from the display and find that there are times when the attendees are available. If you can use a different location (perhaps the cafeteria, with a portable projection unit), you can schedule your meeting.

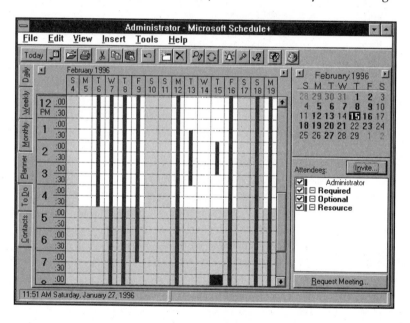

Once you've found the right time for your meeting, you can have Schedule+ send invitations to all attendees, and you can include agenda and other materials with the invitations.

The invitation appears in the recipient's Microsoft Exchange inbox with a special icon that allows users to quickly distinguish it from other messages. The user can accept, tentatively accept, or decline the invitation just by pressing a button on the message form. Schedule+ automatically sends the appropriate message back to the person who called the meeting.

If the user accepts the meeting, the meeting information is automatically entered into their appointment book.

At any time, you can keep track of each person invited to the meeting and see whether that person has accepted, declined, or tentatively accepted the invitation. If the meeting is canceled or moved, you make the change in your Schedule+ calendar, and Microsoft Exchange automatically notifies everyone who has been invited.

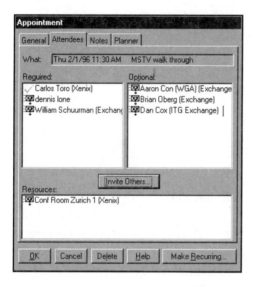

Control Tasks and Projects

Schedule+ helps you manage your own tasks as well as those of your workgroup or project team through personal and shared to-do lists and through integration with Microsoft Project.

Personal To Do List

The To Do list function in Schedule+ is a far cry from the paper-and-pencil list of things that are hanging over your head day after day. With outlining, sorting, and filtering capabilities, Schedule+ can even help you change some of those items from "to do" to "done."

Adding to the list is simple: Just go to the day when something is to be done and type a brief description of the item in the To Do list. The To Do list is visible from any calendar view. Tasks due on the selected day are shown at the top of the To Do list. You can also choose the To Do tab to see a list of all tasks for all days.

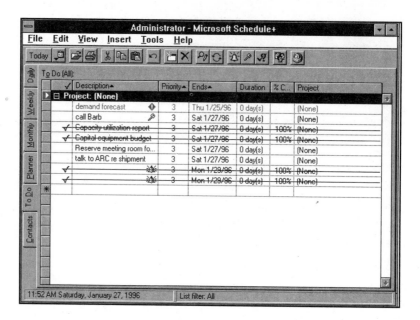

When you complete a task, double-click the description in the To Do list. A check mark appears next to the description so you can easily tell what has been done and what remains to be done. If an item is not completed by its due date, it is automatically carried forward to the next day and highlighted in red to indicate that it is overdue.

You can group tasks by project, date due, or priority, and you can enter recurring tasks. Reminders can be set for any task, and tasks can be marked as private. You can record time spent and percent of completion for each task, as well as other notes and contact and billing information.

Schedule+ has three tools for helping you organize your tasks:

✗ Outlining: You can create multilevel outlines of tasks, grouping work items in many different ways. For example, in the following illustration, the To Do list has been outlined by project to give a quick overview of the tasks associated with each project. Each of the projects can be expanded or collapsed to reveal the underlying task entries.

✗ Sorting: You can sort on any column in the To Do list by clicking on the column header. Up to three columns at a time can be selected for sorting, and each can be sorted in either ascending or descending order.

✗ **Filtering:** You can apply filters to limit the range of tasks that are displayed. For example, you can show only completed tasks, or overdue tasks, or tasks not yet started.

Shared To Do Lists

A powerful aspect of the To Do list is the ability to share tasks with other users. User permissions for tasks are set the same way as user permissions for appointments. That makes it easy for tasks to be shared within a team or between an executive and an assistant. Of course, users always have complete control over their tasks, and can designate any task or group of tasks as private so no one can view specific To Do list items.

Enhanced Project Planning

Microsoft Exchange offers advanced project planning and task delegation through its integration with Microsoft® Project. And, because only the project manager needs the Microsoft Project software, you can save money while you direct your team.

By using Microsoft Project with Schedule+, you can send out three types of electronic forms:

✗ **Send Task Request:** Sends all project tasks to team members for their confirmation. Team members using Schedule+ can add these project tasks to their To Do lists with the click of a button.

✗ **Send Task Updates:** Sends only project tasks that have changed. Team members can update these project tasks on their To Do lists with the click of a button.

✗ **Request Task Updates:** Sends out a request for status on all tasks the team member is responsible for.

When a team member responds to the request for status, you can update the Microsoft Project file from the electronic form. Comments made by team members are stored in the notes fields of the respective project's tasks, along with a date for audit trail purposes. Using Microsoft Exchange electronic forms saves a great deal of re-keying, and it maintains a log of who committed to do what, and when.

Access Anywhere, Anytime

Schedule+ users can work with their calendar even while away from the network. Users can view all appointments and tasks, make additions or modifications, and enter meetings in their calendars. A user who is away from the network can make a shared copy of their schedule available to others to schedule meetings and tasks. The next time the user logs on to the network, the shared calendar is automatically reconciled with the user's copy.

The Foundation for Activity Management Applications

Microsoft Schedule+ can act as a foundation for sophisticated activity management applications.

For example, a user of a customer tracking application based on Microsoft Exchange and Schedule+ might schedule a call on an account based upon the availability of the members of the account team. The customer tracking application could present the schedules of the team members by directly accessing their Schedule+ calendars. Once an appropriate time for the call has been determined, the tracking application could schedule the time for all of the team members involved either by directly accessing their calendars or by sending them a request for the account call.

Schedule+ also works with a variety of hand-held devices, such as the Sharp® Wizard palm-top computer and the Timex® Data Link Watch, allowing users to easily download appointments, phone numbers, anniversaries, and To Do lists from Schedule+.

Time Zones

Because the business community is truly global, time zone management is a key part of Schedule+. If you schedule a conference call using automated scheduling software, the system must recognize that certain team members are in different time zones and schedule events accordingly. It is also helpful to be able to view multiple time zones, such as when you are traveling in one time zone and dealing with business affairs in another.

The combination of Schedule+, Microsoft Exchange Server, and Windows NT Server allow for very efficient and automatic time zone management that can even be used with other applications such as Microsoft Project.

The 7 Habits of Highly Effective People[1]

You can use this scheme of time management to integrate your business, professional, and personal lives together using Schedule+ as the central scheduling agent to keep you on track.

The 7 Habits of Highly Effective People provide a holistic, integrated approach to personal and interpersonal effectiveness. Habits are patterns of behavior that involve three overlapping components: knowledge, attitude, and skill. These three components are learned rather than inherited. We can make or break our habits.

7 Habits Overview

The 7 Habits are habits of effectiveness. Because they are based on principles, they bring the maximum long-term beneficial results possible. They become the basis of a person's character, creating an empowering center of correct maps from which an individual can effectively solve problems, maximize opportunities, and continually learn and integrate other principles in an upward spiral of growth.

The 7 Habits are an orderly sequence of growth, moving from Private to Public Victory.

Habits 1, 2, and 3 lead to Private Victories—the victories that allow us to achieve self-mastery and dominion over self.

✗ In **Habit 1:** Be Proactive. We recognize that we are free to choose.

✗ In **Habit 2:** Begin with the End in Mind. We identify our personal mission and goals.

✗ In **Habit 3:** Put First Things First. We act on our priorities.

Habits 4, 5, and 6 lead to Public Victories—the victories that allow us to achieve success with other people.

---

[1]*Covey, Stephen R. The 7 Habits of Highly Effective People. New York: Simon & Schuster, 1986. Copyright © 1989 by Stephen R. Covey.*

✗ In **Habit 4:** Think Win-Win. We look for alternatives that allow everyone to win.

✗ In **Habit 5:** Seek First to Understand, Then to Be Understood. An attitude and a skill of listening deeply for complete understanding.

✗ In **Habit 6:** Synergize. We discover a creativity that people can experience when they explore their differences together.

✗ In **Habit 7:** Sharpen the Saw. This is the habit that calls the others forth. It comprises simple daily activities that implant the principles of effectiveness in our minds.

The habits form a continuum because the Private Victory must come before the Public Victory. Until we have developed self-mastery, it is difficult, if not impossible, to achieve success with other people. Taken together, the 7 Habits cultivate personal character, which is the foundation of effectiveness.

Chapter

The Microsoft Exchange Server

You want a messaging system that's powerful enough, flexible enough, and open enough to meet your needs now and in the future? Get a LAN-based system.

You want a messaging system that's easy to administer? Get a host-based system.

You want both? Get Microsoft Exchange Server.

A Complete Messaging Infrastructure

Until now, you've had to choose between host-based and LAN-based systems, each of which had some benefits and some limitations. Host-based systems provide powerful administration, but lack integration with personal computer-based applications on the user's desktop. LAN-based systems, on the other hand, let users continue using their PC applications, but they're more difficult to manage because of their distributed nature.

Now there's Microsoft Exchange Server.

Microsoft Exchange Server gives you the benefits of both host- and LAN-based systems. It's the first system that combines distributed, organization-wide messaging; group scheduling; electronic forms; and information sharing with powerful centralized management capabilities.

Microsoft Exchange Server is:

✗ **Easy to manage:** A graphical administrative interface with a single view of the organization makes it easy to manage the components of Microsoft Exchange Server. Management is further simplified by a fault-tolerant database, automatic routing and directory replication, and automated alerts and monitors.

✗ **Easy to integrate with existing systems:** Microsoft Exchange Server not only supports cross-platform clients (Windows, Windows for Workgroups, Windows NT, Windows 95, MS-DOS, Macintosh®, OS/2®, and UNIX®), but its network-independent protocol support enables it to work cooperatively with existing systems, including working seamlessly with Novell NetWare.

✗ **A secure foundation:** By taking advantage of the security of Microsoft Windows NT Server and supporting RSA Data Security, Inc., digital signature and encryption, Microsoft Exchange Server offers a highly secure system.

✗ **Information sharing anytime, anywhere:** The innovative replication technology that is part of Microsoft Exchange Server gives users location-independent access to information.

✗ **Global connectivity:** Microsoft Exchange Server supports rich connectivity through X.400 and to the Internet. It also supports the existing family of Microsoft Mail gateways, as well as a range of third-party gateways.

Inside Microsoft Exchange Server

Microsoft Exchange Server is a comprehensive system with everything you need to manage organization-wide communication. The server components include a directory service, information store, message transfer agent (MTA), connectors, and a system attendant. The Microsoft Exchange Server components run as Microsoft Windows NT Server services and work together to:

✗ **Store and maintain** all information about the organization and each of its sites in the Microsoft Exchange Server directory.

✗ **Control** who can access information from the directory and how the information can be used.

✗ **Provide** a structured repository of information that enables users to submit, retrieve, and manage information such as electronic messages and documents.

✗ **Receive, deliver, transfer, and route** messages throughout and beyond the organization.

✗ **Monitor** the state of the servers and their connections.

✗ **Ensure** that all the servers within and across sites have the same directory information.

✗ **Manage** replication schedules and replication conflicts.

The Microsoft Exchange Server Administrator program is used to manage the server components of Microsoft Exchange Server. This diagram shows how the server components work together.

Administrator Program

One key advantage of Microsoft Exchange Server is its easy manageability across large, geographically dispersed organizations. A graphical system administration application allows you to centrally manage all Microsoft Exchange Server components—including recipients, gateways, and servers—across an entire organization.

The Administrator program displays the Microsoft Exchange Server organization in a hierarchy that makes it easy to navigate to, and manage, the elements at each level.

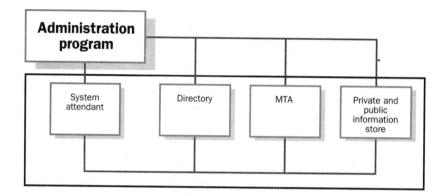

In this example, the organization consists of multiple Microsoft Exchange Server sites. An administrator can view all the components of a server simply by clicking it. The components of the highlighted server ("SIERRADOG") are shown in the right pane of the window.

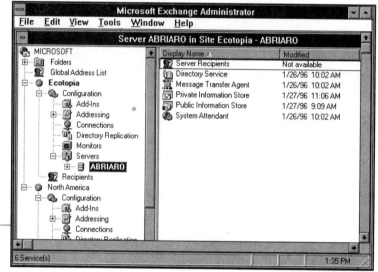

Directory

The Microsoft Exchange Server directory provides a unified, structured view of all users and resources in the organization and keeps track of information about message recipients in the Microsoft Exchange Server organization. This includes information on the recipient mailboxes, distribution lists, and public folders. The recipient's profile can be customized to contain whatever information you want. If, for example, you wanted to add the recipient's birth date to their profile, you could easily create a birth date attribute that could be searched by the Microsoft Exchange Client.

The directory also maintains configuration information used by other Microsoft Exchange Server components to map addresses and route messages. Users access the directory through the Microsoft Exchange Client and use it like a telephone book to obtain information about users and other system components.

Directory Service

The Microsoft Exchange Server's directory service (DS) replicates directory databases between servers in a site and between sites, ensuring that directories are synchronized throughout the Microsoft Exchange Server organization. You can add a recipient at *any* server in a site and the change will be replicated automatically to all other sites. Fault-tolerant replication features enable the DS to synchronize directories even after a catastrophic failure, such as a critical hardware failure.

Within a site, replication is multimaster and event-driven. When one server's directory is updated, the changes are communicated automatically to the other servers in the site. Between Microsoft Exchange Server sites, replication of directory modifications and new entries happens on a scheduled basis. "Bridgehead" servers are defined at each site, and directory update mail is passed between the bridgehead servers. Each bridgehead server is then responsible for replicating the changes to the other servers in the site.

In this diagram, the Microsoft Exchange Server's directory service automatically replicates directory information to the other Microsoft Exchange Servers in the site and routes directory changes to the other Microsoft Exchange Server site at scheduled times.

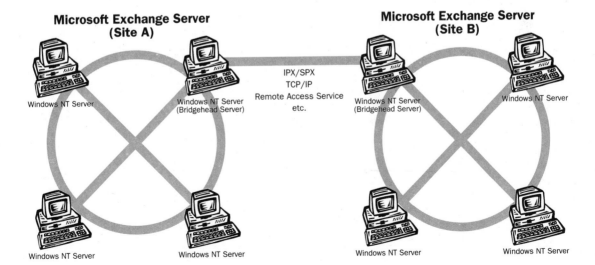

Windows NT Server and the Microsoft Exchange Server Directory Service

The Microsoft Exchange Server's directory service has messaging-specific features that extend the directory service provided in Windows NT Server. Each Microsoft Exchange Server mailbox, public folder, and distribution list is associated with a Windows NT user account. Windows NT Server and the Microsoft Exchange Server directory services work together to simplify this association. When you modify a user in Windows NT Server, you can apply the same change directly to Microsoft Exchange Server. When you create a new user in the Windows NT User Manager dialog box, you have the option to create a Microsoft Exchange Server mailbox using the actual Microsoft Exchange Server property sheets. When you delete a Windows NT account, you can also delete the user's Microsoft Exchange Server mailbox.

The Windows NT User Manager also has an option to modify Microsoft Exchange Server mailbox properties. By selecting Properties from the User Manager Exchange menu, you can access the Microsoft Exchange Server mailbox properties directly from User Manager.

Select Properties from the Exchange menu of Windows NT User Manager to see mailbox properties.

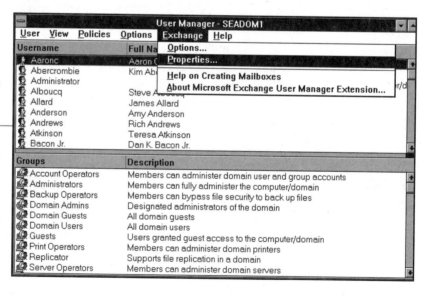

To save time and trouble, Windows NT user accounts can be created or deleted automatically by using the Microsoft Exchange Server directory importing facility.

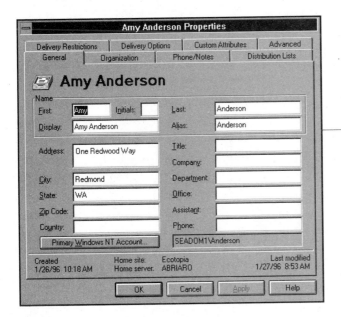

Microsoft Exchange Server properties page brought up from the Windows NT User Manager.

In addition, Microsoft Exchange Server includes an extraction tool that enables you to set up mailboxes very efficiently. Instead of creating a mailbox for each existing account, one by one, you can use the Microsoft Exchange Administrator program to import a list of the existing accounts into the Microsoft Exchange directory and create mailboxes for all of them at the same time.

Directory Synchronization Service

The Directory Synchronization service (DX) synchronizes Microsoft Exchange Server, Microsoft Mail for PC Networks, and other e-mail system directories. The DX is based on the Microsoft Mail for PC Networks directory synchronization model and is fully backward-compatible with Microsoft Mail's directory synchronization.

The DX can act as both a directory synchronization requester and a directory synchronization server. This functionality enables the directory synchronization load to be split between two directory synchronization servers, as shown in the following two diagrams:

The Microsoft Mail directory synchronization model today: one dirsync server and multiple dirsync requesters.

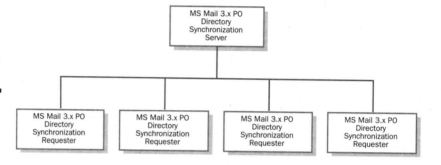

Because the Microsoft Exchange Server DX can function as both a directory synchronization server and requester, adding a single Microsoft Exchange Server computer allows the directory synchronization load to be split between two dirsync servers.

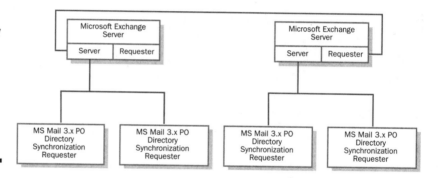

System Attendant

The Microsoft Exchange Server system attendant performs maintenance tasks such as:

✗ **Assisting** the monitoring tools by gathering information on the services running on each server within a site.

✗ **Monitoring** the state of messaging connections between servers. The system attendant can be configured to monitor links from one server to another within a site, between sites, or between mail systems.

✗ **Logging** information about messages sent for message-tracking purposes.

✗ **Building** the routing tables in a site.

✗ **Generating** E-mail addresses for new message recipients.

Message Transfer Agent

The Message Transfer Agent (MTA) provides the engine for routing and transferring data to other servers or to foreign systems. It is the foundation of the Microsoft Exchange Server communication infrastructure and is designed for reliable data transmission across multiple sites and networks. The MTA helps ensure system availability throughout the organization and beyond.

The MTA uses three core components for routing and transferring data to other servers or foreign systems:

1 The Microsoft Exchange Server Site Connector

2 The Dynamic RAS Connector

3 The X.400 Connector

Microsoft Exchange Server Site Connector

The Site Connector is the most efficient way to connect two sites for two reasons:

1 It uses remote procedure calls (RPCs) to set up and control site-to-site communication. There is no translation of system messages, because they aren't sent as messages.

2 Messages take fewer "hops" to get to their destinations. A Site Connector in site A can make a direct connection to an MTA in site B rather than having to send a mail message, which may have to hop to a site bridgehead server and from there to the MTA.

Site Connectors require permanent connections with higher bandwidths than the other connectors, but they are easier to configure. The use of RPCs means you do not have to configure a new network transport for the Site Connector; it will use the existing transport.

Site connectors use whatever LAN transport you have (except DLC and TP4). They are easy and fast to set up because they don't require complicated configuration or a specific transport.

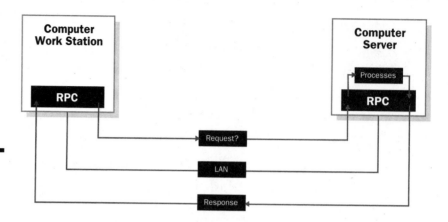

Remote Access Service Connector

The Dynamic RAS Connector is a special case of the site Connector. It uses RAS (asynchronous communication) instead of a permanent network connection between Microsoft Exchange Server sites. You can tell Microsoft Exchange Server when the connection should be made, and it will make the connection to the other site at that time.

Remote Access Service technology is the software built into Windows NT Server 3.x that allows a Windows NT server to act a network node for a number of remotely connected users. The remote connection is made from home, hotel, or wherever to the RAS server via a modem and a telephone line. The remote node is then connected to network resources, in this case Microsoft Exchange Server, via the normal LAN connection. The RAS server converts the telephone signals into LAN signals and vice versa.

X.400 Connector

The X.400 Connector conforms to the 1984 and 1988 X.400 MTA standard. It is typically used when there are low-bandwidth network connections between your sites, when you want to take advantage of your existing X.400 backbone, or when you want to access a public X.400 system. You can schedule when connections should be made, and you can control message size through the connector. You can also control how messages are routed through the Microsoft Exchange Server topology.

Microsoft Exchange Server supports X.400 over these transports:

1 TP0/X.25

2 TP4/(CLNP)

3 TP0/RFC 1006 to TCP/IP

By supporting a full suite of the most popular, reliable, and secure networking transports, Microsoft Exchange Server allows you to choose the one that best meets your needs while providing the flexibility of simultaneously supporting a wide array of messaging options. Companies can communicate with sites that are geographically dispersed and with other companies that use different networking protocols. You can also configure different transports on the same server.

The X.400 Connector supports the following textual body parts:

1 International IA5 (US, German, Norwegian, Swedish)

2 T.61 (Teletex)

3 ISO 6937

4 ISO 8857-1

This support makes it possible for most language characters to be used and transferred, enabling seamless interoperability between different mail systems across national boundaries.

The X.400 Connector also supports these binary body parts:

1 BP9—provides support for embedding messages and forwarding messages based on the X.400 standard.

2 BP14—(1984 specification) provides support for simple transferring of binary attachments.

3 BP 15—provides support for the 1988 X.400 standard for sending attachments.

4 File Transfer Body Part—(1992 specification) (includes file name, size, properties, and other information.)

5 Other X.400 body parts are converted to MAPI binary attachments.

A single Microsoft Exchange Server computer with the X.400 Connector provides compatibility with 1984, 1988, and future MTAs, and the body part conversion can be selected for each MTA connection. That gives you the flexibility to communicate via X.400 with companies that are at different stages of implementing X.400 technology.

Other Native Microsoft Exchange Server Connectors

Internet Mail Connector

The Internet Mail Connector allows Microsoft Exchange Server users to communicate with Internet users through the Simple Mail Transfer Protocol (SMTP) and Multipurpose Internet Mail Extensions (MIME). Because it is a fully integrated component of Microsoft Exchange Server, messages received from a foreign Internet system are indistinguishable from messages received within the organization. Users can even send and receive attachments with their mail messages.

The Internet Mail Connector supports messages in these formats:

✗ **Plain Text format (RFC 822)**

✗ **Multipurpose Internet Mail Extensions (MIME) format (RFC 1521)**

✗ **Microsoft Mail Server format (RFC 1154)**

✗ **UUENCODE and UUDECODE**

Microsoft Mail Connector

The Microsoft Mail Connector provides seamless connectivity to Microsoft Mail for PC Networks, Microsoft Mail for AppleTalk Networks, and Microsoft Mail for PC Networks gateways. It uses a "shadow" post office that is structured like a Microsoft Mail 3.x post office. A Microsoft Exchange Server site appears to your Microsoft Mail Server as just another Microsoft Mail postoffice. The Microsoft Exchange Server site can connect directly to an existing Microsoft Mail postoffice, allowing you to replace—not just supplement—an existing Microsoft Mail MTA. No additional software is required.

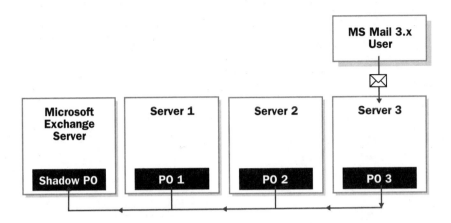

Information Store

The Microsoft Exchange Server information store provides a server-based, structured repository for storing information created by users. It is a database designed to store, and provide quick access to, heterogeneous data such as mail, attachments, electronic forms, images, and voice messages. Microsoft Exchange Server provides a number of tools to help you manage the information store. These tools help you:

✗ **Impose** storage limits for public and personal folders to manage the amount of disk storage used on the server.

✗ **Set** age limits and automatically delete from the information store anything that is older than these limits.

✗ **Establish** security on individual personal and public folders.

✗ **Create** schedules for public folder replication.

The server-based information store has two databases, one for storing private folders for users' mailboxes, and another for storing public folders, including offline folders. (The third type of folder database—personal folders—is typically stored on a user's personal computer.) Microsoft Exchange's replication facilities enable you to automatically distribute information stored in public folders to various locations.

Information Store	Where Information can be Stored	
	Local machine	**Microsoft Exchange Server computer**
Private folders		X
Public folders		X
Personal folders	X	X
Offline folders	X	X

Public Folder Replication

One of the key strengths of Microsoft Exchange Server is its ability to distribute and synchronize shared information. This ability is supported through the Microsoft Exchange Server replication system, which enables you to have multiple synchronized copies of folders in different locations regardless of whether you are connected over a LAN, WAN, X.400, or Internet backbone. Replicating information in this way has three key advantages:

1. Synchronized copies of a public folder can reside on multiple servers, distributing the processing load and improving response time for users accessing information within the folder.

2. Synchronized copies of a public folder can reside at several geographically separated sites, dramatically reducing the amount of long-distance (WAN) traffic necessary to access information.

3. If a server holding one copy of a public folder becomes unavailable, other servers holding synchronized copies of the same folder can be accessed transparently, greatly increasing the availability of information for users and resulting in a highly reliable system.

From the users' perspective, Microsoft Exchange Server offers the unique benefit of location-independent access to shared information. With replication, the physical location of folders is irrelevant to users, and Microsoft Exchange Server hides the sophistication of the public folder replication process. Users need not be aware of where replicated folders are located, the number of replicated copies, or even that replication occurs at all. They simply find information much more available and accessible than ever before.

Management of public folder replication is very simple. The Microsoft Exchange Server's public folder replication is message-based. The administrator only has to select the servers that will receive replicas of the public folders. Microsoft Exchange Server does the rest.

Replication Control

Microsoft Exchange Server gives you a high degree of control over the entire replication process. A number of replication options can be set, including the times at which replication occurs and how information is replicated or distributed around the organization. For example, if you have a large document-library folder that is stored at a headquarters office, you may want to replicate only certain subfolders to servers located in the branch offices.

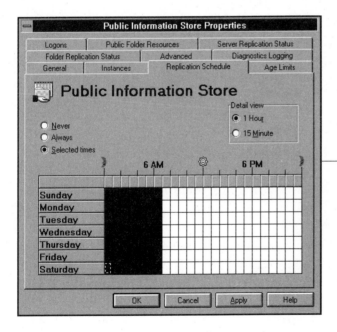

The administrator's interface for folder replication. Notice how the scheduling grid makes the process of setting replication times easy.

The Microsoft Exchange Server Topology

Understanding the Microsoft Exchange Server topology will give you a better understanding of the technology behind Microsoft Exchange Server. For administration, security, and communication purposes, the Microsoft Exchange Server topology is organized into a three-tiered hierarchy. This hierarchy starts with the Microsoft Exchange Server organization, which includes one or more Microsoft Exchange Server sites. Each site can contain one or more Microsoft Exchange Server computers.

The Microsoft Exchange Server Organization

All Microsoft Exchange Server sites in the organization are combined into a single Microsoft Exchange Server organization.

Microsoft Exchange Server Sites

Microsoft Exchange Server-based computers can be grouped into one or more sites for unified administration, security, and communication services. From the Microsoft Exchange Server Administrator program, the administrator can manage everything that is associated with the site—from the users, distribution lists, and public folders to the connectors and gateways.

Sites are the key to how Microsoft Exchange Server makes administration easy. Within a site, message routing and directory replication between servers happens automatically. Administrators simply have to add the server to the site.

Sites usually correspond to geographical areas in an organization's network that are connected by a low-bandwidth line or a backbone connection. A company with 10 sales offices, for instance, could have one site per sales office and have one or more sites for the headquarters. Alternatively, this same company could have one site that encompassed all the sales offices. The advantage of having one large site is that all of the offices can be centrally managed, even if the offices span physical locations. In that way, the company would benefit from a unified information-sharing infrastructure that could be managed from a single location.

While a Microsoft Exchange Server site typically comprises the same set of groups and users as a given Windows NT security domain, a site can span multiple security domains. For example, a corporation's finance and human resources departments may have the same communication needs as other departments but far more demanding security needs. These departments could be configured in separate Windows NT security domains with specific access privileges, yet remain in the same Microsoft Exchange Server site (provided that the two Windows NT domains "trust" each other) to allow centrally administered communication.

A trust relationship is the computer version of, "A friend of Harry's is a friend of mine." When you set up a trust relationship between two domains, you're telling the trusting domain to accept any user who is logged on to the trusted domain. A trust relationship can be two way, in which both domains trust each other's users. It can also be one way, which is like one domain saying, "You can trust my users, but I don't trust yours." Computers aren't always egalitarian.

Domain 1   Domain 2

Microsoft Exchange Server

The server components of Microsoft Exchange Server include the directory service, public and personal information store, message transfer agent, and system attendant, all of which are hosted on a computer that runs Windows NT Server version 3.51 or later. We refer to this computer as the Microsoft Exchange Server-based computer.

The Microsoft Exchange Server Directory Information Tree

The Microsoft Exchange Server Directory Information Tree (DIT) represents the Microsoft Exchange Server topology and illustrates the relationships among the organization, site, and servers. As the following illustration shows, the organization is at the root of the hierarchy, the sites are under the organization, and the servers are under the sites. In this example, "Microsoft" is the name of the organization, "Apps-WGA," "Office," and "WSPU" are the names of the sites in the Microsoft organization, and "DABONE," "damen-dog," and "SIERRADOG" are the names of the servers in the WSPU site.

The Microsoft Exchange Server Directory Information Tree (DIT).

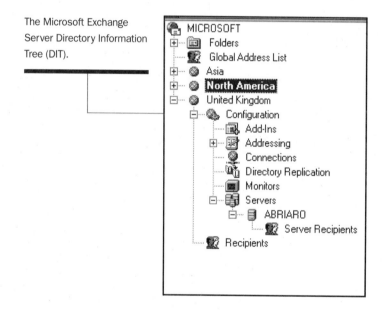

Chapter 5

Microsoft Exchange Server Administration

I t's tempting to think of the cost of an application
as just the cost of the software, plus maybe some
specialized hardware and installation costs. But for
a traditional, LAN-based, shared-file e-mail system,
the real cost is hidden. It's the cost of administering the
system—adding, removing, and moving accounts;
making sure everyone has the right directories;
reconfiguring the system when the organization
changes; and so on.

Microsoft Exchange, on the other hand, was
designed to be easy and inexpensive to administer.

Reducing the Cost of Ownership

The total cost of ownership for client-server communication systems is very heavily weighted by the cost of support and operation. It is estimated that more than 72 percent of the costs of implementing client-server architecture come from keeping the system running smoothly. The capital cost of the hardware and software is less than 15 percent.

We'll tell you more about developing Microsoft Exchange applications in Chapter 8.

A product can reduce the total cost of ownership by decreasing the need for user support and by decreasing the need for development staff. Reducing the need for user support mainly means designing a sensible user interface. The Microsoft Exchange Client, with its familiar Windows look and feel and its close integration with Windows Office applications, gives the user a comfortable, easy-to-learn interface.

Microsoft Exchange Server reduces the need for an expensive development staff in two ways. First, it makes it easy for users to develop their own workgroup applications with little or no programming. Second, when applications are needed for the organization, they can be built upon existing workgroup forms and folders using high-productivity tools such as Microsoft Visual Basic.

But the biggest ongoing cost factor by far in the cost-of-ownership equation is administration. The overhead of administration—estimated to have more than doubled in the last ten years—can wipe out much of the gain in user productivity achieved by installing the system in the first place.

Microsoft Exchange Server helps reduce this cost in many ways:

✗ **Account management** is integrated with Windows NT Server, so you can learn and use just one tool.

✗ **The Windows NT Server** security model allows multiple levels of administrative responsibility, so you can place control at the most appropriate level.

✗ **Comprehensive tools** for modeling and optimizing the system come with the product, so you can test your design assumptions before you implement them.

In this chapter, I'll show you how Microsoft Exchange Server helps administrators work more efficiently. We'll look at the tasks the administrator has to perform and the tools built into Microsoft Exchange Server to help them do those tasks.

The Microsoft Exchange Administrator Program

Microsoft Exchange Server includes a graphical system administration application that allows you to centrally manage all Microsoft Exchange components—including recipients, gateways, and servers—across an entire organization.

The Administrator program displays the organization in a hierarchical structure that makes it easy to navigate and manage the elements of each level. Because the administration of Microsoft Exchange is really management of objects in the directory, navigating the directory tree is the same as navigating your Microsoft Exchange topology. A graphical display allows the administrator to see and access the tree to gather information and to perform account and configuration management.

Here's how it would look in the Microsoft Exchange Administrator window:

Microsoft Exchange Server components are treated as objects. Containers are objects that contain other objects. By selecting objects in the Administrator program hierarchy, you can expand branches to display additional objects in the container. For example, selecting the Recipients container displays its contents.

In this example, the organization comprises multiple Microsoft Exchange sites with many servers in each site. But to the administrator, everything is available on the single screen.

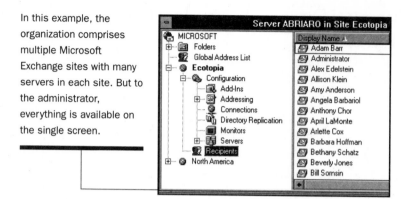

The Administrator program's primary job is to provide access to this directory view. The hierarchy that you see when running the Administrator program is how the data is actually stored in the directory database. Think of the Administrator program as a portal into the directory. The program also allows a user with appropriate privileges to view and set controls on objects in the directory, including users and their mailboxes, connectors, monitors, the information stores, and the message transfer agent.

Single-Seat Management View

A large, geographically dispersed Microsoft Exchange system can be operated from a single point, greatly reducing operating and support costs. As long as one computer can connect over the network to the servers running Microsoft Exchange, one administrator can add users, change account information, and configure the system from this single point.

Microsoft Exchange is designed around the directory service that we introduced in Chapter Four. Because each Microsoft Exchange server has a copy of the organization-wide directory, an administrator can view the entire administrative world in Microsoft Exchange merely by connecting the administration program to any Microsoft Exchange server in the organization. That means they can see all the servers, all the user accounts, and all of the other objects that make up your messaging network in one place and at one time.

Organization

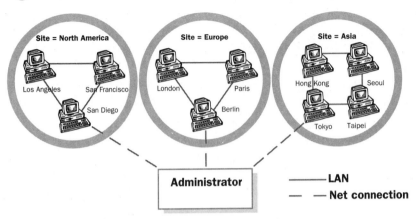

Centralized or Decentralized Object Management

A single Microsoft Exchange Server comprises a number of objects. Some of those objects belong to the user; others facilitate connectivity, communication, and team collaboration. All of them can be managed through a single Administrator program that can simultaneously touch each instance of an object—not just on a single server, but on all servers throughout the organization.

The benefit of central object management is that it enables a single team to operate the entire infrastructure from a central location. Central management brings all the benefits of centralized control, security, and account management previously associated only with host-based messaging.

However, decentralized management is an option. Some companies prefer to operate a highly decentralized environment with different management domains controlling different aspects of the system. The administration model in Microsoft Exchange allows this as well.

Containers in the Microsoft Exchange directory are objects within Windows NT Server. You can apply a set of permissions to each container with an access control list. By grouping servers, connections, monitors, and directory replication into a separate Configuration container, it is possible to set permissions to allow one group of administrators to add, modify, and delete users in the Site Recipients container but not allow those administrators to get into the Configuration container.

You use the Administrator program to manage everything in your organization or site by manipulating the structure of the organization hierarchy or changing the properties of individual objects. The overall structure of your organization is determined by how objects are linked and how their properties are defined.

The following figure shows the objects you can use to build your organization and gives a brief description of each object. Many of the objects correspond to optional components, such as the objects in the Connector container, and are only used on an as-needed basis.

 Organization—The root or starting point of the Microsoft Exchange Server directory hierarchy.

 Folders

 Public Folders—A container for information that can be shared among many users.

 System Folders—A container for special system in formation used by applications such as Schedule+ 7.0.

 Global Address List—Contains all the recipients in the organization.

 Mailbox—A private repository for e-mail and other information. Users must have a mailbox to send and receive e-mail.

 Site—A group of one or more Microsoft Exchange Server computers connected to the same local area network.

Configuration container—Contains configuration objects such as the Monitors, Servers and Directory Replication.

Add-Ins—This container holds services that do not require a mailbox such as application services. Used primarily by Microsoft partners to create special, add on capability.

Addressing container

 Details Templates—Contains localized templates that can be used to define how details are displayed on objects.

 **E-Mail Address Generators**

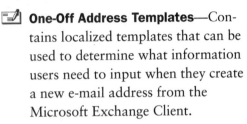 **One-Off Address Templates**—Contains localized templates that can be used to determine what information users need to input when they create a new e-mail address from the Microsoft Exchange Client.

Connections container—Contains the connectors that define the site to site communications over which mail travels.

Directory Replication container—Describes the replication relationships between two sites.

Monitors container

 Link Monitor—Monitors the status of messaging links between Microsoft Exchange Server computers and servers in other systems.

Server Monitor—Monitors the status of Microsoft Exchange Server and/or Windows NT services running on one or more servers.

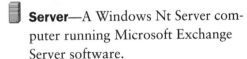 **Servers container**

Server—A Windows Nt Server computer running Microsoft Exchange Server software.

Server Recipients—Contains all the recipients that have this Microsoft Exchange Server computer as their home server.

Directory Service—Stores all the information available about an organization's resources and users such as servers, mailboxes, and public folders.

Message Transfer Agent—Delivers messages to their destination by moving them from one server to another.

Private Information Store—Contains all mailboxes for users who have this Microsoft Exchange Server computer as their home server.

Public Information Store—Contains all public folders (and their contents) that have this Microsoft Exchange Server computer as their home server.

System Attendant—A general maintenance service that must be running in order for Microsoft Exchange Server processes to run.

Recipients—Listing of all recipients that are defined in this Microsoft Exchange Site.

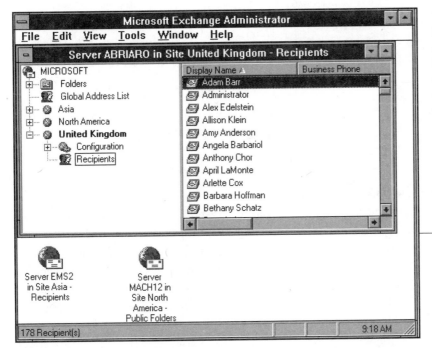

The right-hand pane of the Microsoft Exchange Administrator interface lists all the mailboxes, distribution lists, custom recipients, and public folders that exist in the site. An administrator can double-click any of these objects to change its attributes.

Microsoft Exchange Server Administrative Tasks

Microsoft Exchange Server has been designed so that administrative tasks can be grouped into three categories:

- ✗ **Configuration**
- ✗ **Maintenance**
- ✗ **Monitoring**

Different configurations require different divisions of tasks, and tasks performed by each type of administrator sometimes overlap.

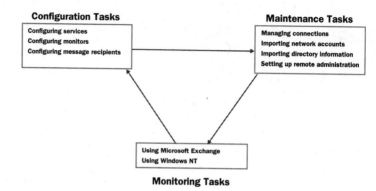

Configuration Tasks
- Configuring services
- Configuring monitors
- Configuring message recipients

Maintenance Tasks
- Managing connections
- Importing network accounts
- Importing directory information
- Setting up remote administration

Using Microsoft Exchange
Using Windows NT

Monitoring Tasks

Configuration

Configuration means creating a system that can send, receive, and access information and messages. Configuration tasks include configuring components, monitors, message recipients, and connections.

In this section, I'm not going to tell you *how* to configure each of these items. That would take far too long, and that probably wouldn't be very valuable information to you right now, anyway.

What is important is that Microsoft Exchange Server gives you so much flexibility in how you configure your overall messaging system. That's what I want to talk about here.

Configuring Components

The Microsoft Exchange Server Setup program installs various components that run along with, and are similar to, Windows NT services. The required components include:

✗ **Message transfer agent (MTA)**

Provides the addressing and routing information for sending messages and other information through the system.

✗ **Information store**

Maintains and organizes information and messages.

✗ **Directory service**

Maintains Address Book information and exchanges this information between Microsoft Exchange servers and other sites.

✗ **System attendant**

Monitors the other Microsoft Exchange services and performs tasks such as calculating routing information, logging data used for message tracking, and other administrative tasks.

Optional services include:

✗ Directory exchange

The directory exchange periodically exchanges recipient information with remote mail systems or other databases of recipient information.

✗ PC interchange

PC interchange handles the connection between Microsoft Mail version 3.2 running on Intel-based machines and Microsoft Exchange Server.

✗ AppleTalk interchange

AppleTalk interchange handles the connection between AppleTalk networks and Microsoft Exchange Server.

The Private Information Store, Public Information Store, Directory, Directory Synchronization, and Message Transfer Agent objects reside in the Server container on the Microsoft Exchange Server. They exist whether or not the Microsoft Exchange Server is connected to other servers, sites, and mail systems.

Directory synchronization needs to be activated only for directory exchange with other mail systems. Directory and public folder replication between sites and mail connectivity between sites and with other mail systems are controlled through the Administrator program.

Private Information Store

The private information store provides central storage for all of the mailboxes that exist on the server. Users have the option to store messages on their local machine in personal folders, but it's better for them to use the server-based private folders for security, management, and backup purposes.

Public Information Store

On each server, the public information store stores data that can be replicated throughout the organization. Through the Administrator program, you can customize replication so that some data is replicated everywhere while other data is centralized on key servers in each site. Replication of data can be tightly controlled, and detailed status screens are available at all times, so the administrator can track the dissemination of this data throughout the enterprise.

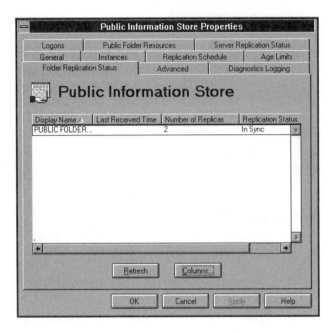

Directory

The directory includes all the routing information required by a server as well as a wealth of customizable user information.

While it's not exactly appropriate to think of Microsoft Exchange as a corporate-wide directory, it can serve as a repository for a wide range of data about each employee that goes far beyond the address books of today's e-mail systems. Microsoft Exchange gives you the flexibility to design directory details to suit your needs.

The Administrator program allows the entry of up to 22 predefined attributes and 10 custom attributes about each user.

From the administration standpoint, the directory contains much more than just mail addresses. It also contains a roadmap of the entire Microsoft Exchange Server organization.

The Microsoft Exchange Server directory is replicated across the organization so each server has a complete copy of the directory. This allows servers to be seen by the Administrator program regardless of their actual location in the network and without the need for a direct network connection to each server. Automatic replication of directory information between servers in a site means that servers do not need to be configured.

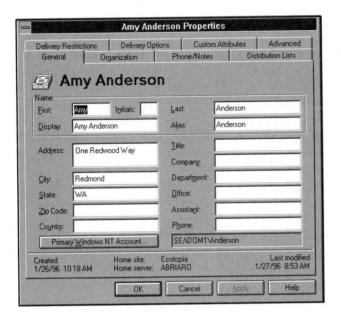

Directory Synchronization

Directory synchronization is currently perceived as the single biggest weakness in LAN-based messaging. Microsoft Exchange removes this weak link and provides a process to keep directories synchronized automatically on a daily basis. The benefit is the ability to communicate quickly and easily with users on a wide range of different messaging systems.

Through the use of the published application programming interface (API) for Microsoft Mail for PC Networks Directory Synchronization, Microsoft Exchange can interface to existing directory gateway servers.

Message Transfer Agent

The message transfer agent delivers all data between two servers in a site and between two bridgehead servers in different sites. The MTA is standards-based, supporting the 1988 ITU-TS X.400 specifications to communicate between sites. This enables customers to use public X.400 systems as a backbone and reduces the infrastructure costs of implementing a globally distributed system.

Access Control

Microsoft Exchange Server offers flexible access control with the permissions model. This model enables you to allocate access and modification rights to other mailboxes, allowing management of the Microsoft

Exchange system to be shared among a series of administrators at varying levels.

In the Windows NT security system, *security descriptors* are attached to *every* object in the system, including files, services, and applications. Windows NT provides these facilities to Microsoft Exchange Server, giving Microsoft Exchange administrators a high degree of access control over all system resources. This allows for groups of objects in the hierarchy to be assigned to lower-level administrators.

For example, the messaging system is closely tied to the communication systems and networks in place at the company, yet the personnel who are trained and experienced with configuration of these subsystems may have little knowledge of the storage requirements for e-mail information in the system. In the past, one administrator account would have privileges for all levels of messaging system management. Now, with Microsoft Exchange administration, you can subdivide the management so that, for example, one account can handle mailbox administration, another account can handle storage maintenance, and a third account (or set of accounts) can handle the communication configuration duties.

From the first time you start Microsoft Exchange, the Windows NT Server account validation is in effect. Before you begin setting up a Microsoft Exchange Server computer, three types of accounts are required:

✗ **Service account:** Used to start services. The service account needs to be recognized by all the Microsoft Exchange Server computers in the organization as having logon as a service privilege. This account is used for setup.

✗ **Admin account:** Used when creating accounts in Windows NT Server and in Microsoft Exchange Server. This account and its privileges are applied to the newly created mailbox accounts. This admin account should be the member of a group of administrators to avoid losing access to objects if the one and only account with privileges is inadvertently deleted.

✗ **User account:** Used to apply user permissions to the mailboxes in Microsoft Exchange Server. Because a user account can be totally integrated with the network logon account, user accounts have user privileges on the system.

Configuring Monitors

Microsoft Exchange Server monitors include the server monitor, used for evaluating server performance, and the link monitor, used for checking connections. These monitors can be run from any Windows NT server or workstation running Microsoft Exchange Server.

Configuring Message Recipients

Message recipients are named and configured through the use of property sheets displayed in the Administrator program. Message recipients include the following:

✗ **Mailbox**

A logical arrangement of messages and other items.

✗ **Distribution list**

A list of recipients usually created to expedite the repetitive sending of messages and other items.

✗ **Custom recipient**

A recipient outside the messaging site, local postoffice, or organization (for example, an Internet recipient with an SMTP address).

✗ **Public folder**

A special folder that a group of users can share for exchanging information.

Administration Tools for Integration and Migration

The tools that assist administrators of the Microsoft Exchange organization act primarily upon the directory. Tools fall into the these categories:

✗ **Integration**

✗ **Migration**

Integration tools are used to import information such as foreign electronic mail system address lists and template information into the Microsoft Exchange directory. These tools normally work in conjunction with the connectors to other systems to allow Microsoft Exchange Server users to communicate easily with the those systems. The directory synchronization between Microsoft Exchange Server and a remote mail system is an example of an integration tool.

Because Microsoft Exchange gets its security from its integration with the Microsoft Windows NT Server 3.5x network operating system, accounts are assigned in the Windows NT Server 3.5x User Manager for Domains.

When you install Microsoft Exchange, the extension to the User Manager is called when creating accounts to facilitate creating network and mail accounts simultaneously. This also allows you to assign privileges to the account for the network and mail.

The Microsoft Exchange Administrator program also includes a tool for extracting a list of users from the already created Windows NT Server account list and then creating mailboxes in Microsoft Exchange from this list. You can select a default user account as the master for creation of all other accounts so that the privileges and access control can be set. The user account and password are inherited from the Windows NT Server account and are used for creation of the mailbox.

You can also take advantage of a tool for reading the NetWare bindery and extracting a list of the users into a file that can then be imported into the Microsoft Exchange directory. To use this tool, you must have a valid NetWare user ID and password and must know the path to the server that holds the list of users to be added to the Microsoft Exchange directory. This tool also lets you create a Windows NT Server account and a Microsoft Exchange mailbox when you are importing.

Microsoft Exchange includes several integration tools. Import and export tools take formatted file input and create entries in a Microsoft Exchange directory, or they extract information from the Microsoft Exchange directory and put it into standard file formats (such as comma-separated values).

A set of directory APIs in the Microsoft Exchange Server Software Developer's Kit allow organizations to automate the process of adding, modifying, and deleting objects in the directory. Using this functionality, an organization could link its Microsoft Exchange directory with an employee database.

Microsoft Exchange Server also contains a migration wizard that will help you migrate users to the Microsoft Exchange information store. This wizard converts the following mail systems:

✗ **Microsoft Mail for PC Networks (Microsoft Mail, PC Mail)**

✗ **Microsoft Mail for AppleTalk Networks (MacMail, Starnine Mail)**

✗ **IBM® PROFS®/OfficeVision®**

✗ **DEC™ All-In-1™ IOS**

✗ **cc:Mail™**

✗ **Verimation® Memo**

You can use migration tools to move users and the data associated with them to Microsoft Exchange Server. These tools can help you convert user accounts, passwords, privileges, mail messages, folders, and other attributes of a mail user on the foreign mail system to their equivalent in Microsoft Exchange Server.

Seamless Migration of New Users

When users are migrated to Microsoft Exchange Server, their display names remain unchanged in the Address Book, so other users don't need to change the way they communicate with migrating colleagues. Custom recipients appear in the Address Book and can be mailed to and included within distribution lists in exactly the same way as recipients on the Microsoft Exchange Server. Custom recipients are created, managed, and deleted using the same commands as with mailboxes and distribution lists. This eases the administrative burden and lower the cost of managing the system as the user population grows.

Data Migration

Ease of data migration is a key factor in reducing the cost of moving to Microsoft Exchange from an existing mail system. Because most companies already have an electronic mail system, moving a user also means moving data, mail messages, and schedule information as well as account information. Microsoft Exchange takes this into consideration with a full set of migration tools that allow the administrator to move users and data from other systems.

This is key to providing a productive installation for users: They can carry on with their daily tasks the same day they move to Microsoft Exchange.

Transparent Coexistence with Other Systems

There is also a set of coexistence tools for those systems where users cannot be moved en masse. Some strategies will require that systems coexist with Microsoft Exchange, with hires or transfers being set up on the Microsoft Exchange system while existing users continue to work on the existing system until equipment or software can be upgraded.

The addresses of recipients can appear in a format that clearly identifies them as users of another mail system, or they can appear indistinguishable from the addresses of Microsoft Exchange Server users. This option is particularly useful when users will be migrated to Microsoft Exchange Server gradually over time (sometimes known as the "whither on the vine" strategy for migration). For instance, representing the IBM PROFS user population in the Microsoft Exchange Server format in the Address Book creates a consistent view for Microsoft Exchange users, while the PROFS users will view Microsoft Exchange users as if they were residing on the PROFS system.

Mail Recipient Objects

Five types of objects are represented in the Recipients container: Mailboxes, Custom Recipients, Distribution Lists, Mailbox Agents, and Public Folders.

Mailboxes contain information about users, such as name, phone numbers, e-mail addresses, primary Windows NT account, where that person fits into the organization (who their manager is and who reports to them), and advanced properties such as message transfer size limits, information store limits, and whether the mailbox will be visible or hidden in the directory.

Custom recipients are almost identical to mailboxes and contain information on users outside the Microsoft Exchange system, typically gateway recipients. Custom recipients do not have an information store associated with them.

Distribution lists (known as aliases or groups in Microsoft Mail 3.*x*) contain lists of users grouped together and designated by some function (managers, students) or activity (skiers, hikers). Distribution lists (DLs) can have properties associated with their directory entry. Properties can include whether the DL is visible in the directory and whether users can see the list of names inside the DL, and they can restrict who can send to the DL (so that not everyone could send to an "entire company" DL). In the case of very large distribution lists, you can even designate a DL expansion server.

Mailbox agents, also called Auto Assistants, can be thought of as processes that run on the server on behalf of a user or group of users. Examples of mailbox agents include the Out Of Office Assistant and the Microsoft Exchange Anonymizer on a suggestion box public folder. These mailboxes are processed by a computer program, rather than a person.

Public folders are the bulletin board and application containers in Microsoft Exchange Server. They can be created, modified, and deleted in the Microsoft Exchange Client or from the Administrator program. Like other objects, they have properties that can be modified, such as whether the public folder is visible in the directory, what views are associated with it, what forms the public folder uses, and what Auto Assistants operate on the folder. From the Administrator program, it is possible to set the replication schedule and locations for a public folder. Microsoft Exchange Server also uses public folders to perform some of its tasks, such as moving Schedule+ free/busy information or making the offline Address Book available to users.

Mailboxes

The mailbox is the fundamental user object on a Microsoft Exchange Server. Mailboxes can be created manually through the Administrator program or in the Windows NT user manager. This can be done while the Windows NT user account is being created, or several mailboxes can be created as a batch from a data file through a directory import facility in the Administrator program. This level of automated mailbox creation reduces the cost of introducing new users or groups of users to the system.

Since mailbox objects are also network resources, the administrator can assign other system users access privileges to a mailbox. For example, you could create a mailbox called **SALES** and assign user privileges to that mailbox to all of the members of the sales department. Then you could publish the e-mail address SALES@company.com in all of the company sales brochures and ads. All mail sent to this address would be routed to the mailbox, and anyone in the sales department could access this mail and respond to it. The person getting the response would receive a mail message from SALES@company.com no matter who at the company actually responded.

You could use the same capability to lower administration over-head and speed the assignment of mailboxes to new users. Just create a set of mailboxes, such as mailbox1, mailbox2, and so on. When a new person is hired into the company or needs access to the mail system, the administrator can simply assign an existing mailbox to the new user rather than having to create a new one each time. These are just two of the ways that administration in Microsoft Exchange is geared toward saving time and energy.

Distribution Lists

Distribution lists are groups of users that can be addressed as one. A large mail system usually includes many thousands of distribution lists, often totaling more than the number of single mailboxes. These distribution lists are created through the Administrator program, using the same commands and terminology as for creating mailboxes. But unlike existing systems, the DLs in Microsoft Exchange are designed to be distributed and managed across the entire system.

For example, if I create a distribution list that contains members from other servers in my system, those members can be expanded from any server in the system rather than only being expanded at the server where the DL was created. In many shared-file mail systems, when I create a DL called SALES at Postoffice One, that DL is then distributed as an e-mail address only. If a user of Postoffice Two wanted to know who the members of the DL called SALES are, they would have to ask the administrator of Postoffice One to expand the list and tell them—by mail, fax, phone, or yelling down the hall—who the members are. Fortunately, Microsoft Exchange replicates the DL object along with all the detail information regarding members so that anyone with access privileges can see who the members are.

Management of distribution lists can be assigned, on a case-by-case basis, to owners among the user population, enabling an element of decentralized control within a centralized model. Distributed management also facilitates departmental distribution lists, allowing members to be added to a team-specific distribution list that can be controlled at the team level. It is even possible to design a system where users can add themselves to DLs and cut out the management layer altogether.

Custom Recipients

Custom recipients are addresses of users on other mail systems that appear in the Microsoft Exchange Server address book because they are used so frequently by members of the Microsoft Exchange Server system. Business partners, vendors, and others can be included as part of the Exchange directory and presented to users in a common address book that is replicated across the enterprise.

Public Folders

Public folders are user objects that exist on a Microsoft Exchange Server and are managed through the Administrator program. Public folders and their behavior are critical to the distributed information model in Microsoft Exchange. They're so important that they have their own separate information store. While they are created by the client interface, public folders become containers of stored information that must be managed the same as any other file storage system.

To refresh your memory about public folders, review Chapter 4.

With the Administrator program, you can set the access control scheme, control the storage requirements, and—most important—manage the distribution of the information contained within the folders across your organization.

Configuring Connections

The Administrator program allows you to connect Microsoft Exchange Server systems with each other and with other mail systems through X.400 and SMTP or MIME.

Single Connectivity Infrastructure for All Types of Data

This connectivity facilitates the exchange of mail messages and replication of data and directory information within a Microsoft Exchange Server organization as well as the exchange of messages with other mail systems. You are creating one topology that will be used for all communication to, from, and within your Microsoft Exchange system.

The connectivity options are configured using the Administrator program.

In the past, if you wanted your e-mail system to exist in an environment of disparate operating systems and communication protocols, you needed several levels of architecture to get it to work. It wasn't just a problem of getting the hardware and software to work together. There was also the problem that different parts of the system were administered by different people, maybe even in different departments. The network infrastructure was handled by one group, the network operating

A signifies the Administration tool. The other system uses a different tool for each part. Microsoft Exchange uses one tool for *all* parts.

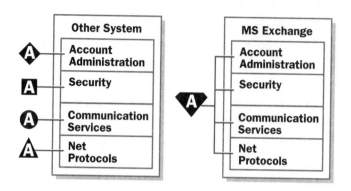

system belonged to someone else, and e-mail was assigned to that guy in the corner. The components of the system weren't designed to facilitate easy administration.

Microsoft Exchange fixes all that. Microsoft Exchange and Windows NT not only talk to each other, they actually like each other. Because they cooperate so nicely, and because their administrative tools are closely integrated, they remove a lot of the burden of setting up and operating your messaging system.

Customizable Topology

A group of Microsoft Exchange Servers that are connected together through high-speed LAN connectivity is known as a *site*. A site can be as small as one server or as large as hundreds of servers. There is no theoretical limit to the number of servers in a site. The benefit of this design is that servers can be logically grouped together. The logic in this case can be aligned along several different paths. For example, a company may already have a clearly defined administrative model. Let's say the company has a CORPORATE level and below that, SALES, MARKETING, ENGINEERING, SUPPORT and HR divisions.

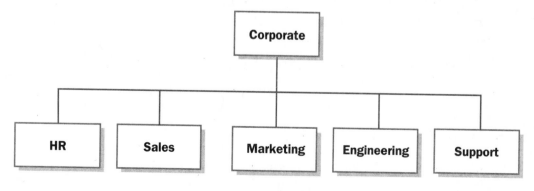

It would be easy to map Microsoft Exchange directly to this type of organization. Employees in the corporate office would be on servers in a site called CORPORATE. People in the other parts of the company would belong to other individual sites that corresponded with their organizations. The reason for this type of structure is that each site would be an entity that could be managed in a distributed fashion, and users who most often work together would be grouped together on servers. This is, of course, a somewhat simplistic example, but it illustrates the flexible architecture of Microsoft Exchange as it pertains to management and administration.

Chapters six and seven cover sites in greater detail. The point I want to make here is that the administrative model of Exchange is as flexible as the rest of the architecture and allows the maximum number of management strategies to be implemented.

Servers Added Automatically to Existing Topology

One of the major administrative headaches of a shared-file mail system is adding a new postoffice to an existing network. Generally, this requires touching each and every other postoffice in the entire enterprise to add information about the new server and the routing information to allow mail to reach this new destination. In the multiple-hub scenarios that are often designed to overcome the limitations of the technology, this job can become overwhelming.

Each Microsoft Exchange server has the ability to add itself automatically at installation time to an existing site. The setup program is pointed to an existing Windows NT server running the Microsoft Exchange Server software, and the new server is added to the site. The new server inherits a copy of the directory. Upon completion of this replication, the server is a fully qualified server in the site with full knowledge of all user containers and the routing information.

Connectivity Options in Microsoft Exchange Server

All of the transport objects that enable connectivity to other sites and other mail systems reside in the Connections Container on the Microsoft Exchange Server. These objects can be accessed directly through the Administrator program.

Chapter 6 covers these options in much more detail.

Microsoft Exchange Server connectors are installed during server setup, and they add themselves and addressing templates to the directory automatically. These connectors are viewed the same way by the Administrator program regardless of the type of connector they are.

There are a number of objects that reside in the Connections Container on a Microsoft Exchange Server that enable connectivity:

✗ **Microsoft Mail Connector** connects Microsoft Exchange Server to Microsoft Mail 3.*x*.

✗ **Internet Mail Connector** connects Microsoft Exchange Server to SMTP mail systems and is MIME compliant.

✗ **X.400 Connector** connects Microsoft Exchange Server to X.400 systems. Note that the X.400 Connector can work over different transport stacks, such as OSI TP4 (Ethernet), Eicon TP0 X.25, TCP/IP, and RAS.

✗ **Site Connector** is a special connector for expeditious intersite communication.

Because these connectors become objects in the Microsoft Exchange directory, they are replicated along with template information to all Microsoft Exchange Server computers in the organization and can be accessed by all users who have appropriate privileges.

Server processes that need configuration, such as message transfer agents, are also viewed as directory entries that have properties. All are configured and managed using the same commands in the Administrator program. The configuration of connectors, message transfer agents, mailboxes, folders, and other Microsoft Exchange Server entities all happens by viewing and modifying properties of these objects in the directory and then replicating the information via directory replication. In most cases, a change need be made only on one Microsoft Exchange Server computer and it will be replicated across the organization.

The exchange of all site-to-site information—from user-to-user messaging to team data replication to route monitoring—is handled through mail messages. This greatly simplifies the management of the rich functionality of Microsoft Exchange Server by providing a single infrastructure for administration purposes.

The Site Connector

The Site Connector enables remote procedure call (RPC) connectivity between two sites that exist on the same local area network. RPC connectivity makes the Site Connector fast, easy to configure, and efficient.

The X.400 Connector

The X.400 Connector allows for three different connectivity options—TCP/IP, TP4, and X.25—between Microsoft Exchange Server and other X.400-compliant mail systems and between two different Microsoft Exchange Server sites. The X.400 Connector not only supports both 1984 and 1988 X.400 communication but it also includes support for the latest X.400 protocol, File Transfer Body Part (FTBP). Microsoft expects to be the first vendor in the world to support this standard in a commercially available product. The X.400 Connector also enables backboning between two remote sites using a public X.400 service such as MCI® or Sprint®.

The Internet Connector

The Internet Connector allows for a variety of Internet and SMTP connectivity options including support of MIME. It also enables backboning between two remote Microsoft Exchange Server sites using the Internet or other SMTP systems.

The Dynamic RAS Connector

The Dynamic RAS Connector enables dialup connectivity between two sites.

Flexibility and Choice

You can use any combination of these four connectors when building a global infrastructure with Microsoft Exchange Server. The benefit of this choice is that it enables you to design the Exchange implementation using your existing environment.

Microsoft Exchange uses the built-in Remote Access Service that is part of Windows NT Server.

Maintenance

All of the configuration tasks we've just talked about can also be thought of as maintenance tasks, because you have to keep doing them from time to time. Here are a couple of other maintenance tasks:

✗ **Backing up** the system.

✗ **Managing** custom forms.

Online Backup of Directory and Information Store

Microsoft Exchange Server includes an enhanced version of the Windows NT Backup application. This version includes all the standard file and directory backup functionality of earlier versions as well as the ability to back up and restore Microsoft Exchange Server directories and information stores.

The enhanced version of Windows NT Backup recognizes Microsoft Exchange Server computers. When you start the application on a Microsoft Exchange Server computer, you immediately get a view of all the Microsoft Exchange Servers in your organization. If you aren't running from a Microsoft Exchange Server computer, you only need to specify the name of one server in the organization and Windows NT Backup displays the entire hierarchy of servers in your organization. The result: You can back up and restore any or all Microsoft Exchange Servers in your entire organization from one seat.

The backups are done while the server is online, so no downtime is necessary to secure your data. The Windows NT Backup program backs up the directory and information store as objects. You do not need to know which files make up the services; you only need to specify which server(s) and which components you want to back up.

Functionality is included to perform full, differential, incremental, and copy backups. Microsoft Exchange backup functionality is also included in the command-line mode of Windows NT Backup, so backup jobs can be batched and scheduled.

Storage Control and Data Replication

Microsoft Exchange Server uses two types of communication for replication of directory information:

✗ **Remote procedure** call (RPC) within a site

✗ **Mail message** across site boundaries

Replication simplifies the tasks of adding a server and new users to the organization. The new servers are automatically detected, and replication occurs as a natural part of the installation process so that new servers receive information on other users and resources in the organization. Other Microsoft Exchange Server computers are also made aware of the new server.

The Microsoft Exchange Server administrator can control many aspects of the system that relate to storage of data. For example, they can set rules for term of storage, size of storage, and other per-user attributes for server mailboxes.

The administrator can also control where replica folders are maintained. When a folder is created as a public (shared) folder, the data is stored by default on the server where the folder is created. The existence of the folder is contained in the directory and replicated across the organization, and RPC connection to the home server (the server where the folder was created) is required for data access. As a result, it can be advantageous for the administrator to position the data on servers other than the home server.

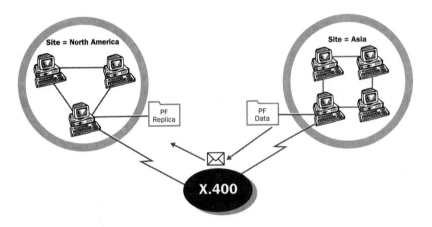

In this figure, there is no LAN network connection between Site Asia and Site North America, so replication is through a mail message carried by a public X.400 system. In this case, the server administrator decided to position a replica of the folder data created in Site Asia on a server in Site North America.

Microsoft Exchange Server administrators must also be able to monitor the operation of the Microsoft Exchange Server components in the organization. Although monitors provide much of this functionality, occasionally more is needed. To help you monitor the system, Microsoft Exchange Server supports message tracking. This feature allows an administrator to identify, follow, and document the path a message takes as it travels through the system. For example, if it is necessary to prove that a certain message was delivered, message tracking can help. Microsoft Exchange Server message tracking looks only at the headers of the messages (To, From, Date, Subject), not the message contents.

Forms Management

Many users of LAN-based messaging systems have been reluctant to introduce mail-enabled applications into their organizations because of the administration overhead of maintaining and operating these applications. Microsoft Exchange Server implements forms management directly into the Administrator program.

Forms are generally kept in the Organizational Forms Library. This library, which appears in the recipients collection when the Show Hidden command on the View menu is chosen, is a special hidden public folder. Replication of this folder, which allows users throughout the enterprise to compose and read custom forms, can be set the same as any other public folder, so distribution of forms occurs through the normal replication process and does not require an additional level of management.

Control Access to Forms

Managing access to the Organizational Forms Library is done with the Forms Administrator. Permissions can be set on the Organizational Forms Library. There are three useful roles that can be assigned to a user or group of users via a distribution list. Someone with the *owner* role may not only use forms, but may also add, modify, or delete forms from the library. A *reviewer* may use forms from the library but may not add, modify, or delete forms. Finally, someone who is assigned the role *none* is prevented from accessing the Organizational Forms Library.

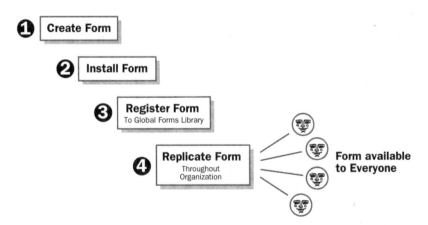

Access to the Organizational Forms Library is "all or nothing"—if you have access to the library, you have access to all forms in it. But there are ways to make forms available on a limited basis.

One way is to install the form in the personal libraries of those people who are permitted to use it. This is done with the Microsoft Exchange Client's Forms Manager.

For some applications, you may want to allow only a few people to compose forms but allow everyone to read and respond with them. The survey application that ships with Microsoft Exchange is an example. The survey application uses two forms—the Compose form, which is used for designing surveys, and the Read/Respond form. The Compose form is installed in a limited-access public folder to which only authorized survey creators have access. When a survey is sent out to the organization, the Read/Respond form is available in the Organizational Forms Library to everyone (assuming the default role in the Organizational Forms Library is set to reviewer).

Monitoring

In a distributed environment, it is essential to be aware of the status of servers everywhere in the enterprise. If one or more servers is down or performing poorly, it can adversely affect the productivity of a large number of users. As a result, administrators need to be able to quickly obtain system feedback and statistics on servers—regardless of their location.

Microsoft Exchange Server includes several monitoring tools that enable you to stay aware of the overall health of an organization-wide Microsoft Exchange system. That helps eliminate problems before they occur, and it facilitates expansion planning. It also saves time that would otherwise be spent searching for problems.

Microsoft Exchange provides a complete monitoring system with all of these capabilities:

- ✗ **Queue monitoring**

- ✗ **Server monitoring**

- ✗ **Link monitoring**

- ✗ **Performance monitoring**

- ✗ **Alerts**

- ✗ **Logging**

In addition to these tools, you can also use the Windows NT Event Viewer, Server Manager, and Performance Monitor to display information.

✗ **Event Viewer** displays event logs that record errors, security audits, and other significant events for problem diagnosis.

✗ **Performance Monitor** displays performance statistics that indicate such things as queue activity, processor utilization, memory usage, and server throughput.

✗ **Server Manager** displays usage statistics such as who is currently accessing a server or workstation and from what access point.

Queue Monitoring

The most immediate indicator of possible service interruption somewhere in your organization will be a buildup of message queues on the various services that are responsible for transferring messages. The following illustration shows how queues for multiple services on multiple servers can be monitored on a single screen.

A view of Queue Monitoring in Microsoft Exchange Server.

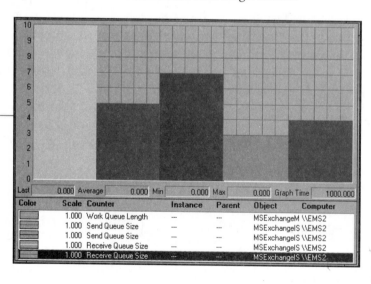

Color	Scale	Counter	Instance	Parent	Object	Computer
	1.000	Work Queue Length	---	---	MSExchangeM	\\EMS2
	1.000	Send Queue Size	---	---	MSExchangeIS	\\EMS2
	1.000	Send Queue Size	---	---	MSExchangeIS	\\EMS2
	1.000	Receive Queue Size	---	---	MSExchangeIS	\\EMS2
	1.000	Receive Queue Size	---	---	MSExchangeIS	\\EMS2

Server Monitoring

Microsoft Exchange Server's monitoring capabilities let you monitor the directory service, the MTA, and the Microsoft Exchange information store on any server in the organization. Server monitor allows you to:

✗ **Select** servers to monitor.

✗ **Configure** the services to be monitored on each server.

✗ **Specify** recipients for alert notifications.

✗ **Change** settings for monitoring frequency, notification frequency, and notification types.

You can easily build a view of a group of servers and view their status at a glance, without having to search for each server in the hierarchy. You can give Monitor Only rights to someone in your organization so they can view how the system is behaving,

All of the Microsoft Exchange Server processes are active Windows NT Server processes that can function and report on their state of operation. The processes are:

✗ **Microsoft Exchange Directory**

✗ **Microsoft Exchange Directory Synchronization**

✗ **Microsoft Exchange Information Store**

✗ **Microsoft Exchange Internet Mail Connector**

✗ **Microsoft Exchange Internet Mail Transport**

✗ **Microsoft Exchange Message Transfer Agent**

✗ **Microsoft Exchange System Attendant**

✗ **Microsoft Mail Connector Interchange**

✗ **Microsoft Mail Connector (PC) MTA**

The Microsoft Exchange System Attendant is the active process that provides for monitoring and reporting of events at the server level.

The monitoring capability enables you to set up an automatic escalation process if a service stops. For example, if the MTA service on a server stops, the monitoring system can be configured to automatically restart it or to notify specific individuals who could take appropriate action.

In this illustration of the monitor window, an upward arrow represents fully functional servers with all services running normally. A downward arrow indicates that one or more of the services on that server has stopped.

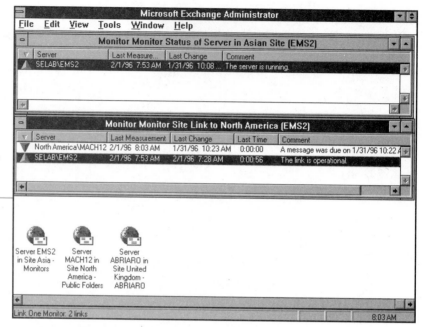

You can configure monitors with an escalation procedure that can alert a console (put up a warning dialog box) through the Windows NT Server Alerter service, restart a server, generate a mail message, or launch a custom application, such as one that would page someone.

Link Monitoring

With the increased need to communicate across geographical boundaries or with other organizations, many organizations must maintain connections to multiple sites or multiple companies. Microsoft Exchange allows you to establish a single, uniform information-sharing system that transparently spans multiple locations and allows users to exchange information anywhere, anytime.

In an extended network that spans multiple sites, it's important to be able to monitor the status of connections between these sites. Monitoring intersite links helps you to prevent problems from happening and to respond quickly when they do occur. In Microsoft Exchange, monitoring the status of inter-site connections is handled by the link monitor. You can even monitor connections to sites that do not have Microsoft messaging systems.

The link monitor checks connections by sending a test message, called a *ping,* from one server to the other servers. Those servers automatically return the message to the sender. The link monitor measures the round-trip time of the test message. You can specify notification options, frequency of pings, and thresholds of time for the round trips.

Like server monitoring, link monitoring can be configured to send alerts and warnings and to execute escalation processes if a connection fails. Setting up and managing link monitors is exactly the same as managing server monitors.

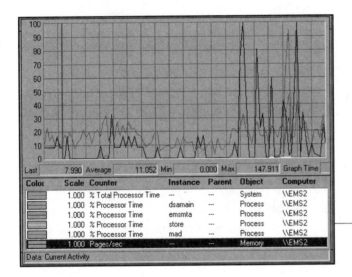

You can access this information from any Windows NT-based server on the network through the Performance Monitor's graphical interface. An easy-to-read, real-time graph like this shows performance statistics over time.

Performance Monitoring

The Windows NT operating system includes several tools that make it easier to obtain complete system statistics and information. One of these tools is the Performance Monitor, which lets administrators obtain statistics on more than 300 system characteristics, including processor, memory, disk, and network.

Because the Performance Monitor is extensible, it can be configured to provide information about the Microsoft Exchange server. The following table shows some statistics that can be accessed through the Performance Monitor.

Directory	MTA	MTA Connections	Information Store
Access permission errors	Messages/sec	Associations	Access permission errors
Browse operations/sec	Message bytes/sec	Bytes received/sec	Browse operations/sec
Reads/sec	MMI connections	Bytes sent/sec	Reads/sec
Replication updates/sec	Work queue size	Messages received/sec	Replication updates/sec
Threads in use	Connectors	Queue size	Threads in use
Writes/sec	Clients		Writes/sec

For example, you can view the number of access permission errors, browse operations, and reads/writes on the Microsoft Exchange directory and the Microsoft Exchange information store. Using this data, you can easily determine the load and activity of users requesting addresses or updating directory information.

The Performance Monitor also lets users view statistics on message throughput and connections between servers. In the following illustration, an administrator observes statistics on the directory, the MTA and the information store. This provides critical information that enables organizations to identify potential performance bottlenecks and eliminate problems before they occur. It also helps administrators to plan for future expansion.

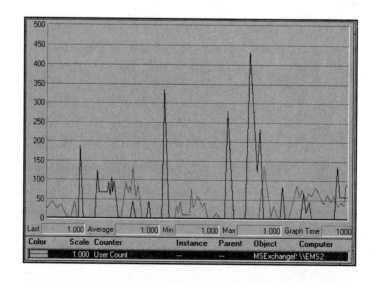

Alerts

When a system event occurs, an *alert* can be sent to designated users or administrators. For example, if the work queue size of the MTA exceeds an administrator-defined threshold, the system will send an alert to a specified administrator. Alerts are important for maintaining the availability of the system because they notify the right people about problems that have occurred or about potential problems that are likely to occur.

Microsoft Exchange includes a flexible alerting mechanism that lets you specify whether an alert should be sent as a network or e-mail alert. *Network alerts* are sent to a specific machine or user logged on to the network. They appear in real time and require immediate attention from the receiver. An *e-mail alert* is sent as a message and is received in the inbox of the designated user.

Alerts can be based on the information in the server monitor, the link monitor, or the Performance Monitor. These three system components cooperate closely with the Microsoft Exchange alert mechanism.

An escalation process can be established for any alert. For example, when a message queue reaches 1,000 messages, all administrators could be notified over the network. At one minute past this event, a specific administrator could be sent a network alert and a mail message. At five minutes past, the administrator could be paged with an installed pager gateway.

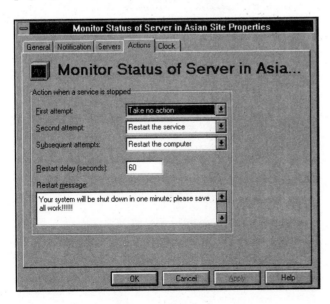

An example of an escalation process to take action when a service stops. The first step might be "take no action," the second step could be "restart the service," and the third step could be "restart the computer." A time delay for executing these actions gives each action a chance to succeed before moving to the next action.

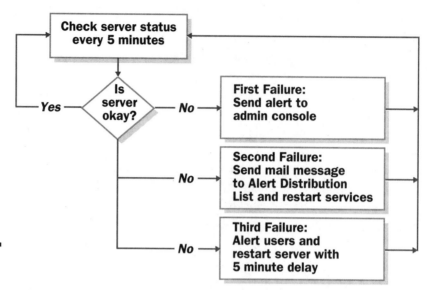

Logging

The Windows NT Server operating system offers a logging facility in which application, security, and system events can be recorded. Administrators can view these events with an easy-to-use graphical tool called the Windows NT Event Viewer. The Microsoft Exchange services utilize this facility to report information on system status.

Date	Time	Source	Category	Event	User	Computer
1/31/96	9:44:55 AM	MSExchangeMTA	Security	9297	N/A	EMS2
1/31/96	9:36:20 AM	MSExchangeMTA	Security	9297	N/A	EMS2
1/31/96	9:25:41 AM	MSExchangeMTA	Security	9297	N/A	EMS2
1/31/96	9:14:53 AM	MSExchangeMTA	Security	9297	N/A	EMS2
1/31/96	9:06:23 AM	MSExchangeMTA	Security	9297	N/A	EMS2
1/31/96	8:58:51 AM	MSExchangeMTA	Security	9297	N/A	EMS2
1/31/96	8:51:56 AM	MSExchangeSA	General	5000	N/A	EMS2
1/31/96	8:51:25 AM	MSExchangeMTA	Security	9297	N/A	EMS2
1/31/96	8:49:57 AM	MSExchangeSA	General	5000	N/A	EMS2
1/31/96	8:49:27 AM	MSExchangeDS	Security	1175	Administrator	EMS2
1/31/96	8:39:19 AM	MSExchangeMTA	Security	9297	N/A	EMS2
1/31/96	8:36:37 AM	MSExchangeAdmin	Replication Config	2022	N/A	EMS2
1/31/96	8:31:49 AM	MSExchangeMTA	Security	9297	N/A	EMS2
1/31/96	8:23:26 AM	MSExchangeMTA	Security	9297	N/A	EMS2
1/31/96	8:1(					EMS2
1/31/96	8:0(					EMS2
1/31/96	7:51					EMS2
1/31/96	7:41					EMS2
1/31/96	7:29					EMS2
1/31/96	7:20					EMS2
1/31/96	7:11					EMS2
1/31/96	7:01					EMS2
1/31/96	6:49					EMS2

Event Viewer - Application Log on \\EMS2

Log View Options Help

Event Detail

Date:	1/31/96	**Event ID:**	2022
Time:	8:36:37 AM	**Source:**	MSExchangeAdmin
User:	N/A	**Type:**	Information
Computer:	EMS2	**Category:**	Replication Configuration

Description:

Calling the knowledge consistency checker on server 'EMS2'.

There are five types of events: error, warning, information, success audit, and failure audit. Types cannot be combined; each event must be a single type. The icon on the left side of the Event Viewer screen indicates the type of event.

For an audit (security) log, only the date, time, category, user, and computer are shown.

You can easily focus on only certain types of events in the Event Viewer by applying filters. For example, you can view only failure audits. The Event Viewer also allows you to filter events based on the source of the event. Events generated by Microsoft Exchange services usually fall into these groups:

✗ **Field engineering events**

✗ **Internal configuration errors**

✗ **Directory access errors**

✗ **Internal operating system errors**

✗ **Internal processing errors**

Icon	Event Type	Meaning
🛑	Error	Significant problems, such as a loss of data or loss of functions. For example, an Error event might be logged if a service was not loaded during Windows NT startup.
①	Warning	Events that are not necessarily significant but that indicate possible future problems. For example, a Warning event might be logged when disk space is low.
ⓘ	Information	Infrequent significant events that describe successful operations of major server services. For example, when an Information Store program loads successfully, it may log an Information event.
🔒	Success audit	Audited security access attempts that were successful. For example, a user's successful attempt to log on to the system might be logged as a Success Audit event.
🔑	Failure audit	Audited security access attempts that failed. For example, if a user tried to access a network drive and failed, the attempt can be logged as a Failure Audit event.

Chapter

6

Planning Your
Microsoft Exchange World

The idea of changing to a new messaging system can be daunting, especially if you had a system in place for some time and you have users who are accustomed to its features. An image of jacking up the building and installing a new foundation comes to mind. You may be wondering whether the benefits of the new system will be worth the cost and trouble of making the switch.

Migrating to a new system may not be fun, exactly, but it doesn't have to be painful. With careful planning and the right tools, others have done it, and you can, too.

Can I Have It?

There are two basic questions about Microsoft Exchange that you need to answer for yourself:

1 Is it what I need?

2 Can I have it?

I've spent the last four chapters giving you data for figuring out the answer to the first question. You must have come up with at least a tentative, qualified "yes," or you wouldn't be reading this chapter.

Now for the second question. Maybe I should rephrase it this way: "Will the costs (in terms of money, disruption to operations, strain on the IS organization, user acceptance, training, support, and so on) of acquiring and installing Microsoft Exchange be acceptable?"

I can't address all the financial costs in this book, because there are too many variables involved. But I can offer plenty of information in this chapter and the next to help answer the rest of the question. I'll cover the steps that our experience has shown us are essential for planning and implementing a new messaging system. Microsoft has developed a set of 12 steps that, if followed, will lead to a successful implementation. I will also provide hints along the way as to the potential "gotchas."

This chapter looks at the messaging system across the entire organization. In the next chapter, we'll look more closely at what goes on inside an individual site. In Chapter Nine, you'll hear from a number of adopters of Microsoft Exchange about their experiences with the product.

Strategy: Shotgun or Wither on the Vine?

There are two high-level strategies for implementing a new messaging system:

✗ **Immediate migration**

✗ **Coexistence**

Some people refer to immediate migration as "single-phase migration." I call it the "shotgun strategy." Whatever you call it, in this strategy, all users are switched over to the new system as quickly as possible. This is the simpler approach, and it might be the right choice for your organization if:

✗ **There is little** or no data to move from the old system.

✗ **All hardware** and software required to run Microsoft Exchange Server and Client are in place.

✗ **The group** responsible for Microsoft Exchange implementation has the resources to move everyone at once.

The second strategy is to move the new system gradually, in several phases spread out over time. That's called the "multiphase migration" or "coexistence" approach. (I call it the "wither-on-the-vine" strategy because, eventually, the old system "dies off" and is replaced by the new one.)

The chief difference with this strategy is that there is a period where both the old and new systems will be in use. That adds a level of complication: figuring out how to get the systems to work together. During the period of coexistence, you must support both systems, maintaining directories and accommodating feature differences across the two systems.

However, this might be the better choice for your organization if:

✗ **Not all** departments can upgrade at the same time.

✗ **You need** to free up hardware in early phases for redeployment during later phases.

✗ **It would require** too much system down-time to move everyone at once.

The main point is, no matter which strategy you choose, planning carefully will be the key element contributing to the success of the move to Microsoft Exchange.

A Step-by-Step Approach

The migration team at Microsoft has broken the planning and design process down into twelve steps. Depending on your circumstances, you may approach these steps more or less formally. Large organizations may need to spend an appreciable amount of time on each of them, and may even have to break some down into sub-steps. Smaller organizations can probably work faster and may be able to combine some steps. However you do it, you must work your way through all of the steps. Skipping a step is an invitation to trouble.

The twelve steps are:

Step 1: Assess user needs	What types of applications and services will your users require?
Step 2: Identify your company's geographic profile	Is your company in one city, one country, or is it worldwide?
Step 3: Assess the underlying network	What is the available network type and bandwidth? What protocols, transports, and operating systems are being used?
Step 4: Choose a Microsoft Windows NT domain topology	What is the appropriate Windows NT domain topology for your organization?
Step 5: Determine the number of sites and site boundaries	Based on factors such as network bandwidth, network traffic, cost, performance, and the Windows NT domain model, what is the appropriate number of sites and appropriate size for each site in your organization?
Step 6: Define the naming conventions	What naming scheme will you use for your organization, sites, servers, mailboxes, distribution lists, public folders, and custom recipients?
Step 7: Link sites	What type of link will you use to connect sites? How will you connect your sites?
Step 8: Plan sites	How many servers will each site have?

Step 9: Plan servers	What are the hardware requirements for each server?
Step 10: Plan connections to other systems	What type of connectivity to other systems do users need?
Step 11: Validate and optimize the design	How do you validate and optimize your design?
Step 12: Plan the roll out	What steps are required to implement the plan?

A Microsoft Exchange Server organization consists of Microsoft Exchange Server computers that are grouped together into sites. Designing a Microsoft Exchange Server topology is the process of conceiving and drawing plans for the number of sites, site boundaries, number of servers per site, and the links between them.

Designing a Microsoft Exchange Server organization—one with a logical number of sites, each of an appropriate size and connected by adequate links—requires a detailed analysis and basic understanding of a number of factors, including the available network bandwidth, type of physical links, amount of internetwork traffic, types of network transports and protocols, operating systems in use, and costs. Much of this information is not normally within the purview of the messaging system personnel. Right from the very early stages of planning, you should be thinking in terms of a team rather than an individual. If you are a smaller company and you do not expect your implementation to grow beyond one server, you will still find yourself with many of these same concerns, only on a smaller scale. You may also find yourself with several hats to wear.

Dun & Bradstreet®

Dun & Bradstreet® Case Study

To illustrate the process of planning for the deployment of Microsoft Exchange Server, I've included excerpts from a case study that describes Dun & Bradstreet's experience.

Dun & Bradstreet needed a stable e-mail platform that would scale to an entire organization. They also wanted a platform they

(continues)

(continued)

could use to develop internal applications and automate routine business processes. They chose Microsoft Exchange Server to become their standard e-mail server for their Corporate and Shared Services centers and recommended Microsoft Exchange Server to various associated divisions.

Dun & Bradstreet operates in a distributed environment. They require strict security restrictions between departments. Individual business divisions require administrative control and access to divisional resources. These divisions also maintain their own IS departments. Dun & Bradstreet requires their messaging system, therefore, to reflect both their divisional security structure, by providing a secure workgroup environment, as well as their corporate messaging structure, by providing fast, reliable communication across the entire organization.

Step 1: Assess User Needs

The first step of implementing Microsoft Exchange Server is to identify the types of applications and services your users require, such as e-mail, scheduling, public folders, and connections to the Internet. After identifying user needs, you can associate them with the features available in Microsoft Exchange Server. You can then use this data to determine how to categorize users; what software, hardware, and training they need; how much server disk space they need; what kind of public folders need to be implemented; how much traffic they'll generate (based on message volume); and so on.

For instance, if you expect your users to be heavy users of public folders, you may want to dedicate specific Microsoft Exchange Servers to act as public folder/bulletin board servers. That makes it easier to manage and back up public folders and also provides better performance to those users who just access the e-mail facilities of Microsoft Exchange Server.

Step 2: Identify Your Company's Geographic Profile

The geographic profile includes all locations where your company has facilities, whether they are clustered in a small region or dispersed over a large area. Use a map or diagram to identify the geographic profile for your company. This is useful as a visual aid for identifying physical locations, types of users at each location, and available network connections.

Microsoft Exchange is flexible enough to allow you to map your Microsoft Exchange hierarchy to your geographic profile. There are other factors that must be taken into account in order to determine if this is the best way to organize Microsoft Exchange. By the end of this chapter, you will have all the clues you need to determine that.

Step 3: Assess the Underlying Network

The underlying network is one of the most important factors affecting your Microsoft Exchange Server topology. As a result, it is extremely important to understand all aspects of the network. Site boundaries, site links, message routing, directory replication, and system administration are some of the areas affected by network topology. The key elements are:

- ✗ **Size**
- ✗ **Bandwidth**
- ✗ **Type and links**
- ✗ **Traffic patterns**
- ✗ **Transports and protocols**

Network Size

A Microsoft Exchange Server organization can span networks of different sizes: a single local area network (LAN) that connects a few computers for sharing files and printers; a mixed network of LANs that connects computers company-wide; a metropolitan-area network (MAN) that connect LAN segments within a campus, industrial park, or city; or a wide-area network (WAN) that links all the computers of a global company.

Designing and configuring networks of different sizes requires different considerations. For example, for a large network, you may need to set up multiple sites. You should consider how to move data—directories and public folders— between sites over WAN links. You need to configure the organization to provide the information and messaging services (such as local access to public folders) at the LAN level, where users create and receive information. On the other hand, a small company with a small network may have just one or very few sites, so it may not require considerations such as how data will be replicated over a WAN link.

Chapter Seven goes into more detail about how to assess your network.

Network Bandwidth

Network bandwidth is the data transmission capacity of a network link. Within a site, servers generally require higher-bandwidth connections. Between sites, Microsoft Exchange Servers communicate via store-and-forward e-mail connections, which can require less bandwidth. When configuring links between sites, an awareness of the available bandwidth will enable you to choose the most appropriate site link (or links), set directory and public folder replication schedules, and establish costs.

Net Available Bandwidth

Net available bandwidth is the bandwidth that is left after other applications have taken what they need. The net available bandwidth—not the total available bandwidth—on a network link between two servers is the decisive factor for determining whether servers can be placed at the same site.

For example, if you have another network application that must coexist with Microsoft Exchange Server, you should be aware of bandwidth consumption by that application. Network protocols that require interactive acknowledgments or broadcasts can also contribute to bandwidth consumption.

Microsoft Exchange is inherently efficient in its use of bandwidth. As I stated previously, using remote-procedure calls (RPC) to generate action at the server on behalf of the client means that far less data needs to be transferred between the workstation and the server. There are also benefits in using RPC instead of file transfers from server to server.

In Microsoft Exchange, there are five types of events that require bandwidth on the network:

✗ **E-mail** message traffic

✗ **System** message traffic

✗ **Replication** of directory information

✗ **Offline** folder synchronization

✗ **Replication** of public folder data

Remote Procedure Calls

All Microsoft Exchange services communicate through remote procedure calls. RPCs can use named pipes, NetBIOS, or Windows Sockets to communicate with remote systems. This allows servers to communicate with each other efficiently and independently of the type of network. RPC supports the following network protocols:

✗ IPX/SPX through Microsoft NWLink

✗ NetBEUI

✗ TCP/IP

You should also take into account the bandwidth that could be consumed if users attach large voice, video, and image files to their messages. Messages themselves consume little bandwidth compared to these attachments.

Connection Cost

To provide some guidelines and examples of bandwidth costs, this shows the relative costs of some common network links in the United States. The cost is based on bandwidth and availability. For example, both the dial-up PPP (point-to-point protocol) lines and dedicated PPP lines have the same bandwidth (up to the speed of the modem used.) However, dedicated PPP lines are more expensive because they are available 24 hours a day.

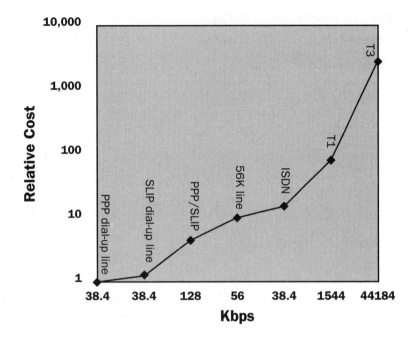

Network Type and Links

I said earlier in this book that a site is a logical grouping of Microsoft Exchange servers. It's up to you to figure out the best way to arrange sites. Network type and links are critical factors in that determination. You can think of Microsoft Exchange sites mapping onto the existing network topology based upon the number and type of links.

Characteristics of Common Network Links

The following tables list the most common network links in three categories: low- to medium-bandwidth, medium- to high-bandwidth, and very-high-bandwidth. Generally, sites should be designed so their servers can connect through links in the medium- to high- and very-high-bandwidth range. Be aware that some of these links are available in ranges of bandwidth rather than just at a discrete bandwidth. For example, frame relay links come in a range from 64 to 512 kilobits per second (Kbps). If you have a 64 Kbps frame relay connection between two servers, you may want to consider placing them in different sites. On the other hand, if they are connected at 512 Kbps, consider placing them in the same site.

Low- to medium-bandwidth connections

Network link	Bandwidth	Common use	Description
Dial-up phone line	2.4, 19.2, to 38.4 Kbps	Single user, remote connections to LANs and WANs	Copper, voice-grade wire. Bandwidths of up to 38.4 Kbps are possible with high-speed modems configured with the same encoding and compression technology on both ends.
X.25 (leased lines)	19.2, 56, and 64 Kbps	WANs	Provides permanent connections between LAN segments. X.25 is an international standard for sending packets over public data networks. Access to an X.25 network is through leased or dial-up lines.
Frame relay (leased lines)	64 to 512 Kbps	WANs	Provides permanent connections between LAN segments. Frame relay is a method for sending packets over private and public data networks. It provides better performance than X.25 because it reduces some of the overhead used in X.25. Sprint, CompuServe, Tymenet, Williams Telecommunications, and other carriers offer frame relay services.
Fractional T-1	64 Kbps	WANs and redundant links	A fraction of a T-1 line. Fractional T-1 allows people to buy T-1 service in 64 Kbps channels at an affordable price. Channels can be added to expand band width up to a full T-1 line.

Medium- to high-bandwidth connections

Network link	Bandwidth	Common use	Description
Integrated Services Digital Network (ISDN)	128 to 150 Kbps	LANs and WANs	High-speed, digital dial-up lines based on the Integrated Services Digital Network standard. Personal computer users benefit the most from these lines. They provide reasonably fast connections to data services, databases, and international networks.
T-1	1.544 Mbps	High-use WAN links	A high-quality digital line that runs over two twisted copper wires. T-1 is commonly used to build private voice and data networks. Its bandwidth of 1.544 Mbps can be divided into twenty-four 64 Kbps channels, each carrying one voice or data transmission.
ArcNet	2.5 Mbps	LANs	ArcNet links have a star or bus topology and use a token-passing access method with coaxial cable.
Token Ring	4 or 16 Mbps	LANs	Token ring links have star and ring topologies and use a token-passing access method with shielded or unshielded twisted-pair cable.
Thin Ethernet	10 Mbps	Single LANs	Thin Ethernet links have a linear bus topology and use a carrier-sense multiple-access with collision-detection (CSMA/CD) access method with thin or twisted-pair cable.
Thick Ethernet	10 Mbps	Multiple LANs	Same as thin Ethernet but with thick cable.
Fiber optic	10 to 100 Mbps	High-use MAN links	Fiber optic cable that usually follows the Fiber Distributed Data Interface (FDDI) standard. It is used for backbone connections in MANs. Large networks with many LAN segments and heavy traffic benefit from FDDI fiber optic cable.

Very-high-bandwidth connections

Network link	Bandwidth	Common use	Description
Satellite connections	128 Kbps to 1.544 Mbps	Wireless WANs (many of them use backup connections)	Wireless connections that provide global data links. AT&T Tridom®, Comsat General Corporation, and GTE Spacenet Corporation offer satellite links.
Microwave connections	1.544 Mbps	Wireless LANs	Wireless connections that use waves at the microwave frequency.
T-3	44.184 Mbps	High-use WAN links	Similar to T-1 but it has higher bandwidth and can be divided into 28 T-1 channels.
Synchronous Optical Network (SONET)	51.8 Mbps to 2.5 GBps	WANs	High-speed, fiber-optic connections defined by the SONET set of standards. SONET is an underlying transport network (similar to Ethernet) with a maximum band width that is equivalent to 48 T-3 lines.
Asynchronous Transfer Mode (ATM)	100, 200, and 400 Mbps up to 9.6 GBps	WANs LAN-to-WAN connections	Data transfer technology that provides a way to simultaneously send packets of information from many sources across a high-speed line, where they are reassembled and transferred to each destination point. ATM supports voice and video. ATM can use existing fractional T-1, T-1, T-3, or SONET as its physical medium.

Network Traffic Patterns

Network traffic is the amount of data that travels through a link. Network traffic patterns are predictable trends of data flow through a link over a period of time. Knowing or predicting network traffic patterns through a link allows you to determine whether the total available bandwidth will be enough to handle bursts of traffic during heavy use of the network.

If network traffic exceeds the available network bandwidth, client/server response becomes unpredictable. To prevent this, monitor network traffic by measuring the network bandwidth utilization (how close a network link is to full capacity) and total packets per second (how close bridges and routers are to full capacity.)

Monitoring network traffic requires specialized tools such as dedicated network monitoring software (such as Microsoft System Management Server) or a packet sniffer. On small networks, the Windows NT Performance Monitor can be used to monitor certain counters to get an idea of the traffic generated by certain processes. Here are examples of some useful counters.

This counter	Measures	Use it to estimate
Bytes total/sec	The number of bytes per second that each server sends and receives.	The overall network traffic to that server. If it is close to the maximum available bandwidth for the link, the link is nearing its capacity, and you should add a new segment to the network.
Messages/sec (Microsoft Exchange MTA)*	The number of P-1 messages processed by the MTA per second.	The amount of traffic generated by message flow (number of messages.)
Message bytes/sec (Microsoft Exchange MTA)*	The content size of P-1 messages in bytes processed by the MTA per second.	The amount of traffic based on message size.
Reads/sec (Microsoft Exchange DS)*		The amount of traffic generated by directory replication.

Note: The three counters marked * become Windows NT Performance Monitor variables after Microsoft Exchange Server is installed.

Chapter Three covers the ability of the Microsoft Exchange Client to work in remote locations and then come online with the server via a slow link.

Network Transports and Protocols

You should know what type of network transports you have so you can configure the site links appropriately.

For example, to configure Site Connectors in the Administrator program, you do not need to know about or configure network transports because all communications happen with remote procedure calls (RPCs) rather than mail messages. To configure the X.400 Connector, on the other hand, you have to know about the network transport because it only works over TP0/X.25, TP4/CLNP or TCP/IP transport and network protocols.

Another consideration is support for remote clients, for which Remote Access Service (RAS) can be used. RAS supports PPP, which enables any client to use TCP/IP, IPX, or NetBEUI. RAS clients can dial in using standard telephone lines, a modem, or a modem pool.

Network Type and Links

Dun & Bradstreet maintains two high-bandwidth, token-ring LANs at their Corporate Center and their Shared Services Center. These two LANs are connected by T-1 leased lines and are standardized on TCP/IP. The rest of the company is composed of distributed, semi-autonomous divisions. Each of these divisions maintains its own network and Information Services staff. They are often linked to the corporate network by low-bandwidth or dial-up connections.

Step 4: Choose a Microsoft Windows NT Domain Topology

Microsoft Exchange Server relies on Windows NT security to authenticate users and Microsoft Exchange Server services. It is important to choose a Windows NT domain model (or study the existing model, if there is one) carefully because:

✗ **It is very difficult** to change a domain structure once it is implemented.

✗ **Site boundaries depend** on the domain structure in place. If sites span more than one domain, these domains must trust each other so users and Microsoft Exchange Server services can be authenticated across the site.

✗ **You should be aware** of how user accounts and global groups from one domain can be used in another domain, if at all.

Domains and Trust Relationships

A *domain* is a group of servers that share common security policy and user account databases. A user needs only one account to have access to all servers in the domain. The domain can contain single or multiple Windows NT Server computers, as well as other types of servers (such as Novell NetWare servers) and clients (such as Windows NT Workstation, Windows 95, Windows 3.x, and MS-DOS-based clients.)

You can simplify account management by establishing trust relationships between domains. A *trust relationship* is the link between two domains that enables a user with an account in one domain to access resources on another domain. Users from the trusted domain can be given rights and permissions to objects in the trusting domain just as if they were members of the trusting domain. When domain A trusts domain B, it allows domain B to return to domain A a list of global groups and information about users who are authenticated in domain B.

Microsoft Windows NT Server Domain Controllers

Within each domain, there is a class of Windows NT Server computers that authenticate logon requests: the domain controllers.

Primary Domain Controller (PDC)

The PDC stores and maintains the security database for the domain. All changes to the security database must be done on the copy stored on the PDC. There can be only one PDC per domain.

Backup Domain Controller (BDC)

The BDC also stores copies of the domain's security database and serves as a substitute when a PDC goes down. If this occurs, one of the backup domain controllers can be promoted to PDC. Because the PDC replicates all changes to the backup domain controllers automatically, the BDCs will have an up-to-date database, and the domain will continue to function.

For more complete information on planning your Windows NT Server domains, see the Microsoft Windows NT Planning document on the Introducing Microsoft Exchange CD.

Choose a Microsoft Windows NT Domain Model

There are four Windows NT domain models: single-domain model, complete-trust model, single-master-domain model, and multiple-master-domain model. The appropriate model depends on your administrative resources and the size of your network. If a domain model is already in place, determine which one, how it is structured, how trust relationships are set up, why that model was chosen, and where the domain controllers are located.

Single-Domain Model

The single-domain model is the simplest Windows NT security domain model. As its name implies, the network in this model has only one domain in which all Windows NT users are created. No trust relationships are necessary. This model is best for organizations with smaller numbers of users in which trust among the organizational groups (departments, divisions, and so on) is not an issue. However, if you anticipate growth in your organization, you might want to consider the multiple master model.

> **YourCo, Inc.**
> All user accounts,
> global and
> local groups

Single Domain Model

Advantages	Disadvantages
Best model for companies with few users and resources.	Poor performance if the domain has too many users and groups.
Centralized management of Windows NT user accounts.	No grouping of users into departments.
No trust relationships to administer.	No grouping of resources.
Windows NT local groups should be defined only once.	Browsing is slow if the domain has a large number of servers.

Complete-Trust Domain Model

The Windows NT complete-trust domain is a good model for companies that want to distribute management of users and domains among different departments. In this model, every domain on the network trusts every other domain.

This model can support up to 40,000 users for each domain. So, for example, if you have three domains, it can support up to 120,000 users. Because each domain has full control over its own user accounts, this model works well for organizations without centralized management. It is, however, harder to ensure the integrity of global groups the other domains might use.

Complete-Trust Domain Model

Advantages	Disadvantages
Best for companies with no central MIS department.	Not practical for companies with central MIS departments.
Scalable to networks with any of users.	Very large number of trust number relationships to manage.
Each domain has full control its user accounts and resources.	Each domain must depend on over other domains to not put inappropriate users into global groups.
Both resources and user accounts are grouped into departments.	

Single-Master Domain Model

The single-master domain model is for companies where the network needs to be split into domains for organizational purposes. Each organizational group can manage its own resources, but user accounts and global groups need to be defined in the master domain. This model can support up to 40,000 users, all in the master domain.

Only the servers in the master domain have copies of the network user accounts. There should be at least one extra server running Windows NT Server as a backup domain controller in the master domain. Then, if the domain controller fails, the other can take over, and the network can keep running.

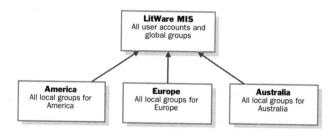

Single-Master Domain Model

Advantages	Disadvantages
Best choice for companies that don't have too many users and must have shared resources split into groups.	Poor performance if the master domain has too many users and global groups.
User accounts can be centrally managed.	Local groups must be defined in each domain where they are to be used.
Resources are grouped logically.	
Department domains can have their own administrators to manage the resources in the department.	
Global groups are defined only once (in the master domain).	

Multiple-Master Domain Model

This domain model is for companies that are organized by groups, departments, or locations and want centralized administration. Because it is the most scalable model, it is good for organizations that anticipate substantial growth. It can support up to 40,000 users in each master domain.

This model is organized in two tiers. The first tier contains the master domains that trust each other. The second-tier domains trust the master domains, but the master domains do not trust them. Because the master domains trust each other, only one copy of each user account is needed, but accounts are split among the master domains.

The administrative requirements for this model can be considerably greater than the other models. Local and global groups may have to be defined several times, and there are several trust relationships to manage.

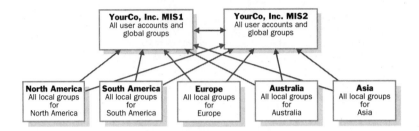

Multiple-Master Domain Model

Advantages	Disadvantages
Best choice for companies with many users and a centralized MIS department.	Both local and global groups may have to be defined multiple times.
Scalable to networks with any number of users.	More trust relationships to manage.
Resources are grouped logically.	Not all user accounts located in one domain.
Department domains can have their own administrators to manage the resources in the department.	

Microsoft NT Domain Topology

Dun & Bradstreet chose to implement a variation of the multiple-master domain architecture within their corporate network to facilitate the enforcement of their security model. This architecture consists of configuring their Microsoft NT Server domains in two tiers. The first tier consists of two master user account domains: STSNA and DNBCC. STSNA contains the user accounts for the employees located at the Shared Services Center in Pennsylvania. DNBCC contains the user accounts for the employees located at Dun & Bradstreet's Corporate Center in New York and Connecticut. No trust relationships were established between the two user account domains. This prevents user accounts from one domain being validated in the other.

The second tier consists of five resource domains. Three of these are regionally defined local resource domains for Pennsylvania, New York, and Connecticut; the other two are public resource domains. STSPA and STSPUB, the local and public resource domains for the Shared Services Division, maintain one-way trust relationships to the STSNA user account domain. User accounts defined in the STSNA domain can access the resources defined in the STSPA and STSPUB resource domains. The remaining three resource domains, DNBNY, DNBCT (local resource domains), and DNBCCPUB (public resource domain), maintain one-way trust relationships to the DNBCC user account domain, which allows users at the Corporate Center access to their regional and divisional resources.

This two-tier domain architecture allows user accounts and groups to be created and administered at the corporate level, while access restrictions and permissions to resources can be defined and managed at the divisional and local levels.

Dun & Bradstreet configured two additional resource domains—DNBSTS and DNBMAIL—to support their messaging system. These resource domains differ from the divisional and regional resource domains in that they maintain one-way trust relationships with both of the user account domains as well as a two-way trust relationship with each other. These trust relationships allow any user with a valid account in one of the two user account domains access to the messaging system. The two-way trust relationship between the two messaging domains facilitates centralized administration of the messaging system.

(continues)

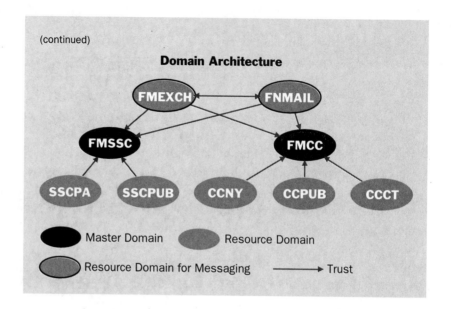

(continued)

Domain Architecture

Choose the Domain Controllers
Consider these factors when choosing your domain controllers:

Number of Domain Controllers
Configure at least one server per domain as a backup domain controller. For a more robust backup mechanism, it's a good idea to have several backup domain controllers in a domain.

Microsoft Exchange Server Computer as a Domain Controller
There is no requirement for a Microsoft Exchange Server computer to be a domain controller. You may decide to host Microsoft Exchange Server on your domain controller based on the type and number of servers you have available and on cost considerations. For performance reasons, however, you may not want to install Microsoft Exchange Server on the primary domain controller.

Physical Location
Make sure your domain controllers have reliable network connections to the servers in the domain. If a domain has servers at different physi-

cal locations connected by a WAN link, each location should have at least one backup domain controller.

Mapping Domains and Sites

Sites can map to domains in different ways. They can map one-to-one, or a site can span several domains, provided these domains trust each other.

There are no special rules to map sites to domains in the four domain models, and it is not necessary to map all existing domains to your sites. For example, if you have a complete trust model, you could place all servers in one of the domains or spread them among all domains. In the master- and multiple-master domain models, you could place all your servers in a single second-tier domain, in a single first-tier domain, or spread them across several first-tier domains. Your choice will depend on how you want to structure administration of the domains and the Microsoft Exchange Server computers that reside in them.

For more information on Windows NT Server and domain planning, see the Windows NT domain planning tool that is part of the Microsoft Exchange Site Modeling tool on the Introducing Microsoft Exchange CD. Also see the Windows NT Resource Kit available from Microsoft Press.

Step 5: Determine the Number of Sites and Site Boundaries

Determining the number of sites and the site boundaries are interrelated processes.

Define Site Boundaries

There are several factors that determine where to draw site boundaries. Some factors are conditions that all Microsoft Exchange Server computers must satisfy in order to be placed in the same site. Others are factors that, while not mandatory, should be considered when

It is important to plan the number of sites and their boundaries very carefully. Once you have created your sites, it is difficult to split or join other sites. Even moving users from one site to another is not a trivial task.

you are planning your site boundaries. These factors include administration, connection cost, security, and performance. There are also less tangible organizational issues that you should consider, such as grouping users who work together in a single site.

Necessary Conditions

Here is an overview of what is required at each Microsoft Exchange Server site.

For more information about remote procedure calls, see the RPC white paper included on the Introducing Microsoft Exchange CD.

Synchronous Remote Procedure Call Connectivity

All Microsoft Exchange Server computers within a site must be able to communicate through synchronous RPCs, the mechanism by which the servers exchange messages and directory information within a site.

A site's physical boundaries can be as large as you like, but they cannot span a connection that does not support synchronous RPCs. For example, if you have a large network spanning North and South America but the network connection between North America and South America does not support synchronous RPC connections (for example, it uses serial dial-up communication via modems), you must define separate sites for North America and South America and have e-mail connectivity between them.

Security

Microsoft Exchange Server uses the Microsoft Windows NT security services to:

- ✗ **Authenticate** servers with one another.

- ✗ **Authenticate** a user's request to log on.

- ✗ **Control** who can access which objects (such as mailboxes and distribution lists).

- ✗ **Determine** which actions an individual can take on an object.

- ✗ **Determine** which events are audited.

Microsoft Windows NT security must be set up in a way that allows the Microsoft Exchange Servers within a site to authenticate each other. This is necessary because all server services within a site must run under the same security context. This is also an administrative consideration. Account access to Microsoft Exchange servers will be a critical factor in determining which accounts have administrative privileges and can administer Microsoft Exchange.

Permanent Connections

Your network must have permanent—as opposed to periodic—LAN connections between Microsoft Exchange Server computers in a site. These permanent connections include LANs, leased lines, and some types of WAN links. Periodic connections are connections that are not available all the time, such as a dial-up connection through a modem.

Often, such connections are used for distant geographic locations that you connect to only a few times a day.

High Network Bandwidth

All servers within a site should be connected through a network link with relatively high bandwidth. The threshold for determining high network bandwidth is somewhat arbitrary. The bandwidth must be enough to handle the volume of data being transferred such as messages, directory replication, and public folder replication. For some installations, links below 56 Kbps may be sufficient, but the threshold for your installation may be higher if you have large volumes of data.

The bandwidth available to connect two or more Microsoft Exchange Server computers will fall into one of the following categories:

Category
No permanent connectivity. The connection is not available full-time and must be established periodically, usually through a modem dial-up line. Servers in this category must be placed in separate sites.
A permanent connection, such as a leased line, with a speed of 56 Kbps or less. Servers in this category generally should be placed in separate sites. This is not a requirement, however. To make your decision, use the performance and cost factors described later in this chapter.
A permanent connection, such as a leased line, with a speed of 128 Kbps to 512 Kbps. At this line speed, servers may or may not be placed in separate sites. To make your decision, use the performance and cost factors described later in this chapter.
A permanent connection, such as a leased line, with a speed of 1 Mbps. At this line speed, performance is less of a concern. Whether you place the server in a separate site depends on other factors, which are described later in this chapter.
Full connectivity; a logical LAN with no bandwidth restrictions. This server should generally be placed in the same site as the other servers to which it can connect.

If you are getting the impression that bandwidth is important, you are correct. In my 20-plus years of networking experience, there has been one constant: No matter how much bandwidth you have, you will always need more.

Other Factors

Site Administration

Many Microsoft Exchange Server administrative services are configured automatically within a site, making it easier for you to administer servers that are grouped within a single site. As a result, you should consider configuring your sites to cover as many servers as possible. Administration is only one factor to consider, however. If your planning indicates it would be better to have more, smaller sites, that should be the guiding principle that you use.

Line Charges

Microsoft Exchange Server computers that are connected over a line with charges based on the amount of data that is sent should be placed in separate sites. This allows you to minimize costs by minimizing the amount of information that is shared by those servers.

For more information on performance, refer to the white paper that is included on the Introducing Microsoft Exchange CD.

Performance

Performance is another important factor to consider when drawing your site boundaries. Performance is a large enough topic to get its own section later in this chapter.

Directory Replication

Within a site, replication is multimaster and event-driven. All Microsoft Exchange Server computers exchange all of their directory information with each other automatically. When drawing site boundaries, consider how directory replication affects cost and performance.

The cost of replicating directory information between two servers is determined by the cost of maintaining the link between those servers and the cost of sending data over that link. If two Microsoft Exchange Server computers are connected through a slow link, consider placing the servers in separate sites so you can control when directory information is replicated. You can then configure directory replication between these two sites so that the slow link is used only occasionally, minimizing cost and improving performance.

Organizational Considerations

In addition to the technology issues, you should consider organizational factors when planning your sites. Grouping people who work together on the same servers and sites will improve overall performance of the system, reduce network traffic, and reduce resource utilization. For example, if members of the research team are located at different sites, you may have to replicate public folder information between the two sites. However, if the research team can be hosted on a single server, replication would not be required.

Determine the Number of Sites

The number of sites will be determined by the site boundaries. With Microsoft Exchange, the number of sites is not a critical factor. That is, if you construct optimum site boundaries, giving due consideration to the factors described above, you will wind up with some number of sites. While having fewer sites will result in less work in configuration and administration, that by itself is not sufficient reason to combine sites.

The overriding goal is to make the overall system as efficient as possible. If splitting a site or combining two sites would improve the overall scheme, then do it.

Step 6: Define the Naming Conventions

Planning the naming conventions for your organization before you install and configure the system is important. Meaningful and logical names make it easy both to use and to administer the system. They also minimize rework caused by unplanned name changes. Names should be mapped to items that are not easily changed because names in Microsoft Exchange, once established, are difficult to change.

When you're planning your naming conventions, consider points such as these:

1 Will the names need to be compatible with existing messaging systems or other applications? Those systems might have more restrictive rules for names (particularly for length) than Microsoft Exchange.

2 Will your organization expand someday beyond the country you're now in? If so, will the names you choose be appropriate in other countries? For example, a site called "US Sales" might prove awkward if you need to expand it to include European operations.

3 Does your organization change frequently? If it does, you might not want to use specific organizational names for sites, because they might change. Consider using more generic names such as "sales" or "engineering."

4 Is there a possibility you might move your business operations? If so, specific geographic names (such as the Amsterdam site) might prove to be a problem when you do.

This isn't an exhaustive list; I'm just trying to point out the kinds of considerations that go into a naming convention. The key is, don't box yourself into a convention that will prove unworkable in the future.

Each object in the Microsoft Exchange Server directory is uniquely identified by a name (the distinguished name), and you must provide the site and organization names when you install and configure Microsoft Exchange Server. A good naming strategy is one that makes it easy for you to add and identify sites, servers, gateways, connectors, users, and all of the other objects. You can base your naming conventions on geography, company structure, building numbers, and so on.

The Microsoft Exchange Server directory name has three levels:

1 Organization

2 Site name

3 Microsoft Exchange Server recipient

(There may be more than one recipient container name in a user's distinguished name, depending on the organization of the Microsoft Exchange Server system.)

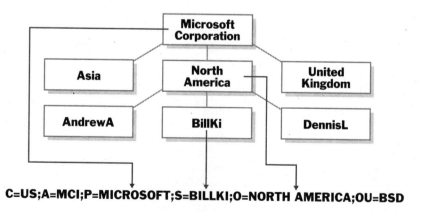

C=US;A=MCI;P=MICROSOFT;S=BILLKI;O=NORTH AMERICA;OU=BSD

Microsoft Exchange Server derives X.400 originator/recipient (O/R) names. Here's how the Microsoft Exchange name elements map to the X.400 name elements:

Microsoft Exchange name elements	X.400 name (label)
	Country (C)
	Administrative management domain—ADMD (A)
Site name	Private management domain—PRMD (P)
Organization	Organization (O)
	Organizational units (OU1, OU2, OU3, and OU4)
	Common name (CN)
	Generation qualifier (Q)
	Initials (I)
Microsoft Exchange Server recipient.	Surname (S)
	Given name (G)
	Domain-defined attributes (DDA)

Even though country is not a Microsoft Exchange Server name element, Microsoft Exchange Server supplies the country for the X.400 name.

As an alternative to the X.400 name derived by Microsoft Exchange, you can explicitly associate any legal X.400 name with any user. The X.400 name can be completely unrelated to the user's Microsoft Exchange name elements. That's particularly handy if your users already have X.400 names and you don't want to have to change them.

The X.400 name must include the country and ADMD (which can be blank) and at least one other element. If the X.400 name derived by Microsoft Exchange Server may not be sufficient to distin-

Additional information about X.400 names is given in Appendix B.

guish the user in the X.400 name space, you'll need to supply additional elements to make the X.400 name unique. For example, if you add the X.400 elements OU and ADMD, a typical X.400 name would look like this:

```
C=US;A=MCI;P=MICROSOFT;S=BILLKI;O=NORTH AMERICA;OU=BSD
```

See the section on Foreign E-Mail Addresses in this chapter and Chapter Five, Microsoft Exchange Server Administration, for more details.)

Organization Name

Choose an organization name that encompasses your entire organization. It must be unique and cannot be changed. When choosing an organization name, be aware that it is used to generate foreign e-mail addresses and the distinguished names of all directory objects such as mailboxes, public folders, and distribution lists. Organization names can contain up to 64 characters, but for practical reasons, you may want to use names that have fewer than 10 characters. This is especially true if you are connecting to legacy systems. In effect, this name is inherited by all of the addresses that are part of the Microsoft Exchange universe, so careful consideration should be given in establishing this name. For example, I might use my company name, because that is unlikely to change over time. Conversely, I would not use a location or city name because the company might move.

Site Names

Sites can be named by geographic location (countries, regions, cities), by physical location (buildings), or by function. The latter is a useful model for accounting purposes in internal divisions. Like the organization name, site names must be unique, cannot be changed, and are used to generate foreign e-mail addresses and directory names. Site names can contain up to 64 characters but, as with the organization name, you may want to choose site names that have fewer than 10 characters, especially if you are connecting to legacy systems.

An example of coexisting with a legacy system might be useful here. Suppose your organization has a number of users who are going to continue to use IBM PROFS as their e-mail system. The naming conventions used in the legacy system (PROFS, in this case) must conform to a two-part HOST/USER name, and neither part of the name may exceed eight characters in length.

If you choose Microsoft Exchange names that don't fit this limitation, the consequences must be carefully measured in advance as part of your planning: Mail might not be delivered, Reply To might not be handled correctly, addresses may get truncated and become difficult for the recipient to figure out. Microsoft Exchange is flexible enough to do the right thing most of the time, but you're still inviting problems if you go outside the lines.

Server Names

The Setup program uses the Windows NT Server computer name for the Microsoft Exchange server name. It is important to plan the names you want to use for your Microsoft Exchange Server computers before you install Microsoft Windows NT Server.

Server names must be unique and cannot be changed without reinstalling Microsoft Exchange Server. They can contain up to 15 characters, but they cannot include any of the following characters:

If you have already installed Microsoft Windows NT servers, Microsoft Exchange will use the server names, but if they include any forbidden characters, they must be changed before you install Microsoft Exchange. Microsoft Windows NT Server does allow you to change the server name, but that is not always a trivial thing, such as in the case of domain controllers. (For more information, refer to your Windows NT Server documentation.)

- ✘ **Bullet**

- ✘ **Currency sign**

- ✘ **Broken vertical bar**

- ✘ **Section sign**

- ✘ **Paragraph sign**

This list of forbidden characters is correct as of this writing for Microsoft Windows NT Server Versions 3.x.

If you are going to run logon scripts, do not use spaces in the computer names of the domain controllers.

To be safe, check your Microsoft Windows NT Server documentation for the latest information on server name limitations.

Mailbox Names

Choose mailbox names that are easy to identify based on your company standards for phone and address books. You might also want to consider coordinating mailbox name conventions with the naming scheme used for Windows NT user accounts or for previous e-mail systems. These names are more flexible because they are designed as a resource that is normally associated with users, who frequently appear, disappear, move, and change their names.

This table shows the fields in Microsoft Exchange Server mailbox names:

Field	Guideline	Restrictions
First Name	The user's first name.	Up to 16 characters. Can be changed.
Last Name	The user's last name.	Up to 40 characters. Can be changed.
Alias Name	A short name to identify the user. This name can be automatically generated when the first and last names are entered. The administrator can customize how the directory name is created through the Options command on the Tools menu.	Up to 64 characters. Can be changed.
Display Name	The mailbox name as you want it displayed in the Administrator window and in the Address Book. For example, you can use First Name Last Name (Daniel Shelly), Last Name, First Name Initial. (Shelly, Daniel B.), or Initial Last Name (DShelly). Whatever you use, be consistent so that all mailboxes are displayed in the same fashion. The display name is a mandatory field and can be automatically created when the first and last name fields are entered.	Up to 256 characters. Can be changed.

I have already mentioned in previous chapters that mailboxes in Microsoft Exchange Server are really network resources that can be shared. I also mentioned that this allows for new ways of using these resources compared to the traditional shared file e-mail system. Mailboxes can be used to display resources such as conference rooms in the Address Book. If you intend to use them this way, use consistent names for these resources. For example, if you use them for conference rooms, you could display them as conference room, building (size of room), as in Tahoe conference room, 2A (20). Whatever you decide, it's best to use the same conventions for all resources.

Foreign E-mail Addresses

To communicate with foreign e-mail systems, Microsoft Exchange Server users (recipients) must have an address in a format that the foreign system can understand. Similarly, users in a foreign system must be represented in Microsoft Exchange Server. A *custom recipient* is a user whose address is on a foreign e-mail system.

A *foreign e-mail address* is the address by which Microsoft Exchange recipients (mailboxes, distribution lists, public folders, and custom recipients) are known to foreign e-mail systems. Based on the site address, Microsoft Exchange automatically generates a Microsoft Mail (PC), X.400, and Internet address for each recipient. You can create, modify, or remove foreign mail addresses by using the Administrator program.

X.400 Addresses

Here are the allowed characters in an X.400 address (X.400 O/R names). These characters are of the Printable String type according to the X.208 Recommendation.

Character	Designation
A, B, …, Z	Capital letters
a, b, …, z	Small letters
0, 1, …, 9	Digits
(space)	Space
'	Apostrophe
(	Left parenthesis
)	Right parenthesis
+	Plus sign
,	Comma
-	Hyphen
.	Full stop
/	Solidus
:	Colon
=	Equals sign
?	Question mark

SMTP

If your organization will be connected to the Internet or other SMTP systems, consider any character restrictions that SMTP imposes on its addressing scheme. You can use only lowercase and uppercase letters (a-z and A-Z) (no distinction is made between lowercase and uppercase characters), numbers (0-9), and the hyphen (-).

Naming Conventions

Dun & Bradstreet has chosen several naming conventions to serve as guidelines in their deployment of Microsoft Exchange Server. These conventions will facilitate administration as well as customer use by allowing users and administrators to easily identify objects in their Microsoft Exchange Organization.

Organization Name

Dun & Bradstreet will use **The Dun & Bradstreet Corporation** as the Organization Display Name for all Microsoft Exchange Server implementations. This display name will be matched exactly in all sites.

In order to maintain brief and easily recognized X.400 and SMTP proxy addresses, Dun & Bradstreet administrators will use **DNB** as the Organization Directory Name.

Site Naming Conventions

Each site must have a site directory name that is unique within the organization. Dun & Bradstreet site directory names will adhere to the following guidelines:

- ✗ They will contain eight characters or less with no spaces, punctuation, or diacritical marks.

- ✗ Where possible, they will remain consistent with current Microsoft Mail network names (such as DBCORP, MOODYS, IMSUSA, NCH, DONTECH).

Dun & Bradstreet will define site display names according to the following guidelines:

✗ The site name will not include the word "site".

✗ The site name will not include the following characters: " / \ ; : .

✗ The site name will refer to a Dun & Bradstreet division and, if necessary, a specific office or region.

Mailbox Naming Conventions

Dun & Bradstreet will use the first initial of the user's first name followed by the user's last name as the standard mailbox directory name. Thus, the standard will be DSmith, where "D" is the first initial of the first name and "Smith" is the last name. Administrators will resolve duplicates with a middle initial or counter (for example, DPSmith or DSmith1).

Dun & Bradstreet will continue to use their current Microsoft Mail mailbox display name standard, which adheres to the following format: Lastname, Firstname Middle Initial.

Custom Recipient Naming Conventions

Where possible, Dun & Bradstreet will use the same naming conventions with custom recipients for external X.400, SMTP, and other gateway mailboxes as they do for internal mailboxes. The only exception is that they will append the address type to the display name, as shown below:

✗ Gallagher, Karin (Internet)

✗ Nash, Mike (MHS)

✗ Mitchell, Linda (X.400)

✗ Haarsager, Gary (PROFS)

(continues)

(continued)

Public Folder Naming Conventions

Administrators will assign display names to public folders that clearly define both their purpose and the scope of their use. Dun & Bradstreet folder names will follow these guidelines:

✗ The word "folder" will not appear in the folder display name.

✗ Acronyms and abbreviations will be used minimally.

✗ Folders specific to a department, group, or division will reference the appropriate group name.

Recipient Container Naming Conventions

Dun & Bradstreet will define four recipient containers in each site. They are as follows:

Container Name	Container Role
Microsoft Exchange Recipients	All Microsoft Exchange users in the site
Microsoft Mail Recipients	All Microsoft Mail recipients (via the Microsoft Mail Connector/ DXA)
Microsoft Exchange Distribution Lists	All Microsoft Exchange Distribution Lists
Private Recipients	All Microsoft Exchange users and DLs not to be shared with other sites

Step 7: Link Sites

Sites can be configured to exchange directory information, public folders, and messages. This section explains how to link your sites and place the connections in your site and how this affects the Microsoft Exchange Server. It is important to understand these details before planning your servers.

The information that is transferred can be controlled by the administrators in either site. Information flow can be slowed if the connection speed between sites is not fast enough to handle the volume of data.

Routing within a site is point-to-point and requires no planning or configuration. Routing between sites or to another e-mail system, however, does require planning and configuration.

Types of Connectors

Site Connector

The Site Connector software is the most efficient way to connect two sites because it uses RPC for site-to-site communication. Site Connectors require permanent connections with higher bandwidths than the other connectors. However, because they use RPC, you do not have to configure a network transport for them.

This table lists advantages and disadvantages of using a Site Connector.

Advantages	Disadvantages
Easy to configure because it does not require configuration of the network transport and because you do not have to schedule connections.	Requires permanent connections of higher bandwidth. Cannot control message size sent through the Site Connector.
Most efficient because there is no message translation and because a message takes fewer "hops" to get to its destination.	Cannot schedule when connections are to be made.

Dynamic RAS Connector

The Dynamic RAS Connector is a special kind of Site Connector. It uses RAS asynchronous communication instead of a permanent network connection between sites. You can configure when the connection should be made, and at that time, Microsoft Exchange Server will make the connection to the other site.

Advantages	Disadvantages
Administrator-controlled dial-up connectivity.	Data transfer is dependent on the speed of the modems.
Works over slow, non-permanent connections.	

X.400 Connector

The X.400 Connector is used when there is no direct network connection between your sites, when you want to take advantage of your existing X.400 backbone, or when you want to access a public X.400 system. For this connector, you must configure one of the following network transports: TP0/X.25, TP4/CLNP, or TCP/IP.

Advantages	Disadvantages
Can schedule when connection happens.	Must configure network transports.
Can control message size through the connector.	May not be able to use this connector if you have bridges/routers that do not support the same network transports on both sides of the bridge/router.
Can control how messages are routed through the Microsoft Exchange Server topology.	Somewhat more complicated to configure than Site Connector.
Uses international standard protocol for message transfer (X.400).	Can be costly if volume of data is high.

To connect two sites, identify a Microsoft Exchange Server in each site to support the connection. Configure the message transfer agent (MTA) on each Microsoft Exchange Server to connect to the other server's MTA or intermediate MTAs through the appropriate network transport.

You can have one or more connections configured between sites. You should consider having redundant routes in your routing strategy for load balancing and least-cost routing. You can assign costs to each route, and the connectors will select the route with the lowest cost. In addition, if one route should go down, messages could continue to be routed through the other connections. The connectors can load-balance routing over the remaining connections based on the their assigned costs.

Microsoft Exchange Connectors

Site Connectors

Dun & Bradstreet will use a Site Connector between the Corporate Center and Shared Services Center sites. This architecture will be a blueprint for future business units containing multiple sites, for the following reasons:

- ✘ It will provide the highest level of performance;
- ✘ It will allow all inter-divisional messages to be routed through the divisional headquarters-based site, emulating the "hub-and-spoke" architecture currently employed in the Dun & Bradstreet messaging network.

X.400 Connectors

Dun & Bradstreet to use X.400 Connectors as their primary connection between business divisions because there are no domain trust requirements. This provides global messaging without compromising the security of the business division.

Internet Connectors

Dun & Bradstreet has chosen to implement an Internet Mail Connector at the Corporate Center for its use and for use by the Shared Services Center. This connector will provide an improved level of Internet connectivity for the Shared Services Center without increasing their administrative load. It will create only a minimal increase in administration for the Corporate Center.

Microsoft Mail Connectors

Dun & Bradstreet will use Microsoft Mail Connectors in both the Corporate Center and the Shared Services Center sites; how-

(continues)

(continued)

ever, only the Corporate Center site will implement Directory Exchange. This will minimize administrative overhead while providing a high-speed messaging link between Shared Service Center-based Microsoft Exchange users and Shared Service Center-based Microsoft Mail applications. When Dun & Bradstreet ports the Microsoft Mail-based applications Microsoft Exchange (planned for the 1996), the Microsoft Mail Connector at the Shared Service Center will be removed.

Dun & Bradstreet will handle all Microsoft Mail directory exchange for both the Corporate Center and the Shared Service Center through the connection at the Corporate Center. They also intend to use this model as a blueprint for Dun & Bradstreet divisions. The divisional headquarters can then use their Microsoft Exchange Servers for directory exchange, thereby reducing the administrative burdens related to maintaining Microsoft Mail directories. This implementation will also decrease the number of Microsoft Mail post offices currently in directory synchronization (currently more than 250), making the Microsoft Mail network more efficient.

The Schedule+ Free/Busy gateway is a component of the Microsoft Mail Connector that exchanges information between Schedule+ 1.0 and Schedule+ 7.0. Dun & Bradstreet will implement this component at both the Corporate Center and the Shared Services Center to facilitate coexistence with current Microsoft Mail users.

Tailoring Traffic Between Sites

Traffic between sites is divided between replication messages and other types of messages. While it is difficult to plan for the precise amount of each type of traffic, you can use some generalities to reduce traffic between sites.

Message Traffic

The number and size of messages users send between sites can vary greatly. While you can't limit the number of messages, you can limit their size to prevent users from sending large enclosures.

Directory Replication Between Sites

Replication is the process of copying new and updated information from one site to another. This includes directory information about mailboxes, distribution lists, public folder addresses and contents, and addresses of users in foreign systems. The first time replication occurs, all information is sent to other sites. After that, only modifications and new entries are exchanged.

By setting connection schedules between sites, you can schedule the flow of messages between them. If your bandwidth is limited, you can adjust directory updates to occur during off-hours so they do not impact message flow.

Public Folder Replication

When a public folder is replicated, all changes are sent to all other replicas of that folder in the organization. Public folder replication can be controlled to send only during off-hours. Replication messages can be limited in size, so large messages do not cause delays in a gateway or MTA transmission queue when traveling over slow links.

In Microsoft Exchange Server version 4.0, the granularity of changes is at the document level. A change to a document will cause the entire document to be replicated.

Instead of replicating a public folder to another site, the administrator can specify a parameter called the *Public Folder Affinity*. Public folder affinity allows users from one site to connect to public folders in other sites. This reduces network traffic caused by replication, reduces required storage space, and reduces or eliminates replication latency, but it can cause *more* network traffic than having additional replicas if items in the public folders are read very often by people in the site.

Plan Communication Between Sites

The most important considerations in planning replication between any two sites are the characteristics of the physical link and the relative importance of sharing information.

For example, when two sites are connected over an expensive link (as defined by speed, cost, or both), you can limit how often the sites connect to exchange mail or directory information and control the maximum size of messages that are sent through the expensive link.

When directory information is critical, you can increase the frequency with which the sites exchange information and you can specify full replication, even if the sites are connected by an expensive link. As I described earlier, you can also specify multiple methods of communication, even if it causes redundancy. For example, if the Systems Network Architecture (SNA) backbone is down, you can link the sites over more expensive phone lines or a public X.25 connection. This happens dynamically and is based upon least-cost routing.

If you are using a permanent connection between sites, but the connection is a slow-speed link, you can restrict directory service replication and traffic by setting a maximum message size. You can augment this bandwidth during the day with a scheduled X.400 connection.

Step 8: Plan Sites

Planning sites involves a number of factors, including determining how many servers are required for each site, where to locate each server, how to administer servers, and how many and what type of gateways your site needs. That's too much information to cover here, so I devoted an entire chapter—Chapter Seven—to this subject and the next.

Step 9: Plan Servers

Planning servers involves determining the function of the server and its software and hardware requirements. For example, you can dedicate a Microsoft Exchange Server for public folders or to expand distribution lists. If you use the advanced security features that Microsoft Exchange Server provides, you will have to determine which Microsoft

Exchange Server computer in your organization will manage your advanced security keys. Hardware and software requirements directly impact the performance of each server. Once again, I'll give you complete information about planning servers in the next chapter.

Step 10: Plan Connections to Other Systems

To connect to other systems, Microsoft Exchange Server supports a number of Windows NT Server gateways as well as the suite of Microsoft Mail Server gateways that are currently available. In addition to rich gateway connectivity, Microsoft Exchange Server natively supports three key connectivity components: the 1988 X.400 MTA described earlier, the Microsoft Mail Connector for rich connectivity with Microsoft Mail users, and the Internet Mail Connector, which connects Microsoft Exchange Server users to the Internet.

For more on connectivity, see the *Microsoft Exchange Connectivity Guide,* published by Microsoft Press.

The following table provides a brief summary of how you can connect your sites to Microsoft Mail and the Internet. The table also includes the network transports they support.

Connector	Network transport	Use this connector to
Microsoft Mail Connector	• LAN • X.25 • Asynchronous • Microsoft Remote • Access Service (RAS)	Take advantage of existing Microsoft Mail 3.x Gateways such as PROFS, SNADS, NetWare MHS, and FAX.
Internet Mail Connector	• TCP/IP	Connect to the Internet or to an SMTP backbone. Supports RFC 822 plus MIME/RFC 1521 extensions.

Planning for these connectivity components is very important, but a detailed discussion of the factors to consider is beyond the scope of this book. Indeed, entire books have been written describing the X.400 connectivity issues.

Step 11: Validate and Optimize the Design

Optimizing the design means:

1 Designing several topology options for both Microsoft Exchange Server and your implementation of Windows NT Server. Each option can include a brief overview of the topology plan, network maps showing the data path, routing diagrams, and an outline of the benefits and the drawbacks for that option.

2 Analyzing, reviewing, and testing each option to develop the best alternative.

3 Modifying your plans as needed to maximize performance and service to users.

You may have to go through this process more than once, trying different options and refining the design.

Check your design against projected loads, error rates, peak-to-average message traffic ratios, and sustainable forwarding rates by various Microsoft Exchange servers. Don't forget to test your assumptions by using the tools provided with Microsoft Exchange Server. Simulating the server load using the load simulation tool will help to validate performance assumptions you have made during the design process. The modeling tool, contained on the accompanying CD, can also assist you in validating your assumptions regarding site layout and connectivity. There is also the Windows NT Server resource kit, which contains a number of tools to assist in the design and validation of your Windows NT Server domains.

Using the Load Simulation Tool

The load simulation tool is a software tool that is part of the administration group in Microsoft Exchange Server. It allows you to compare the performance of various hardware platforms under simulated load conditions you set up to reflect your organization's demands. The load simulation tool can programmatically create a server with hundreds of users who are sending thousands of messages as well as accessing forms and public folders.

The load simulation tool reports on different aspects of server performance, and you can use these reports to compare the likely performance of different platform configurations. This simplifies the task of coming up with a suitable hardware platform based upon real performance.

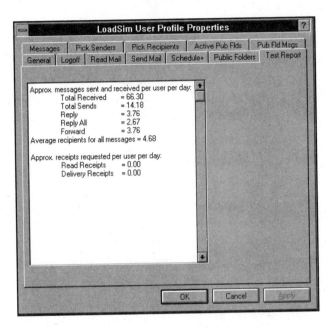

Using the Microsoft Exchange Server Site Modeling Tool

This tool is designed to create models of site layouts in a Microsoft Exchange organization. The models are based upon a complex matrix of network hardware, software, and communication protocol variables. It allows the architect to enter the physical attributes of the organization in a graphic way and to test the connectivity assumptions as they apply to Microsoft Exchange sites.

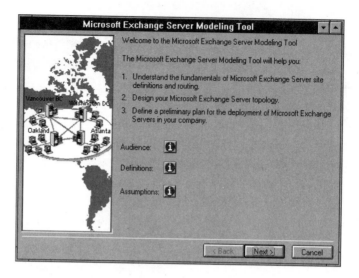

Step 12: Plan the Roll Out

The roll-out plan comprises the steps and procedures you will follow to implement the new system in the organization and migrate users from existing systems to the new system. The roll-out plan is the most important of the 12 steps and yet, if the previous 11 steps have been carefully completed and tested, this should be the easiest step of all to accomplish.

Developing a Roll-Out Plan

There's no one format for a roll-out plan that will fit every organization, because each installation is different. Regardless of its final form, your plan should cover at least the following points:

- ✗ **Timetable**
- ✗ **Clearly defined checkpoints**
- ✗ **Training plan**
- ✗ **List of personnel**
- ✗ **List of responsibilities**
- ✗ **Vendor contact list**
- ✗ **Key support contacts**

Using Migration Tools to Move Users and Data

As mentioned in the chapter on administration, Microsoft Exchange comes with a set of tools that allow for rapid migration of users and their data. Migration includes not only moving a user account from one network system to another, but also creating a new mailbox and collecting data accumulated by the user on the other system as well.

In the case of mail systems, the migration tools allow for moving a single user or an entire user population on a postoffice or host to Microsoft Exchange Server and creating Microsoft Windows NT Server accounts as well as all the necessary user privileges to make the users part of the new mail system immediately.

Migration and Coexistence

Dun & Bradstreet currently uses Microsoft Mail for PC Networks in the standard "hub and spoke" configuration. They will use the Microsoft Exchange Migration Tool to migrate users' existing mailboxes to Microsoft Exchange Server.

Migrations will occur on Friday evenings to ensure that Microsoft Mail directory synchronization is completed successfully and that customer addresses are properly represented in the Global Address List.

Dun & Bradstreet has set a 50-MB limit on disk space for their users' mailboxes on the Microsoft Exchange Servers. Users, therefore, will need to reduce their MMF files to less than 50MB prior to migration.

Dun & Bradstreet will migrate its initial implementation in four stages:

Pilot Group 1
Pilot group 1 will migrate first. This group consists of approximately 15-20 Corporate Systems associates.

Pilot Group 2
Pilot group 2 will migrate next, incorporating approximately 10 remaining associates in Corporate Systems and the Corporate Communications department.

(continues)

(continued)

Corporate Center and Shared Services Center

Dun & Bradstreet plans to migrate the remaining Corporate Center and Shared Services customers at the rate of approximately 20 per night. They will develop and verify a rollout schedule with customers prior to commencement.

Fail-safe

Dun & Bradstreet will maintain the legacy Microsoft Mail postoffices in a disconnected state for one month following completion of each migration. In the event of failure, users can use the Microsoft Mail provider to connect to their old mailboxes for basic messaging functionality. Dun & Bradstreet administrators will instruct users in how to install the Microsoft Mail provider.

Continuing Migration

Dun & Bradstreet will establish the Dun & Bradstreet Messaging Backbone site as a "routing clearinghouse" for all interdivisional messages. This will allow the Dun & Bradstreet Data Services group to centrally manage the Dun & Bradstreet messaging infrastructure. Additionally, this central-site architecture will allow each Dun & Bradstreet division to establish a single connector through which they can communicate with the rest of Dun & Bradstreet.

The three top-level routing post offices (DBCORP/DNBHUB, DBCORP/DNBHUB1, DBCORP/DNBHUB2) will be migrated to Microsoft Exchange servers. Each will run the Microsoft Mail Connector using a Microsoft Mail proxy address of DBCORP/DNBHUB. This will require that the routing tables on divisional hub post offices be updated to reflect all other divisional post offices as indirect via DBCORP/DNBHUB. Each of the three Microsoft Exchange Servers will run at least one instance of the Microsoft Mail Connector External program.

Divisional hub post office servers will route mail through the central site. As Dun & Bradstreet divisions migrate to Microsoft

Exchange Server, these divisional hub post office will become Microsoft Exchange servers, and the Microsoft Mail Connector will be replaced with an X.400 Connector.

All X.400 Connectors to or from the central messaging site will use the TCP/IP transport stack, because the Dun & Bradstreet wide-area network passes only TCP/IP network traffic.

Connector Redundancy

Dun & Bradstreet will establish a Windows NT Remote Access Server in the DNBMAIL domain. They will also configure X.400 Connectors over RAS to and from each divisional top-level site. By setting the "cost" of each of these connectors to 100, Dun & Bradstreet can configure these connectors to not be used unless the primary TCP/IP-based X.400 connector (cost of 1) goes down. This configuration provides an out-of-bandwidth solution for continuing messaging traffic in case of a wide area network outage.

Dun & Bradstreet will establish a Windows NT Remote Access Server in the DNBMAIL domain. They will also configure X.400 Connectors over RAS to and from each divisional top-level site. By setting the "cost" of each of these connectors to 100, Dun & Bradstreet can configure these connectors to not be used unless the primary TCP/IP-based X.400 Connector (cost of 1) goes down. This configuration provides a solution for continuing messaging traffic in case of a wide area network outage.

Chapter

Planning Sites and Servers

I f the Microsoft Exchange topology you designed in the previous chapter represents your organizational world, then sites are cities and servers are neighborhoods within that world. In designing the topology, you determined the number of sites and their boundaries. Now we're going to see what goes on inside the sites. To use our analogy, in this chapter you'll design the messaging "cities" and "neighborhoods" to fit the needs of the people who work there.

Planning Sites

Site and server planning builds on the work you did in planning your Microsoft Exchange Server topology. (I assume you've made at least a draft plan for your company.) When planning your Microsoft Exchange Server topology, you looked at ways to meet your current and future needs, minimize impact on your existing network, and stay within your budget. Site planning has the same goals.

Here are the things you need to think about when you are planning sites and servers:

✗ **Physical network layout.** Locating servers on the same LAN segments as the users reduces traffic across bridges and routers.

✗ **Types of users and their needs.** Planning for server hardware and gateways requires knowing which users plan to use which features of Microsoft Exchange Server.

✗ **Special service needs.** Special services—such as gateways, news feeds, security and other applications—impact planning for server loading and hardware.

✗ **Mobile client access.** Planning for mobile clients includes deciding on the type and quantity of remote services your site must support.

This design work is presented for sites that require more than one Microsoft Exchange Server. If your site requires only one server, this chapter is useful for planning the hardware you need for that server.

I'll cover these points in this chapter.

Network Layout Inside the Site

In Chapter Six, you defined the number and locations of sites in your Microsoft Exchange Server topology and the types of connections among them. Now you can determine the number, type, and configuration of Microsoft Exchange Servers required in each site.

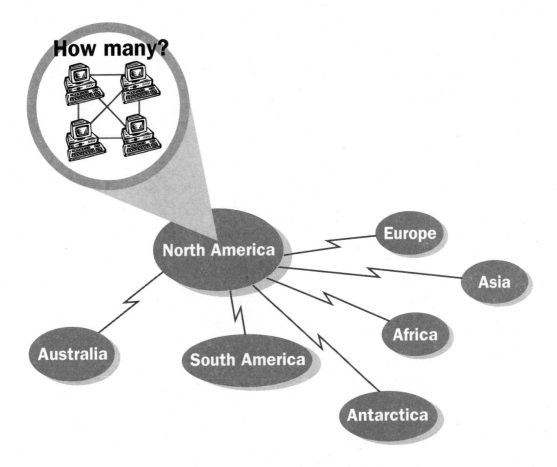

To begin planning your site, you need a description of your site's physical network layout. The physical network is the groundwork on which to lay the foundation for your site. You used information on your physical network in Chapter Six to establish the boundaries of the site. In this section, you will examine the physical network within each of those sites to see the network influences that affect the design of your site.

LAN Segments

All data that moves on a LAN is transmitted, carried, and received. In the simplest LAN, the data travels directly from the transmitter to the receiver. In more complex situations, the data must travel through routers or bridges. Each part of the network that connects into a router or bridge is a segment of the network.

Start your site layout with a drawing of your physical network. If you do not have a wide-area network, or if all your servers are on the same network segment, start with a straight line to represent the LAN.

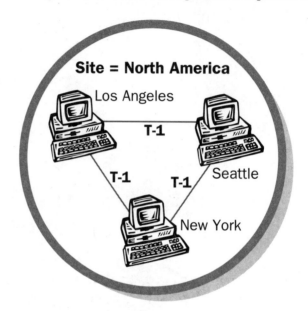

Network and Physical Locations

Every segment of your network is in a physical location. For example, one segment can serve a building or a floor in that building. Add information to your drawing about the location of each segment of the network in your facility, including the number of users it serves. With this information, you'll begin to see appropriate locations for Microsoft Exchange servers.

The users on the first floor are accounting department employees; the second floor is the sales department; and the third floor is the human relations department. The people on each floor work on the same information and communicate most often with members of their own group.

> **Microsoft Exchange Site Topology**
> Dun & Bradstreet chose two primary sites for their initial implementation of Microsoft Exchange. These sites mirror the messaging domains implemented in Microsoft Windows NT Server.
>
> Dun & Bradstreet decided to configure their Microsoft Exchange sites to mirror the business structures they will be supporting. Divisional administrators will map future sites and their relative components to their respective business units.

Defining the Users in Your Site

A description of the people who will be using Microsoft Exchange Server will help you plan for and meet their data needs. In this section, you will add groups of users to your layout, then examine each group's information uses and needs.

Grouping Microsoft Exchange Server Users

Group your Microsoft Exchange Server users by organizational or network location, always trying to group users together with their data. Then analyze each group to see the kind of information they generate and exchange, their public folder use, and their storage and performance needs. Later, when you are determining which users will have mailboxes on a server, this information can simplify performance, load balancing, and budget decisions.

In our example, all the employees in Los Angeles provide data for the service and manufacturing employees located in New York and the shipping department people in Seattle.

One way to start setting up groups is to look at your organization chart or survey each LAN segment. Add groups to your layout with the name of the group and an estimate of the number of people in it. Try to place users into groups that give you some flexibility later in planning your servers.

For example, if your server hardware will support only 150 users per server, keep that figure in mind when grouping users together. In our example, Los Angeles has three hundred people spread across three floors of the building. When the network was designed, the simplest way to group them was to add a server to each floor. It would be most appropriate to think of grouping these folks together in Microsoft Exchange by installing the Microsoft Exchange Server software on each of the three servers.

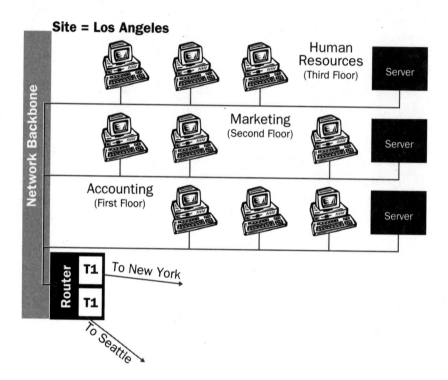

Describing Microsoft Exchange Server Users

Once you have identified your groups, describe them in ways that help you design the site to meet their needs. Here are suggestions for obtaining the information you need for these descriptions.

Message Volume

To make it easy to estimate loads, Microsoft has defined three basic user types, based on real-world usage data on current mail systems.

Parameter	Light User	Medium User	Heavy User
Maximum inbox size (in messages)	20	125	250
Other old mail processing (per day)	5x	15x	20x
Total sends per day (computed average)	7	20	39
Total receipts per day (computed average)	20	56	119

Your mileage may vary, but these are good baseline estimates.

Naturally, there are differences among users in every group. For the sake of analysis, try to determine the average for each group. There are several ways to collect this data. If your current mail system has administrative accounting features, generate a report on current use for members of these groups. If your current mail system allows you to save all sent mail, survey several users in each group to get an idea of how many messages are sent in a day. Another method is to survey people who were out of the office for a day or two to determine how many new messages were waiting for them when they returned. (This survey method can also be used to collect other relevant data, such as how much mail is saved by users.)

Message Storage

Microsoft Exchange Server allows personal folders to be stored either in the server information store, in a personal folder store on the client workstation, or in both. Public folders are always stored in the information store. The Microsoft Exchange Server information store uses a single-instance storage architecture to reduce disk usage; for example, if a user sends one message to ten recipients on a server, each recipient's mailbox gets a pointer to the single shared copy of the sent message.

To further limit disk usage on the server, you can set limits for the total amount of disk space each user is allowed to use, and you can set limits on the number and age of sent and received messages that can be stored.

Even if you decide to set storage limits for mailboxes, the storage needs for each group of users can be different. A survey of your current mail system is a good way to understand current storage use. This survey will help you understand the amount of hardware you need as well. It may indicate that your current hardware does not suit the needs of the user community and will need to be upgraded.

Message Traffic

Categorize data and message flow within your organization and to other systems. In your layout, you can describe each group's typical or expected traffic pattern. Ask the following questions:

Is mail sent mostly

✗ **Within the group?**

✗ **To other specific groups?**

✗ **To other specific sites?**

✗ **To specific gateways?**

You can assume that people in a group will eventually send mail to every other group, but you are looking for major traffic trends. You can get the data if your existing mail system has reporting capabilities that describe this flow. You can also examine the pattern by using a sample survey of sent mail or inboxes.

Messages addressed only to local users require fewer resources to deliver. By understanding traffic between groups, you can plan for groups that most often exchange mail to share the same server and decrease the load on the network and other servers.

Public Folder Needs

Defining the public folder needs for each group will help you later in planning server hardware and software. Besides describing the public folder needs of each group, you should also decide which administrative policies you plan to implement in regard to public folders.

A word of caution: If you do not presently have public folders, you may underestimate how much people will use them once the Microsoft Exchange system is installed. The use of public folders is likely to be greater than you think, especially once users find out how useful they are and how easy it is to develop workgroup applications based on them. Use the following suggestions in making your estimates, and then add a healthy fudge factor to allow for growth.

For each folder a group will use exclusively, estimate:

✗ **Volume of new information:** the number and size of the messages or forms that will be created each day.

✗ **Longevity of information:** how many days this information should be retained. For example, a public folder with weekly schedules and announcements would not need to be retained for more than two weeks, but a customer-tracking application might require data to be kept indefinitely.

✗ **Load:** how many users are going to access this public folder. How many times a day? Will they read all new items? Will they search, sort, and change views?

Public folders do not need to reside on the same server as the users, so a group's public folder use does not necessarily impact the design of its server. However, if their load is high enough, the network traffic they generate may cause you to place their public folder on their server or on another server on the same LAN segment.

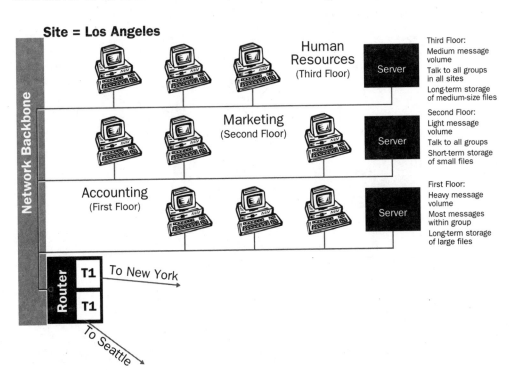

Public Folder Topology

Dun & Bradstreet will implement a divisional public folder tree to increase collaboration and productivity within their organization. This strategy has the benefit of mirroring Dun & Bradstreet's business model as well as allowing individual departments to manage their own public folder resources.

Dun & Bradstreet will create a top-level folder for each division and assign a divisional administrator to it. Only the divisional administrator will have owner permissions on this folder; all other users will have read-only permission. The divisional administrator will create sub-folders on a per-departmental basis and will identify and train departmental administrators as owners of these sub-folders. The departmental administrator will create and manage all folders contained within a department.

This strategy allows divisional and departmental managers, who are more knowledgeable about business content and processes, to administer the public folders they are using. The following diagram details this strategy:

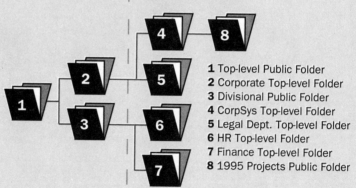

Public Folder Strategy
Divisional Folder Trees
Divisional Admin | Departmental Admin

1 Top-level Public Folder
2 Corporate Top-level Folder
3 Divisional Public Folder
4 CorpSys Top-level Folder
5 Legal Dept. Top-level Folder
6 HR Top-level Folder
7 Finance Top-level Folder
8 1995 Projects Public Folder

When a public folder needs to be replicated to another server or site, the departmental administrator will notify the divisional administrator, who will then replicate the folder to the target server.

This table shows the general kinds of folders Dun & Bradstreet will use, along with their planned replication frequency:

Folder Type	Folder Description	Replication Frequency
Discussion folder	threaded conversations	once per hour
Document library	documents for update	once every four hours
Document library	documents for perusal	once per day
Archive folder	archived discussions	once per week
Broadcast folder	company-wide publications	once per week or month

Additional Services in a Site

All Microsoft Exchange Servers that are members of the same site perform an identical set of core functions, including directory services, mail transfer, and message storage. Some servers can contain additional software or can perform specialized services. Before planning server hardware and its placement on the network, determine which of these services you need in your site. Later on, you'll need to make sure you have enough server power to handle them.

The additional Microsoft Exchange Servers software and services include:

- ✗ **Administrator program**
- ✗ **Client installation points**
- ✗ **Internet connection server**
- ✗ **Public folder storage**
- ✗ **Links to other sites**
- ✗ **Links to Microsoft Mail or other mail systems**

The Windows NT Servers can also perform other tasks that are not directly related to Microsoft Exchange Servers. For example:

- ✗ **Primary domain controller (PDC)**
- ✗ **Backup domain controller (BDC)**
- ✗ **Remote Access Service (RAS)**
- ✗ **Structured Query Language (SQL) Server**
- ✗ **Microsoft System Management Server**
- ✗ **Microsoft SNA Server**

Schedule+ may also be used in the network, and there are some special considerations for doing that. Because the first server in a site has a hidden public folder that contains the free and busy time information for every Schedule+ user both in the site and at other sites, it can influence which server you install first. When a user is trying to schedule a meeting and uses the Planner, Schedule+ reads the free and busy time information from this public folder for each invited recipient who is not the user's home server. The volume of this public folder should be 3 KB per user in the organization. The load on this public folder depends on your use of Schedule+ to schedule meetings with people or resources outside your home server.

If a Microsoft Exchange Server is underutilized, you can designate it to perform additional services. For example, if all servers in the site except one are single processor computers and they each have an equal load of users, the multiprocessor computer is a good choice for processor-intensive activities. If one server has more available hard disk space than others, you can use it as the home server for public folders.

If all your servers use a standardized configuration and have an even user load, distribute these services evenly among all servers in the site. Monitoring your servers after installation is the only way to determine where to add gateways, new users, and public folders.

Planning for Mobile User Access

Some electronic mail programs have separate client programs for mobile access. However, Microsoft Exchange Server allows all clients to access personal and public folders remotely. Clients can be used offline to work with personal and public folders and connect to the server by making a remote network connection with a variety of software and hardware. Once connected to the network, the client can connect to the server, send outgoing mail, synchronize work completed offline and retrieve waiting mail.

In planning your Microsoft Exchange Server site, evaluate the needs of your mobile users. This includes managing remote access, having sufficient modems, phone lines, and ISDN or X.25 connections for the expected volume of traffic, and incorporating flexibility for future growth. Security requirements should also be taken into consideration.

Microsoft Exchange Clients need network access to the Microsoft Exchange Server. If they are at a remote location, they need some means of connecting to the network so they can send RPCs to the Microsoft Exchange Server as if they were on a LAN.

Connecting: Client Side

To connect to the network, Microsoft Exchange Clients can start and end communications programs that are included with the client or network operating system. You do not need to use this software to make the network connection; it is provided as a convenient default.

Client	Default communication
MS-DOS	Shiva, included with the Microsoft Exchange Client
Windows 16-bit	Shiva, included with the Microsoft Exchange Client
Windows for Workgroups	RAS, included with operating system
Windows 32-bit	RAS, included with operating system
Windows 95	Dial-Up Networking, included with operating system

Connecting: Server Side

On the server side of remote access to Microsoft Exchange Server, you have three options:

✗ **Windows NT Remote Access Service**

RAS is built into Windows NT servers and supports connection from RAS and Shiva clients. RAS is a Microsoft product that allows a remote workstation to connect to a network. You can use any of the following connection methods with RAS: modem, X.25 network directly or through a modem and packet assembly and disassembly (PAD), modem pool, ISDN, SNA, security hosts and switches, or RS-232 null-modem cable.

A Microsoft Exchange Server can also host a RAS server. Or, depending on your remote access needs, you could install a RAS server on a dedicated Windows NT server. For more information on the capabilities of RAS, see the Windows NT Remote Access Service documentation.

✗ **Shiva LanRover**

Shiva LanRover supports connections from Shiva and RAS.

✗ **Other**

Any remote access software that is compatible with RAS or the network software that is currently used by your remote workstations.

Assessing Needs

As you plan remote access hardware requirements, examine your mobile user traffic patterns. These factors can affect your decisions:

✗ **Number** of remote clients

✗ **Frequency** and duration of connections

✗ **Volume** of data sent and received

✗ **When** calls occur

✗ **Convenience** for remote clients

✗ **Connection** speed

Several mobile users can be served by one RAS server unless they call frequently. If all mobile users call to pick up mail at the same time, you will need more lines to handle the load (or you can encourage them to spread out their calls over a longer time period).

If you want to support multiple connections in the site, you should decide if you need a *hunt system* in your company's phone system. With a hunt system, a call to a single phone number is switched to an available modem, so you don't have to have a separate phone number for each modem. A hunt system makes it easier and quicker for mobile users to connect.

A more important consideration is the speed of the connections. A remote client connecting at 9600 bits per second (bps) keeps a connection busy longer than a remote client connecting at 19,200 bps. This speed is limited in asynchronous connections by the types of modems used and the highest transfer rates at which the two can connect. In X.25 connections, the speed is limited by either the bandwidth of the leased line or the modem speed of the PAD (if a PAD is used), whichever is lower.

Determining the Number of Connections

If your current mail system supports mobile user access, you can use your experience with these connections as a guide in planning Microsoft Exchange Server mobile user access. This is a good first step, but it may not provide an accurate estimate of your needs. These factors can increase your need for connections:

✗ **All Microsoft Exchange Server** users now have clients capable of mobile use.

✗ **The number** of portable and home computers is increasing.

The following options available for Microsoft Exchange Service can decrease the number of connections needed:

✗ **High-speed** connections, such as X.25 and ISDN.

✗ **Ability** to preview message headers for review before downloading.

✗ **Server-based** AutoAssistants for sorting and forwarding new mail.

   ✗ **Automated** late-night connection features.

   ✗ **Automatic** compression of all messages (but not attachments).

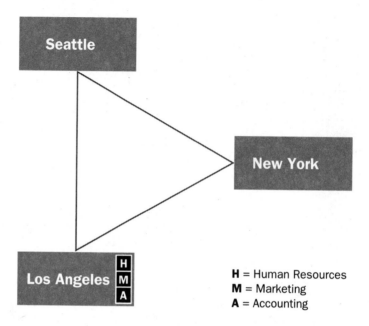

H = Human Resources
M = Marketing
A = Accounting

Planning Site Servers

The number of Microsoft Exchange Servers required for a site depends on the number of users, public folders, and gateways you plan to support and the kind of hardware you plan to use. You can use the scaling information, the site layout you completed, and the recommendations in the following sections to plan your hardware and software requirements.

Performance Factors for Servers

Five key factors affect server performance:

1 **Number** of disks

2 **Speed** and type of input/output subsystem

3 **Amount** of memory

4 **Processor** speed and number of processors

5 **Speed**, type and number of network cards

I'll discuss these factors in this section.

Microsoft Exchange Server includes a system optimization tool that will ensure that you get the most from your Microsoft Exchange Server computer. Based on your system configuration, the easy-to-use optimizer will make recommendations concerning Microsoft Exchange Server file locations, memory usage, and various other system parameters that will affect the performance of your Microsoft Exchange Server. Be sure to run the optimizer when you install Microsoft Exchange Server and whenever you change your system configuration.

Proper planning of your server can increase performance. For example, if you group users who usually send mail to each other onto the same server, the percentage of messages addressed exclusively to recipients on the same server increases. These messages are delivered by *local delivery*. This means that the information store delivers the message and the MTA is not involved, reducing disk and CPU load on the server.

This is an area where you can attain some economies by having larger servers with greater numbers of users. If you group users together carefully, you can minimize network traffic.

Distributing or Concentrating Servers

The way to give the best service to the individual user is to optimize the overall system within the organization and the site. Poor performance on one Microsoft Exchange Server can affect users at other Microsoft Exchange Servers and sites.

There is more than one hardware configuration that can meet the needs of your site. You may want to either implement a greater number of smaller servers or a smaller number of more powerful servers.

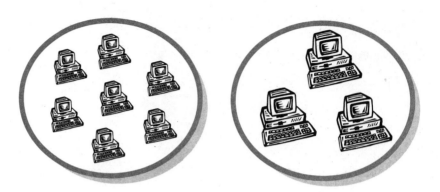

There are advantages and disadvantages to each configuration. The following table summarizes the advantages and disadvantages of using a number of less powerful computers:

Advantages	Disadvantages
Single failure impacts fewer users.	More hardware to maintain.
Can customize each server to the users it serves.	Customized hardware increases support costs.
Generally less expensive to add incremental increases in capacity.	Increases in users or load require more hardware.
More choices in off-the-shelf small hardware available.	Greater network overhead and storage for replicated data.

On the other hand, here are the advantages and disadvantages of using fewer, more powerful computers:

Advantages	Disadvantages
Designed for upgradability of processors and disk arrays.	Fewer vendors from which to choose; may not be able to use hardware that existing mail system is using.
Less network traffic with more users per server; more likely all recipients are on the same server. Also directory service has fewer servers to replicate directory changes resulting in less network traffic.	Network adapter card must be able to handle high volume of user traffic to each server.
Lower overall disk storage requirements because of single instance store architecture.	Information store is larger and takes longer to back up and restore.
Better fault-tolerant designs and error correction possible with more powerful hardware.	Increased vulnerability to a single point of failure.
Reduced administration.	

In some sites, a mixture of large and small servers can best meet the needs of large and small workgroups.

There is no perfect solution, so don't get caught in an endless loop trying to find one. Do the best job of planning that you can, knowing that you can always consolidate or distribute users later if strategies change or you want to adjust loads.

Microsoft Exchange Server Distribution

Corporate Center
The Dun & Bradstreet Corporate Center will be defined as a single Microsoft Exchange site called the Dun & Bradstreet Messaging Backbone site.

(continues)

(continued)

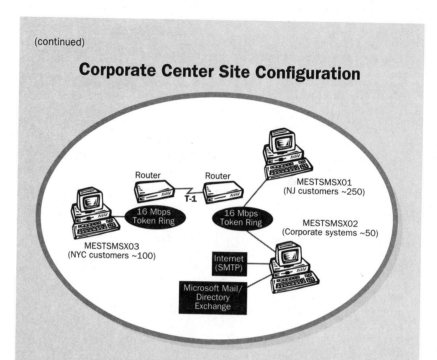

Corporate Center Site Configuration

The Dun & Bradstreet Messaging Backbone site will consist of three Microsoft Exchange Servers: one for customers in the Wilton, Connecticut, location (approximately 250-300 associates); one for the New York City locations (total about 100 associates); and one for Corporate Systems (about 50 associates). The Corporate Systems Server will also act as a staging area for updates, patches and add-ins.

The Corporate Center has ample available bandwidth: The Wilton and Corporate Systems servers will be on the same 16 Mbps token ring LAN. The New York server will also be on a 16 Mbps token ring LAN. These two LANs will be connected by way of T-1 Wellfleet routers. The narrowest bandwidth between any two servers will be 1 Mbps.

Dun & Bradstreet will install a Microsoft Mail Connector and an Internet Mail Connector on the Corporate Systems Server to provide messaging access to SMTP mail systems as well as the Dun & Bradstreet legacy Microsoft Mail network.

Shared Services Center, North America
The Shared Services Center in Allentown, Pennsylvania, will also be its own site, serving an end-user population of approximately 200. It will contain a single Microsoft Exchange server and a Microsoft Mail Connector.

Shared Services Center Site Configuration

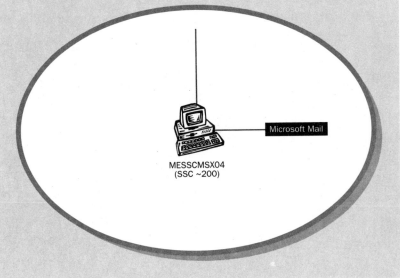

MESSCMSX04
(SSC ~200)

Microsoft Mail

Assigning Users

You can use the general guidelines listed below in designing the servers. However, note that it is impossible to follow all these guidelines at the same time because some conflict with each other. They are presented here as factors to consider in your design so you can make the tradeoffs that fit your site's needs.

- ✗ **Concentrate** mailboxes and groups that most often send mail to each other to take advantage of local delivery.

- ✗ **Make** all the users for a server come from the same network segment. You can gain efficiencies if most of your data does not have to flow outside of a network segment.

✗ **On a WAN,** spread out copies of the client installation points and the Administrator program.

✗ **Spread out** mailboxes (such as administrators' mailboxes) and critical public folders of mission critical people so a single failure doesn't stop business.

✗ **Concentrate** mission critical mailboxes, public folders, and gateways on servers with hot-swappable hardware.

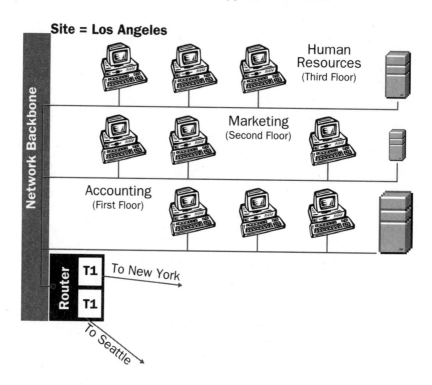

Estimating Server Hardware Requirements

Here are some guidelines for estimating server hardware requirements. Microsoft Exchange Server needs the following system resources:

✗ **System memory** for processing user requests to the directory, for connecting users to their Microsoft Exchange Server mailboxes, and for transferring information to and from the user mailboxes stored on a server.

✘ **Disk space** for the server software and for the Microsoft Exchange Server information store, directory service, and transaction log files.

✘ **Disk transfer** bandwidth to handle the reading and writing of information to disk.

✘ **Fast bus** architecture sufficient to support disk and other I/O requirements.

✘ **CPU processing** time for all the services to handle requests from clients, gateways, and other Microsoft Exchange Servers.

✘ **Network adapter** card bandwidth to handle network traffic. Multiple network cards are possible.

✘ **Optional** outside communication hardware for remote clients.

Adding gateway software to a Microsoft Exchange Server uses additional disk space, disk transfer bandwidth, and system memory. When adding physical network connections to a Microsoft Exchange Server for use by gateways, plan to have extra system memory available to handle peak traffic loads during the times of the day when users connect to and disconnect from the system, and whenever you have scheduled gateway connections.

When choosing hardware for Microsoft Exchange Server computers, plan ahead for future needs. That way, as the number of users and gateways in a site grows, you can reconfigure the existing hardware on current servers instead of adding more servers. There are several ways to make the most of existing server hardware for Microsoft Exchange Servers:

✘ **Increase** the number and speed of the disk or disk arrays.

✘ **Optimize** the input/output system. Disk-intensive processes take more time if the I/O system is slow. Use a fast-caching controller with a high-performance interface such as a PCI SCSI.

✘ **Increase** the amount of system memory for each Microsoft Exchange Server computer.

✘ **Buy** the fastest single processors.

✗ **Replace** disk drives and volume sets with striped drive arrays. Striped, mirrored drives can provide maximum data protection and optimum read access (but they require more disk space).

✗ **Reduce** the number of non-Microsoft Exchange Server software processes that run on the server hardware. Although the Microsoft Exchange Server computer can support other processes, for best performance it is generally best to dedicate the server for Microsoft Exchange Server processes.

✗ **Upgrade** the processors on existing servers or use multiprocessors in existing servers.

Microsoft BackOffice products are fully supported running together on a single server. Still, use good judgment in deciding where to run various processes. Even though it is technically possible to run a number of programs on one machine, performance will begin to suffer at some point.

Select hardware that can be upgraded easily. If a bottleneck is identified after installation, you can eliminate it with a minor upgrade rather than a new server or change in site layout.

For example, many RAID arrays allow you to add to or upgrade the disk drives within them. Some computers have slots to add additional symmetric processors. Computers have different limits on the maximum amount of RAM that can be installed. Even if you don't need this capability immediately, it can make it easier to handle future growth.

System Memory

Microsoft Exchange Server executables are multithreaded processes that run as Windows NT services. Each process allocates and de-allocates system memory dynamically and can use as much system memory as the server hardware has available.

When physical memory is exhausted, new processes and programs are forced to use *virtual memory*. Virtual memory is simulated RAM created by using a portion of the hard disk as a swap file. This slows down the processes and programs that use the virtual memory and those that need to read and write to the hard disk.

For optimal performance, your Microsoft Exchange Server computers should have at least enough physical system memory to avoid constant heavy use of virtual memory. You should consider increasing server memory as client usage of the server increases and as more services are run on the server.

Use the Microsoft Exchange Optimizer to optimize memory usage on your Microsoft Exchange Server computer. If you add physical memory (RAM) to your Microsoft Exchange Server computer, you should rerun the Optimizer.

Disk Usage

Over time, the size of the Microsoft Exchange Server's information stores grow. The files increase in size as the following increase:

✗ **Mailboxes**

✗ **Distribution lists**

✗ **Public folders**

✗ **Gateways**

✗ **Remote users**

✗ **Mail messages**

✗ **Public folder items**

✗ **Outbound mail** in queue for gateway or other site

To control hard disk needs and improve performance, you can set some administrative policies:

✗ **Impose** storage limits on all users to limit the size of their mailboxes.

✗ **Limit** the maximum age for material in public folders to decrease their volume.

✗ **Impose** storage limits on public folders.

✗ **Limit** the maximum message size.

If your needs grow beyond your initial estimates, you can adjust your available disk space later using these strategies:

✗ **Add** another Microsoft Exchange Server to the site and add new users to it.

✗ **Move** a group of mailboxes to a new Microsoft Exchange server in the site.

✗ **Move** public folders to other Microsoft Exchange Servers in the site and do not replicate them within the site.

✗ **Consider** dedicating a Microsoft Exchange Server for public folders.

✗ **Increase** frequency of connections to other sites and systems to keep outbound queues small.

✗ **If you have** a lot of MTA traffic, consider dedicating a Microsoft Exchange Server to routing those messages.

✗ **Monitor** the amount of disk space that is allocated to individual mailboxes and ask specific users to delete outdated mail messages. If disk space is a problem, consider preventing users from using the Sent Mail folder because it can get very large over time. You could also consider the Clean Mailbox option in the Microsoft Exchange Server administration program to delete old messages from the personal folder store.

✗ **Add** hard drives. Windows NT Server enables you to configure multiple physical drives into one virtual drive or volume set. Before installation, partition one drive into drive C for Windows NT Server and drive D for Microsoft Exchange Server. You can later add a second hard drive and expand drive D to include some or all of the second drive. You can connect up to 32 hard drives to form one volume set. However, drive C cannot be expanded into a volume set with this method, so it is important to plan ahead before Windows NT Server is installed.

If your computer has multiple disk drives, consider some of the other available disk administration options before installing Microsoft Exchange Server:

✗ **Disk striping**

Disk striping creates a virtual drive over two or more hard drives and can greatly improve private and public information store I/O performance. When writing to a file, some of the data is written to each hard drive in the virtual drive to reduce the writing time. Reading gets a similar boost in speed by reading simultaneously from multiple sources.

✗ **Disk striping with parity**

Disk striping with parity requires at least three hard drives. This is similar to basic disk striping because the read and write operations to a file are spread out over the hard drives. However, for each piece of data that is written to a hard drive, a parity stripe is also written. If one hard drive in the virtual drive fails, the data on that drive can be recreated from data and parity stripes on the other drives. This takes more hard disk space to save information stores of the same size, but it provides fault tolerance.

✗ **Disk mirroring**

Disk mirroring makes a duplicate copy of the hard drive on a second drive. If the first drive fails, all the data is on a second drive. This does not improve the write operation speed, but it does improve reading speed because you can read from either of the two drives. It also provides the fault tolerance of disk striping with parity without requiring three hard drives. After Microsoft Exchange Server is installed, disk mirroring is the only option you can implement without backing up all the data and reformatting the drives.

When you decide on a storage solution, use the Microsoft Exchange Optimizer to benchmark your I/O subsystem and have it recommend locations for relevant Microsoft Exchange Server files. If you are adding new disks to your Microsoft Exchange Server computer, you can also use the Optimizer to experiment with I/O setup.

Processors

Microsoft Exchange Server benefits from symmetric multiprocessor support in Windows NT. If processing speed is limiting your Microsoft Exchange Server's performance, consider purchasing a faster processor. If you are already using the fastest processor for your server, consider adding additional processors.

Your Microsoft Exchange Server computer needs enough processing power to handle requests from clients, other servers in the site, and optional special services such as gateways, links to other sites, RAS servers, and file servers for client installations.

Not all servers need multiprocessor support, and not all hardware is easily upgradable to multiprocessor support if it is needed later. Plan your processor choices accordingly.

Network Connections

A Microsoft Exchange Server must have at least one physical connection to the network. You may want your Microsoft Exchange Server to have multiple network adapter cards, 32-bit adapter cards, or PCI adapter cards. You can maximize network throughput with multiple, high-speed network cards. Server hardware that separates I/O on different channels will also help optimize network performance.

Microsoft Exchange Server Architecture

Hardware Platform
Dun & Bradstreet's selected hardware platforms for Microsoft Exchange Servers are as follows:

	Large Servers (150+ Mailboxes)	Small Servers (up to 150 Mailboxes)
Make/ Model	Compaq® ProLiant® 4x000 or XL-class server	Compaq ProLiant 4x000 or XL-class server
CPUs	2 Pentium® processors	1 Pentium® processor

	Large Servers (150+ Mailboxes)	Small Servers (up to 150 Mailboxes)
RAM	128 MB	64 MB
Disk Space	8 GB	4 GB
RAID	Level 5	Level 5

Disk Array Configuration

Dun & Bradstreet has implemented the following disk configuration:

Disk Array Configuration

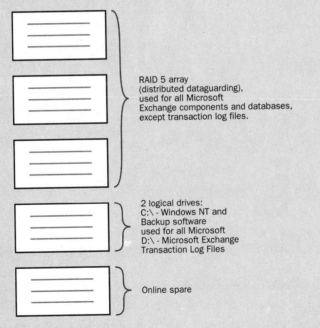

RAID 5 array
(distributed dataguarding),
used for all Microsoft
Exchange components and databases,
except transaction log files.

2 logical drives:
C:\ - Windows NT and
Backup software
used for all Microsoft
D:\ - Microsoft Exchange
Transaction Log Files

Online spare

Dun & Bradstreet uses the same configuration for both large and small servers. Drive sizes are 2.1 GB for the small server (for a total of 10 GB, including online spare), and 4.3 GB for the

(continues)

(continued)

large server (for a total of 20 GB, including online spare). Running the Microsoft Exchange Optimizer after Microsoft Exchange Server setup (and before installing user mailboxes) can help locate and resolve any other tuning issues.

Software Installation

Dun & Bradstreet will install the following software on each of their messaging servers:

✗ **Windows NT Server 3.51:** Required by Microsoft Exchange Server 4.0

✗ **Microsoft Exchange Server 4.0:** Customized installation involves complete setup of all server and administration programs. Client software will not be installed on Microsoft Exchange Servers.

✗ **Backup Software:** Dun & Bradstreet will use Windows NT Backup with the Microsoft Exchange backup extensions. When Arcada® software releases its version of Backup Exec for Microsoft® Exchange, Dun & Bradstreet will evaluate it as their standard backup software.

The Microsoft Exchange Client (Win 16) will be the standard messaging client at Dun & Bradstreet.

The Question—How Many Users per Server?

"How many users per server does Microsoft Exchange support?" sounds like a simple question. It would certainly make our lives a lot simpler if we could just say, "N," where N is some number that was derived by unspecified means and that everyone just accepts. But in the real world, it's impossible to give an unqualified answer to this question. The only short answer, I'm afraid, is, "It all depends."

Determining the number of users who can be supported comfortably on a given Microsoft Exchange Server configuration is an involved task. In an ideal world, we could simulate the organization on various server configurations to get an exact performance figure for each one. Then you could just pick the one that comes out on top. In the real world, however, people mean different things when they talk about "users," "servers," and "support," and a perfect simulation is often impossible.

I know I won't win any friends if I just say "it all depends" and leave it at that, so I'll give you the best information I can based on tests run by the Microsoft Exchange Performance Team. If you've got your own simulation resources, this chapter, along with associated information on the accompanying CD, gives you a head start toward producing your own customized answer to the users-per-server question.

If you want to understand the performance of Microsoft Exchange Server, how server performance relates to users, and how that relationship is measured (or how to measure it yourself), study this information carefully.

RC1 Benchmark Test Results

Based on performance tests with Microsoft Exchange Server RC1, single Microsoft Exchange Server computers with the following configurations will support 120 to more than 1,500 users with an acceptable level of response. This assumes that Microsoft Exchange Server is the only application that is being run on that computer.

Configuration	Approximate number of users
486/66 processor, 24 MB RAM, 1x1 GB disk (1 server)	120 light users
Pentium 66 MHz processor, 32 MB RAM, 1x1 GB disk, 1x1 GB (2 server)	320 light users
Pentium 90 MHz processor, 64 MB RAM, 1x2 GB, 4x2 GB (2 server)	1,560 light users
Pentium 66 MHz processor, 32 MB RAM, 1x1 GB, 1x1 GB (2 server)	160 medium users
Pentium 90 MHz processor, 64 MB RAM, 1x2 GB, 4x2 GB (2 server)	400 medium users

The benchmark testing and recommendations are based on Microsoft Exchange Server RC1. Because these recommendations are for RC1 configurations, they may change due to the performance work that is currently in development.

If you need a quick start, the Users per Server Test Results section of the Performance White Paper on the accompanying CD contains the users per server data and charts generated by the Microsoft Exchange Performance Team. This data, provided for a few predefined user and server configurations, can be used for presentation, as a reference for capacity planning, or as a comparison point for custom-generated users per server data.

To understand the predefined configurations, you should examine the user definitions used to generate the results; these are laid out in the LoadSim Canonical User Definitions section. While the data alone can be useful, I strongly suggest you invest the time to read this entire document and understand the ideas and methods used to generate the users-per-server numbers. This understanding will allow you to use the users-per-server data more effectively; it can also help you produce high-quality users-per-server data by providing a starting point for defining and running your own customized tests.

Understanding *The* Question

Let's take a closer look at the factors that go into the answer to *The* Question. Then I'll talk some more about how to go about answering it.

What is a "User"?

Users vary widely in their Microsoft Exchange-related activities. Usage patterns and activity levels depend on many factors, including business and personal use of messaging, scheduling and workgroup activities, geographical dispersion, and corporate culture. A user may receive hundreds of messages each day or only one or two. They may originate 50 or more a day or only one per week. Some users may interact with the server for 12 hours at a time while others may only connect once a week for a few minutes. They may read hundreds of messages in dozens of public folders every day or none at all.

No two users are exactly the same. In a given user community, a small percentage of the users may generate a disproportionately large percentage of the total load on a server because they are more aggressive users of the system.

What is "Load"?

Load is generated by users connected to the Microsoft Exchange Server system, or by other servers, either in the organization or outside it (via various connectors). The load generated by other servers is in turn caused by users connected to those servers, so all of the load generated in the system as a whole comes from users. The load a specific user places on a specific server generally falls into two categories: user-initiated actions and background actions.

User-Initiated Actions

User-initiated actions are those operations the server performs as a direct result of a user's action and are generally synchronous from the user's point of view. For example, opening a standard unread message in a personal folder in the server information store requires processing time on the server to receive and interpret the open request, evaluate any access restrictions, retrieve the message from the database, mark the message as unread, update the unread count for the folder, marshal the information and return the requested message properties to the client, and generate a folder notification to the client (to notify the client the message has now been read). All of this happens in the time it takes for the remote procedure call (RPC) issued by the client application to return control to the client. The actual time the user perceives the operation taking will be this time plus any additional processing time needed by the client application to draw the window, unmarshal and display the message properties, and so on.

When a user interacts with the server directly, the actions they perform place some immediate load on the server for some length of time. User-initiated actions are the single most significant contributing load factor on Microsoft Exchange Servers that directly support users (as opposed to servers acting primarily as a backbone or gateway server) and are directly proportional to the number of users actively interacting with the server.

Background Actions

In addition to the work it may do to satisfy synchronous user-initiated actions, a Microsoft Exchange Server performs asynchronous or background actions on behalf of users. Accepting, transferring, and delivering messages; making routing decisions; expanding distribution lists;

replicating changes to public folders and directory service information; executing rules; monitoring storage quotas; and performing other background maintenance tasks are all examples of the work a server may do asynchronously on behalf of users, whether they are connected or not. This work is called "asynchronous" because the time it takes does not directly influence the users' perception of the speed of the system, at least not as long as the actions are completed within some reasonable amount of time.

In general, the load due to background actions is also proportional to the number of users on the server. However, other factors, such as whether the server acts as an inter-site connector or hosts a messaging gateway, can have a large impact. On a Microsoft Exchange Server that acts purely as a gateway or backbone machine and does not directly host any users at all, the load due to user-initiated actions is essentially non-existent and the load on the machine can be considered to be entirely due to background actions.

Loaded or Unloaded?

When the Microsoft Exchange Server software services a user-initiated action or performs background actions, it uses each of its system resources—CPU, memory, disks, and so on—to some degree over some period of time. For example, responding to an open message request from a client may require several milliseconds of CPU processing time, one or more disk accesses, and enough memory to hold the code and data necessary to perform the operation. When these actions are separated in time, 100 percent of the server hardware can be dedicated to each action. Each action completes as fast as possible and does not need to wait for hardware resources to become available. When actions are spaced out in time and the machine is essentially idle between actions, it is said to be *unloaded*.

When many users are initiating actions close together in time, or a large number of background events are occurring, the server hardware resources are divided among the various operations. Bottlenecks occur when the code servicing a particular action must wait for hardware to become available in order to complete its tasks. The server is then said to be *under load*.

Just What is a Server?

Definitions of "server" vary widely as well. One organization with large, centrally located or well-connected sites may wish to use a small number of very expensive, high-end, multiprocessor server machines with gigabytes of RAM and dozens of disk drives, hosting as many users per server machine as possible. Another may be interested in using many hundreds of inexpensive, lower-end machines to tie together their many small, geographically dispersed locations.

Many organizations consist of locations of different sizes and levels of connectivity and have several different requirements with respect to servers and the users they host. All customers want the most cost-effective solution not only in terms of hardware, but also with respect to maintenance costs, administration costs, bandwidth costs, floor space, etc.

Practical Limits

Microsoft Exchange Server has no explicit limit on the number of users you can put on a single server. There may, however, be practical limits not directly related to server performance that may prove to be the limiting factor on the number of users a given server can support.

For example, at present there is a 16 GB limitation on the size of the public and private information store databases (32 GB total). Depending on your disk-management policies and the ways people use the system, this could become the limiting factor for how many users can be placed on one server.

There may also be practical limits dictated by the time it takes to back up a very large server database.

However, in general, the main factor in determining the number of users a given server will support is the load each user places on the server.

Why Did I Ask?

By now, you are probably wondering where this is leading. I want to make several points:

✗ **First,** it should now be clear that *The* Question is a very complex one. The first thing you need to do is to understand the factors that go into the answer.

✗ **Second,** Microsoft understands the complexity and the importance of *The* Question. We've done a lot of work studying *The* Question, and we have a lot of information—as well as some very useful tools—that can help you answer it.

✗ **Third,** understand that deriving *The* Answer that's best for your organization is as much art as science: There is no "N." Do the best you can at measuring your environment and your users. Run a pilot installation if you can. Then come up with your own "N," knowing that you'll probably have to do some refining as time goes by.

Chapter 8

The Microsoft Exchange Application Platform

For a lot of organizations—perhaps including yours—a great e-mail system isn't enough. Your success may depend on being able to capture, store, recall, and deliver information where it's needed, when it's needed. You need to respond quickly to changes in the organization, the market, and the world. You need to encourage innovation and responsiveness at all levels of the organization. To do these things, you need a messaging system on which you can base applications ranging from simple workgroup forms to complex, organization data warehousing systems.

Power to the Group

Today, we hear a lot about "groupware" and "workgroup computing." While not precisely defined, those terms are usually used to describe software that helps people share information, plan and coordinate work, and operate more effectively and efficiently. Notice that the emphasis is on the workgroup, not on the organization as a whole.

E-mail was the first, and is still the most important, workgroup application. (Even though e-mail systems are usually installed company-wide, the great majority of messages are between users in the same or "adjacent" workgroups.)

Scheduling was and is the next most important tool for increasing the efficiency of the workgroup.

In the previous several chapters, I told you a lot about what Microsoft Exchange can do. I hope you're at least beginning to agree that Microsoft Exchange lives up to the slogan, "e-mail done right." If your organization needs a capable, flexible, easy-to-administer e-mail system, Microsoft Exchange is for you.

But Microsoft Exchange is more than just a great e-mail system. As computer power continues to permeate the organization, we continue to change the way we think about information and how we handle it. From the original concentration in the mainframe, remote in time and space from the information consumer, we're moving the means to capture, store, transport, recall, and manipulate information right to the user's desk.

Microsoft Exchange facilitates this movement with its application development tools and facilities. In this chapter, I'll describe those tools and facilities and show how they can serve as the application platform that will help your organization achieve the goal of "information at your fingertips."

What is a Microsoft Exchange Application?

A Microsoft Exchange application is somewhat different from a traditional computer application. Instead of a single executable program with supporting files, a Microsoft Exchange application usually has two main parts:

Microsoft Exchange folders: Folders serve as containers for information and associated forms. They can also be used to control who has access to specific information.

Microsoft Exchange forms: Forms serve as the means to enter and view information. The standard message form is used to display message information; other forms can be tailored to display other specific kinds of information.

Microsoft Exchange applications also rely on Microsoft Exchange to transport information and keep it updated throughout the workgroup or organization, and the Microsoft Exchange Client serves as a tool for displaying folder contents.

The Application Continuum

It will help us to understand the benefits of Microsoft Exchange as an application platform if we think of applications as falling on a continuum that has several indexes. One index is the size of the user group; it ranges from the individual to the entire organization. Other indexes are shown in the following illustration:

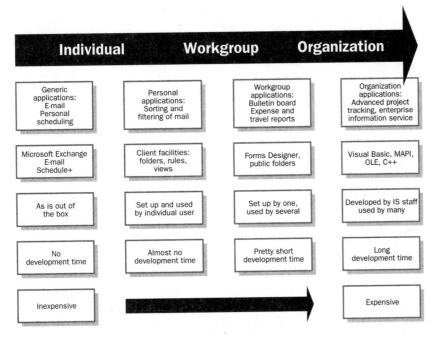

Mail and scheduling can be thought of as "generic" applications, meaning that their basic functions and interfaces can be the same regardless of the characteristics of the group that is using them. Thus, the basic functions of Microsoft Exchange and Schedule+ will work equally well for the engineering group, the sales group, the manufacturing group, and any other group in the organization.

Individual applications are simply the things individual users can do with the inherent features in Microsoft Exchange, such as using a public folder to create a discussion bulletin board, or using rules in Microsoft Exchange to automatically file incoming information according to who originated the file or when it was originated.

Workgroup Applications

Beyond this basic level, there are lots of other applications that groups could use: contact tracking, status reporting, general administration, and so on. These are examples of "workgroup computing," which is the term often used to describe applications that enable people to share information, plan and coordinate work, and operate more efficiently.

These applications share several characteristics:

1 They're pretty simple applications.

2 To be most effective, they need to be tailored to the specific needs of the group. (What works for one group won't necessarily work for any other group.)

3 Because they are simple, they may not appear to be very significant, so it may be hard to get management to spend money to develop them. (Unless there happens to be a "power user" in the group who enjoys programming and has the time to do it, the group may have to do without the application.)

4 They have the potential to make a major improvement in the efficiency and effectiveness of the group.

Organization Applications

At the other end of the application continuum are the organization-wide, often mission-critical, applications. This is where the corporate IS department spends its time and money—usually, a lot of time and money.

An organization might have one or more applications designed to handle hundreds of thousands of transactions per day—airline reservations, catalog orders, inventory management, and the like. Almost certainly, every organization has—or needs—applications to improve the flow of information into, within, and out of the organization. This latter category comprises the kinds of applications we're interested in here.

The Microsoft Exchange Application Platform

The continuum view is useful because the facilities of Microsoft Exchange support the full range of applications from the workgroup to the organization. Applications that are based on Microsoft Exchange can originate at any point on the continuum, and they can "grow" as needs dictate. Microsoft Exchange helps you bridge the gap between ad-hoc workgroup applications and full-blown organization solutions.

For example, a simple "home-made" workgroup application for keeping track of sales leads in a single department could provide the basis for an enhanced contact-tracking system that could be used throughout the company. When a workgroup application based on Microsoft Exchange forms needs more capability, or when it needs to be scaled up to serve other parts of the organization, you can use Visual Basic to extend the functionality without having to reinvent any of the forms.

In the following sections, we'll describe the tools and facilities for application development that are included in Microsoft Exchange.

Developing Workgroup Applications

Stand-Alone and Folder-Based Applications

There are two basic types of Microsoft Exchange workgroup applications: *stand-alone* applications and *folder-based* applications. The job you need to do will determine which kind of application you create. Some sophisticated applications may involve elements of both stand-alone and folder-based applications.

A stand-alone application uses forms to send structured information from one user to another. The form is not associated with any particular public folder, and the form is generally sent directly to the recipient's mailbox. Stand-alone applications can be used for things like telephone messages, routing slips, and travel authorization requests.

With folder-based applications, information is sent to custom public folders, where it is stored, organized, and made available for others (with the proper authorization) when they need it. The steps used to create folder-based applications are the same as those used to create stand-alone applications, except for the additional step of creating the public folder for the application. Examples of folder-based applications are a discussion database, a bulletin board, a document library, or a customer tracking system.

Personal Applications

The application continuum illustration at the beginning of this chapter shows personal applications at the low end of the development scale (beyond simply using the product straight out of the box). Personal applications (okay, maybe it's stretching the point to call them "applications") are anything you can do with the Microsoft Exchange forms, folders, filters, and views for your own use. In fact, a personal application could be every bit as complex as a workgroup application, but most often, they're simple forms and straightforward folder arrangements that help you do your job, and they usually don't involve public folders.

Typical Workgroup Applications

Microsoft Exchange provides a number of facilities for creating and running workgroup applications:

- ✘ **A tool** to create custom electronic forms.

- ✘ **The capability** to group and organize forms based on the information they contain.

- ✘ **Public folders** to hold the forms.

- ✘ **The ability** to replicate public folders to other servers, making the information available to anyone across the company.

- ✘ **Security** to protect folders from unauthorized access.

- ✘ **Rules** for specifying actions that take place automatically when a form is put into a folder.

These forms, views, folders, permissions, and rules are used to create Microsoft Exchange applications. Here are some of the kinds of workgroup applications you can make with the native capabilities of Microsoft Exchange—and without any programming:

Routing Forms

Users can easily create person-to-person routing forms. For example, a sales manager could design a form to gather weekly sales data from sales people. The sales people—whether permanently connected to the network or mobile—could simply fill out the preaddressed form and send it back to the sales manager.

A routing form might look like this:

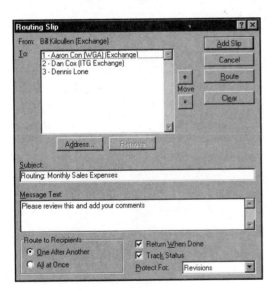

Discussion Groups

With Microsoft Exchange, it's easy to set up a discussion, or "bulletin board," application. All it takes is a public folder where you and your coworkers can carry on a discussion. Anyone can browse the messages already in the folder and add their own messages, either in reply to what someone else said or to start their own topic.

You can create a discussion public folder on any topic. For example, you could create a product feature folder where the product team can hold conversations on what features to include in an upcoming product.

Users won't have to search backward through a long list of mail messages to find out who said what, and you can avoid the network-clogging glut of redundant messages that result from a lengthy mail discussion among a large group of people.

Here's what the user might see in a discussion group folder:

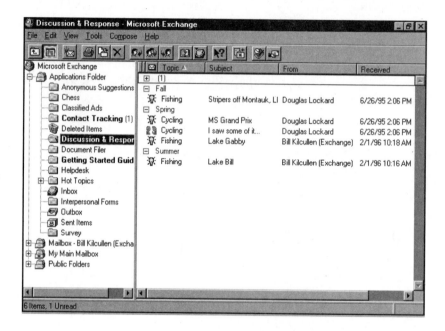

Microsoft Exchange even provides a generic form for posting messages to a public folder, so a discussion database can be built quickly.

Reference Repositories

Most groups need a central repository where users can go to find information such as product specifications, project plans, standard operating procedures, an employee handbook, monthly reports, and sales data.

You can use replicated public folders for this type of application. With replicated folders, updates to the information in the central repository are automatically distributed to all other servers that support the users who need the information.

Here's how product information, entered as posted messages, could be viewed in a public folder application:

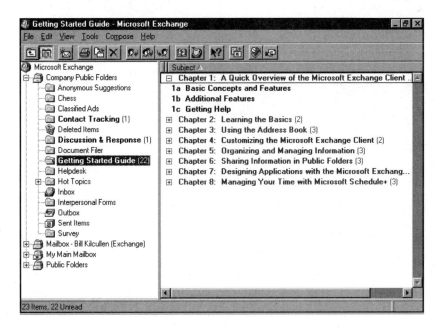

Tracking Applications

In most companies, sales people need to access a number of information sources before making an account call. They may need to call other members of the sales force to determine who last contacted the customer, go through sales orders to find out whether the company has outstanding orders, and keep a mental account history.

Many organizations provide this functionality through the use of third-party products. The Microsoft Exchange sample tracking application brings that functionality into the same user interface as e-mail and other workgroup applications.

For instance, with a customer-tracking public folder, a sales person could go to a single location to look up or enter the last contact with the customer, to review the history of customer contacts and orders, and to study company profile information.

A contact form might look like this:

```
Correspondence Report                                    _ □ X
File  Edit  View  Insert  Format  Tools  Compose  Help

[print] X [icons]  ▲  ▼

Sketchy (Everywear)                  ┌─ Nature of Correspondence ──────┐
                                     │ Medium:  ┌──────────────────┐   │
          Bethany Schatz             │          │ Electronic Mail  ▲ │  │
Item Author: Max Benson (Exchange)   │          │ Phone            │   │
          11/4/95 6:58:55 PM         │          │ Letter/Package   ▼ │  │
                                     │          ○ We Initiated  ● They Initiated │
                                     └─────────────────────────────────┘
Summary:  spoke with Ty

Details:  he's sending some of the clothing our way!              ▲



                                                                  ▼
```

With a form such as this, designed just for the application, sales people can quickly enter information. Check boxes and drop-down lists make it easy to enter standard information.

Microsoft Exchange's ability to show data in various views goes a long way toward turning "data" into "information." For example, sales people could look at contacts arranged according to the person contacted or the product discussed.

I described how to set up folders in chapter 3.

Designing Folders

One of the primary tools used to build Microsoft Exchange applications is the Microsoft Exchange Folder Designer. The Folder Designer, or public folder property sheets dialog box, is built into the Microsoft Exchange Client and is used to set the views, forms, rules, permissions, and other general attributes of a public folder. You don't need to do any programming to create and manage public folders.

bug reports Properties

| Replication Schedule | Distribution Lists | Custom Attributes | Advanced |
| General | Replicas | Folder Replication Status | |

📧 **bug reports**

Folder name: `bug reports`

Address book display name
- ⦿ Same as folder name
- ○ Use this name: `_____`

Alias name: `bug reports`

☐ Age limit for all replicas (days): `____`   Client Permissions...

Notes:

Folder path:
`bug reports`

| Created | Home site: United Kingdom | Last modified |
| 1/27/96 10:17 AM | Home server: ABRIARO | 2/2/96 4:16 PM |

OK   Cancel   Apply   Help

Public folder property sheets let you create and manage folders without programming.

Using the Microsoft Exchange Forms Designer

If your application calls for something more than regular e-mail messages or the standard post-to-folder form, you can use the Microsoft Exchange Forms Designer to create custom forms—without programming. Using the Forms Designer, you simply drag and drop prebuilt screen objects onto a blank "page" to create the desired form. These screen objects include:

- ✗ **Preprogrammed message fields:** To, From, CC, BCC, and Subject

- ✗ **General graphical controls:** labels, text boxes, check boxes, and option buttons

- ✗ **Basic field properties:** style, alignment, color, formatting, tab order, validation, and alerts

- ✗ **Advanced user interface elements:** menus, toolbar with ToolTips, rich-text editor, OLE, help screens, and status bar

To show you how simple it is, you can add printing capability to any form just by dragging the button labeled "Print" onto the form.

When the form is the way you want it, the Forms Designer automatically compiles and installs it.

Wizards guide you through the form design process.

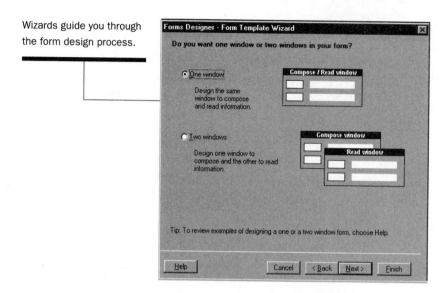

Managing Electronic Forms

After you create forms, the next step is to make them available to users. This involves making sure that the forms are accessible to the right people (and only the right people) at the right time. Stand-alone forms probably should be available to users at any time. Forms that are part of a folder-based application should appear as options when the public folder is opened. Some forms will need to be available only when the client is online; others, such as an order-entry form, may be required even when the user is disconnected from the server.

To ensure that the forms are available to users when they are needed, forms are installed into one of the four form registries described in the following table.

Registry	Description	Advantage
Organization Forms Registry	A public repository for forms that is located on a Microsoft Exchange Server computer. Usually used for stand-alone, interpersonal forms.	Allows forms to be used by anyone who has access to the server. Centralized storage makes management of the forms easy for administrators.
Public Folder Registry	A public repository for forms that is located on a Microsoft Exchange Server computer. Holds forms used in folder-based applications.	Allows forms to be used by anyone who has access to the server and has permissions on the related public folder. Centralized storage makes management easy for administrators.

Registry	Description	Advantage
Personal Folder Registry	A personal repository for forms used with folder-based applications. The repository can be located on a server, but more typically is on the user's local hard drive.	Allows forms to be distributed using a set of personal folders. Easy to distribute to remote users as a .PST file on a floppy or compact disk.
Personal Registry	A personal repository for designated users that holds stand-alone forms. The repository can be located on a server or on the user's local hard drive.	Allows use of forms when the user is offline. Can also provide tight controls on forms that should be limited to specific users.

Developing Organization Applications

Extending Electronic Forms

The designers of Microsoft Exchange had two seemingly conflicting goals in mind when they developed the product. The first goal was to enable users to create applications with no programming required. To meet this goal, they developed the Forms Designer, the Folder Designer, and Microsoft Exchange Client features. However, they had a second, equally important goal of allowing organizations to extend forms-based applications by using traditional programming tools to add advanced capabilities—and to do that without having to start over from scratch.

Here's where the concept of an application "continuum" really becomes clear. Microsoft Exchange lets you start small and grow. It doesn't run out of steam when you want to take an application from the workgroup to the organization.

To make this level of extensibility possible, the Forms Designer not only compiles a form into an executable file, but also generates standard Visual Basic project files such as the .MAK, .BAS, and .FRM files. These Visual Basic source files are automatically stored in the same directory as the associated Forms Designer source file (.EPF file). Using Visual Basic version 4.0, developers can open the .MAK file and add custom "handcode" routines, use APIs or OLE automation, and integrate third-party applications or custom controls to add functionality to the form.

Here are some of the ways the functionality of forms can be extended:

✗ **Use** the data access of Visual Basic or custom controls to populate form fields with information from a database.

✗ **Extend** Microsoft Exchange's validation capabilities and range checking.

✗ **Add** Custom data fields for grid control, masked edit control, and an OLE container.

✗ **Customize** the user interface button controls or make other user interface enhancements.

✗ **Add** dialog boxes or create forms with multiple panels.

✗ **Customize** the standard menus and toolbars.

✗ **Add** calculations or derived fields.

✗ **Customize** field events with procedures such as change(), click(), and gotfocus().

✗ **Include** advanced MAPI functionality.

To the novice developer, the Forms Designer tool provides all of the features required to quickly and easily construct workgroup applications. For advanced solutions, the Forms Designer enables the developer to construct the general framework for the form, then use Visual Basic to extend the functionality and polish the application.

Using Sample Applications

Microsoft Exchange comes with a number of sample applications that are both instructive and useful—and even fun.

Here are descriptions of the sample applications:

Application	Description
Discussion and Response	Provides forms for submitting discussion topics and a response form for responding to a discussion in progress. Views are grouped by discussion topic or by author, and the items in the folder are threaded by conversation.
Hot Topics (Moderated News)	Provides moderated distribution of "news." Items submitted to the folder are diverted to a moderator's subfolder for review. When a moderator approves a submission, it appears in the Hot Topics folder for access by readers. This application could also be used for classified ads.

Application	Description
Document Filer	Store and categorize OLE compound documents such as those created using Microsoft Word, Microsoft Excel, or Microsoft® PowerPoint®. This folder uses the built-in compound document wrapper form, IPM.Document, to promote document summary properties to the Microsoft Exchange Viewer. To file a document, the user drags it from the File Manager and drops it in the Document Filer folder. Views are grouped by author, keyword, and type.
Contact Tracking	Product and service organizations can use Contact Tracking to collect and keep data such as all sales leads in all regions, all qualified leads for one product or service, all outstanding invoices, or a history of all purchase orders, giving every person in the organization access to the data needed to complete every aspect of customer service.
Getting Started	Provides a guide to getting started with Microsoft Exchange. Items in this folder are tutorial in nature with step-by-step instructions for client users. Shows how folders can serve as a place to store and access tutorial information.
Help Desk	Use to manage problem description, triage, assignment, and resolution. Using Microsoft Exchange, help-desk supervisors can track technician productivity, technician expertise, and common product or service trouble spots.
Chess	The Microsoft Exchange forms-based version of the traditional chess game. This application shows how Microsoft Visual Basic, OLE, and Microsoft Exchange can be combined to create graphic applications.
Survey	Use the Survey and Answer forms to design a survey. It contains all types of questions, including multiple choice, true or false, essay, gradient or scale, and ranking. You can also analyze survey results by generating a report in Microsoft Word, using OLE automation.
Anonymous Postings	This sample application provides for anonymous submissions to a public folder by replacing the sender's name in the From field with "Anonymous". The Anonymous Postings application is designed to support forums where people may otherwise be unwilling to post messages.

The sample applications serve several purposes. They show you some of the types of business solutions that can be built on the Microsoft Exchange platform. In addition, because the sample applications also include the source files used to create them, they serve as starting points—modifiable templates—for developers to enhance and customize. Not only do the sample applications make it easy to build custom applications, but they also provide the sample source code for developers to learn more about how Microsoft Exchange applications are built.

The survey application is a good example of how the capabilities of Microsoft Exchange can be integrated with other Microsoft Office products to produce a robust application. From within the survey application, a summary of the information from received survey forms can be output to Microsoft Excel for analysis, to Microsoft Word for use in a report, or to Microsoft PowerPoint for use in a presentation.

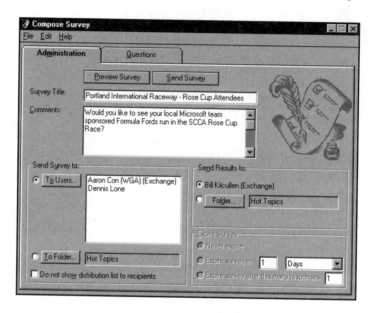

This degree of application integration lets the application designer take advantage of the strengths of each application—and each programming interface, since both Visual Basic and the Microsoft Office applications utilize the same engine—to build a custom solution.

The chess application is a custom application written in Visual Basic that shows the moves that have been made in a chess game played by mail by two Microsoft Exchange users.

The chess game shows how an application can be created to view and navigate through the information in a Microsoft Exchange public folder. The same application could be used to move data into and out of Microsoft Exchange, independent of the Microsoft Exchange Client. It also demonstrates how data can be turned into compelling, quickly understood visual information.

Most significantly, this application shows that the only limit to the customization of an Microsoft Exchange-based application is your own imagination.

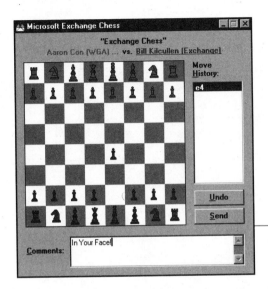

The right side of the chess board shows the moves that have been made so far in the game. Click on one of the earlier moves and the chess pieces rearrange themselves to the positions they occupied at that point in the game.

So when your boss finds you playing chess, you can explain that you're really working on an application to graphically show the flow of products through the factory, or the occupancy levels of apartment complexes through the year, or the history of a project, or whatever. Just don't let on that you're having fun.

Integrating Custom Applications with MAPI and OLE

Microsoft Exchange is built on the open, de facto industry-standard Messaging API (MAPI). There is also an OLE Automation interface to MAPI (OLE Messaging) and an OLE Automation interface to Schedule+ (OLE Scheduling). With these facilities, you (or a third-party solution provider) can integrate custom applications with Microsoft Exchange.

The MAPI subsystem infrastructure upon which Microsoft Exchange is built is shown here:

The MAPI Subsystem

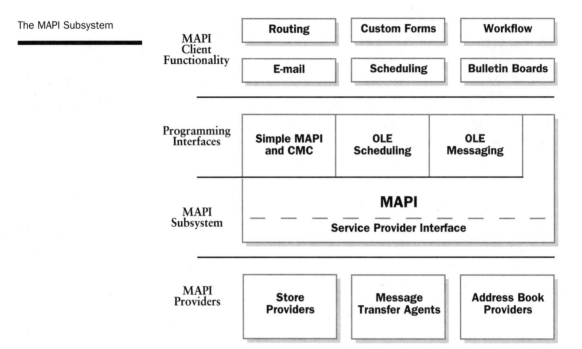

Applications can communicate with the service providers in Microsoft Exchange through the MAPI subsystem, or the MAPI subsystem can initiate contact and then the services can communicate directly.

MAPI-compliant applications span a broad range of messaging and workgroup functions. MAPI can be used by 16-bit applications running on Windows 3.x or by 16- or 32-bit applications running on Windows NT Server or Windows 95.

These applications access the service provider functions they need through a single interface instead of having to work with a specific interface for each provider, much as applications using the Microsoft Windows printing subsystem don't need drivers for every available printer.

Applications that require messaging services can access them through any of five programming interfaces: Simple MAPI (sMAPI), Common Messaging Calls (CMC), OLE Messaging, OLE Scheduling, and MAPI itself.

Requests for messaging services are processed by the MAPI subsystem, either as function interface calls (as in the case of sMAPI or CMC) or as manipulations of MAPI objects (as in the case of OLE Messaging or MAPI itself) and passed on to the appropriate MAPI-compliant service provider. The MAPI service providers then perform the requested actions for the client and pass back action through the MAPI subsystem to the MAPI client.

Each MAPI subsystem interface has its uses:

✗ **sMAPI** contains 12 Windows-based function calls that enable messaging-aware applications to perform basic messaging tasks such as sending e-mail and resolving e-mail names. It provides the programming interface primarily used by Microsoft Mail.

✗ **CMC** provides functionality similar to that available in sMAPI, but has been designed to support cross-platform applications.

✗ **OLE Messaging** is an OLE Automation server that presents a large subset of MAPI functionality to the developer. It enables Visual Basic and Visual Basic for Applications developers to use the messaging and workgroup functionality inherent in MAPI, and permits users to get more use out of their investment in programming VBA as well as their investment in desktop software by integrating those applications into custom Microsoft Exchange solutions.

✗ **OLE Scheduling** is an OLE Automation server that provides Visual Basic and Visual Basic for Applications developers with an interface to the information stored in Schedule+ 7.0.

For example, you could use the Telephone Application Programming Interface (TAPI) and Schedule+ to create an application that sends meeting reminders, including a text message, to a user's pager. Or, using Microsoft Project, you could schedule tasks in both Microsoft Project and Schedule+.

Integration with Microsoft Office for Windows 95 and Schedule+ is especially close, and solutions can be quickly built that integrate them using VBA through the OLE Scheduling interface.

For example, new contact information entered by your sales representative in Schedule+ could be copied to Microsoft Excel for reporting and analysis. Reports could be generated in Microsoft Word based on information in Schedule+.

✗ **MAPI** itself is a Component Object Model (COM) interface that enables MAPI objects such as messages, forms, and folders to be manipulated. It is designed to be used by more complex messaging and workgroup applications. Thus, MAPI will be used by developers desiring a full range of functionality in their applications and the performance that comes from writing directly to an API.

Integrating Third-Party Applications

Third-party programming interfaces can be built on MAPI. Because MAPI is such an open and well-defined interface, a proprietary third-party API can be implemented on top of MAPI without the need to revise the MAPI subsystem itself. Thus, customers can implement their own MAPI solutions that meet their particular needs without incurring the development costs that would arise with other messaging infrastructures.

Companies whose business is building solutions for others will find the Microsoft Exchange Software Development Kit a valuable tool. With this kit, companies can integrate their application with Microsoft Exchange or build a custom gateway to provide a tailored solution.

They can also extend the Microsoft Exchange Client interface to meet their specific needs, add functionality to the administrative module, or access virtually any portion of the Microsoft Exchange infrastructure.

Chapter

9

Postscript

"...there's a huge pent-up demand for Microsoft Exchange."

There's little doubt in our minds that there's a huge pent-up demand for Microsoft Exchange. The Microsoft Mail user base has been clamoring for a client-server solution to help it move beyond the limitations of file-based mail. From everything we've seen, Exchange has the feature set to meet most of that base's demands. We also agree with you that Exchange will serve as a unifying message infrastructure that corporations will use to consolidate their melange of existing e-mail systems. Furthermore, Exchange can only benefit by the fact that NT Server has built up a huge head of steam. The fact that NT Server has been accepted as a reliable enterprise platform will greatly aid Exchange's marketing objectives.

Exchange will have some other shortcomings when it ships. Its weak UNIX support will be among the most notable of these. Generally, though, it has an impressive feature set and does a good job of leveraging NT Server and the other members of the BackOffice suite.

Dwight B. Davis, Editor
Windows Watcher.

"Microsoft Exchange can resolve the shortcomings of their messaging system and enhance the way they do business."

In the past, SQLSoft has had an opportunity to visit many sites for consultation. Most of these sites either have e-mail or want e-mail. We have noticed several things in common with these sites. These sites are experiencing shortcomings with their current e-mail systems that are inhibiting their ability to do business. These shortcomings generally fall under a few different categories:

✗ **Connectivity** within and outside the company

✗ **Administration** of disparate operating systems and mail systems

✗ **Security**

✗ **General** limitations in mail functionality ranging from the inability to send attachments to not being able to effectively use and administer distribution lists

When visiting these sites, we generally take two strategies to resolve the issues. First we will try to quickly improve their current situation by fixing problems with their current technology or training them to more effectively use their current technology. This approach has certain limitations, and in some cases they are positioning themselves to move to a 'next generation' of business systems and are through trying to enhance their current environment. This usually involves more than e-mail. For example, a company may have bought an e-mail system 15 years ago that required a particular operating system to support that functionality. In the course of using that operating system, they may even have started to use [it] for other purposes, such as file and print services. Now this company is in the unenviable position of being limited not only by an outdated mail system, but also by an outdated operating system.

A client may bring me in to discuss their e-mail issues, but it almost always is also a discussion about what the future platform for hosting the enterprise business systems will be. In these discussions, a couple of things seem to be most important: consolidation of operating systems and leveraging of expensive skill sets. These clients have generally already evaluated NT, NetWare, UNIX, and OS/2, and now they are basing their decisions on what can be done with these various operating systems.

The BackOffice suite is very interesting option to these companies because of the ability to implement one OS, and get enterprise functionality. As part of our consulting on their mail issues, we make it clear that with Exchange they can consolidate many of the components that make up their messaging system under NT. Now they can leverage off of what they have learned about NT and have a flatter learning curve in order to implement Exchange. Because of the BackOffice suite, they can also do this for enterprise database functionality with SQL Server and overall management with Server Management System. Because of the consolidated operating system, we also get consolidated security. One logon for e-mail, file and print services, and database connectivity.

Now that the client is interested in NT for the obvious benefits, we can begin to address how Microsoft Exchange can resolve the shortcomings of their messaging system and enhance the way they do business.

The first shortcoming mentioned above is connectivity within and outside the company. With integrated connectivity to a variety of native messaging standards, such as X.400 and SMTP, they can implement one system that can operate with their existing messaging systems as well as outside the company using standard messaging specifications. Most companies don't have the luxury or capability to implement a new messaging system for all their clients overnight. This makes seamless connectivity to existing messaging systems critical for their implementation. We have also found that stability for these outside connections is a major issue. It's interesting to note that several of my clients wish to use beta versions of Exchange to replace their current Internet mail solutions because Exchange, as a beta, is more stable and provides much greater flexibility and performance than what they have now.

The second shortcoming, administration of disparate operating systems and messaging systems, is addressed in a number of ways. First, with Exchange based on NT, administrators already know how to check for errors in Event Viewer; they already know how to gauge performance and troubleshoot using Performance Monitor; and they already know the underlying operations of Security because they already know NT. Exchange merely leverages off components that the client is already very comfortable with using. They feel comfortable knowing that the product is not exactly completely brand new because it is using the technology of NT.

Second, Exchange Administration follows the standards of other BackOffice products in how the product is configured. We have the tree hierarchy, and property pages that clients are comfortable using in products like SQL Server 6.0 and Windows 95. This makes it much easier for an administer to become comfortable working with the Administrator tool. In addition, administration can be done for the entire organization from a single glass. How nice would it be for a mail administrator to be able to connect to an overseas subsidiary and add mailboxs to the system or troubleshoot performance problems. Single-seat administration gives the administrators great flexibility and control of the entire messaging system.

As for the third short-coming, security, most clients are very excited about a couple of things regarding security in Exchange. First is the single logon. For years, our access to messaging has been based on a separate user id and password that is used to access the network. With Exchange, your access to messaging is based on your NT user account. This makes it much easier for users and administrators. Users only have to remember one set of user id and password, and administrators can consolidate their security into one NT Security Accounts Manager Database. In addition, we have the flexibility of individual security on Exchange folders. This makes it possible to differentiate between access security to messaging and access to data within that messaging environment. NT administrators can keep control of overall access to messaging with NT user accounts, and Exchange users can control access to data within folders using Exchange security. This offloads the overhead of controlling all aspects of security from the administrative staff and lets the user take on some of this responsibility, as appropriate.

The fourth shortcoming, general limitations, has been addressed in a variety of ways. Exchange supports rich text formatting in messages, including colors and different fonts, which make it easier to display, interpret, and communicate ideas. The distribution list management in Exchange also far exceeds the capabilities of some earlier systems, providing global distribution functionality and completely automated management of changes to the directory that might effect distribution lists.

SQLSoft has been using Exchange in production since Beta 2. One of the first things that comes to mind in our experience has been stability. Since moving to Exchange, we have not been down once. Before Exchange, our access to Internet messaging was going down once a day at least.

Exchange has also made an impact in the way SQLSoft handles information within the company and in dealing with interests outside the company, such as our clients and an Exchange user group we have started in conjunction with Microsoft called the Northwest Messaging Forum.

We keep track of all dealings with our clients for consulting on a per engineer basis. This made it difficult to keep of track of client visits, because when a different engineer would visit a client, they would keep track of what transpired separately. Using Exchange Public Folders and Office 95 Binder technology, we now keep track of client information such as consulting visits, configurations, and key contacts centrally in a public folder. By using the Binder, we have one "document" that keeps track of drawings of client configurations, standard memos using Word 95, and proposals in Excel. Using the custom views in Exchange and custom properties of the binder documents, I can organize the information for each client in the folder so that it is displayed using an expandable tree hierarchy that is organized by custom Binder properties such as client name. This allows us to share information with everybody and keep it centrally located. When an engineer makes a consulting visit, they transcribe what occurred on that visit as a posted reply to the Binder for that client, so we have a history recorded. The other benefit here is that I don't have to create a folder for each client. That becomes messy after awhile, with the custom view, the hierarchy is grouped by client name.

We also use public folders to disseminate a variety of information within the company, such as staff meeting agendas, policies and procedures, and all of our course setup information for setting up classes we teach. Centrally locating this information greatly reduces disk utilization on our clients, because things like meeting agendas, which are in Word 95, are only stored once, instead of multiple times, as when they were sent to each employee.

Steve Schwartz, Senior Consultant
SQLSoft

"Electronic messaging is arguably Microsoft Exchange's greatest strength."

Microsoft Exchange promises to have a major impact on the messaging industry as the leader of a new class of messaging products which integrate enterprise-wide messaging services, directory services, groupware functionality and a powerful foundation for building workflow and workgroup applications into a single environment. We believe Exchange will allow organizations to significantly improve productivity while reducing administrative costs and complexity.

Electronic Messaging

Electronic messaging is arguably Microsoft Exchange's greatest strength. In terms of client functionality, the Exchange client is clearly designed for end-user ease-of-use. Extensive hands-on testing points out Exchange's superiority in many messaging client features, such as:

✗ **OLE** integration which allows users to drag and drop text and files from message to folder and between messages.

✗ **Message** links to files stored on the NT server.

✗ **The Universal** Inbox for messages from various sources such as X.400, MIME, CompuServe, Microsoft Mail and others.

✗ **View** filtering on the Inbox.

✗ **Message** read/receipt notifications.

✗ **Integration** with the NOS (NT) for single log-in to the network and Exchange.

In addition to client functionality, the Exchange client/server-based architecture is relatively simple to install and configure. One of the Exchange architecture's strengths is its tight integration with the Windows NT Server network operating system. Installation and configuration of the Exchange Server is straightforward, as it 'learns' much of its basic configuration from its integration with NT. The Exchange Server also handles distribution lists particularly well, especially when deleting a user's NT/Exchange account automatically removed the name from all public distribution lists. Another of Exchange's strong points is the inclusion of X.400 and SMTP/MIME MTAs (Exchange Connectors).

For messaging security, Exchange supports public/private key encryption and digital signatures. Exchange's model uses a single Key Management Server for an entire organization. This model focuses on centralizing the management and distribution of keys. Exchange supports U.S. 64-byte and International 40-byte encryption algorithms.

Directory Services

Exchange's X.500-like Directory Service client is superior to other products currently on the market, largely due to its search support. For example, Exchange users can search on any attribute stored in the directory (e.g., a user's telephone number). Other products allow searches only on user names. Additionally, the Exchange use of tab sheets to separate the directory data is another example of well-designed, user-friendliness.

Network Integration and Management

Network integration and management are key areas for enterprise-wide information sharing services. Exchange leverages its tight integration with Windows NT Advanced Server to provide superior functionality in these areas. First, the Exchange Server uses the user account and network topology information managed by NT. This greatly reduces redundancy and simplifies the task of managing accounts and connections in both the NOS and application environments.

A by-product of Exchange's integration with NT Server is its enhanced security. NT's many advanced security functions, such as:

✗ **Account** lock-out after log-in attempts using an erroneous password.

✗ **Limiting** user log-ins to specific workstations and/or specific hours.

✗ **Setting** account expiration dates.

Perhaps the most striking network management functionality Exchange offers is its network monitoring capability. Exchange provides the Link Monitor, Server Monitor and Performance Monitor with each Exchange server. These tools are very simple to install and configure, yet very powerful in their ability to trap and report erroneous conditions across the Exchange network.

Data Replication

Exchange uses an RPC mechanism between LAN-attached servers, and a messaging-based, store-and-forward mechanism between WAN-attached servers. The Exchange replication engine uses the Exchange directory to keep track of folder replicas. Creating replication schedules between servers is very simple in Exchange. Wizards and property sheets walk the administrator through the replication scheduling process, supporting easy point-and-click replication schedule generation.

Remote Client Services

Remote client support for the message Inbox is fully integrated with the Exchange product. Users are able to download message headers without downloading entire messages, and can download copies of messages while leaving the original message in the message store. These features enable users to function efficiently while traveling away from the office.

Workflow Automation

Exchange includes integrated applications such as shared folders, calendar/scheduling and forms management which provide the foundation for a client/server office and workflow automation system for distributed LANs.

A Review of Microsoft Exchange
Sara Radicati
The Radicati Group, Inc.

"Companies need a comfortable balance of access to data versus control...."

Background

Over the past two decades, computing infrastructures have changed dramatically in organizations around the world. Companies have inverted the model whereby all computing and data management was performed by the mainframe or minicomputer, secured and protected against access by anyone without "privilege." Partly in response to this restrictive control of the information and processes necessary to perform one's job, the personal computing revolution was welcomed with open arms by those desperately needing the ability to manage their own mission-critical data.

As a consequence of the rapid proliferation of PC technology, access and manipulation of corporate data has become somewhat independent from formal IS controls. Some industry analysts say that this independence approaches the point where organizations are at risk of losing valuable data because of lack of adequate data protection procedures. We create, share, manipulate, and delete information in every functional area of the enterprise, oftentimes disregarding the impact of those actions on other departments which might benefit from its use. Worse yet, there is little consideration given to the impact of the *loss* of access (through modification, deletion, or inadequate backups) when that data has critical value to other departments in the enterprise. In some respects, while inverting the computing infrastructure model, we have compounded the management problems of the company's most valuable asset: *corporate information.* In every industry there are examples today of the need for better information management:

✗ **Manufacturing:** A batch of parts are manufactured to improper specifications because the shop floor had not been notified of the availability of the latest drawings.

✗ **Insurance:** A group of fraudulent claims are paid because not all employees could be trained on the new review policies in time.

✗ **Financial Services:** Improper trading activity occurred because of the lack of foolproof automated oversight rules.

✗ **ISO/9000:** A company risks the loss of registration because it cannot ensure that proper quality procedures were followed.

✗ **Customer Service:** A valued customer switches to another supplier because their correspondence was lost and never acknowledged.

Companies need a comfortable balance of access to data versus control and IS disciplines. The only way that this can be accomplished is through computing tools which have as their principle design criteria: data protection, secure data access, process management, and above all, ease of use. The department goals with respect to information are very straightforward. They need to ensure that the right information is available, to the proper people, and that the correct procedures are followed—automatically. Yet they need to have the flexibility to control the business processes and information dissemination without waiting for lengthy application development backlogs to clear.

The availability of powerful yet flexible information management and infrastructure tools like Microsoft Exchange coupled with easy-to-use applications such as Keyfile's workflow software will provide customers with significant competitive advantage in solving these all-too-common business problems. Let's examine how the department's goals are met through the combination of these products.

Right Information

In every department, information constantly changes. Documents easily can be rendered worthless (or even damaged) if all of the information relevant to a decision is not available to the decision maker. Additionally, information is not of just one data type. Decision support information can be a piece of customer correspondence which has been scanned as an image, or a word processing document, or a spreadsheet, or mainframe data record, or any combination of these. The automated information sharing facility of Microsoft Exchange through its public folder mechanism ensures that the people who need the information have it—no matter what the data type.

Proper Access

Information is only a valuable as its integrity. Microsoft Exchange provides data management which is secure from loss, protected [from] unauthorized access, while remaining easily available to those who need it. By providing this sound environment, developers who provide customer solutions within the Microsoft Exchange architecture, know that their solutions, on the one hand, are protected by the robust Microsoft technology infrastructure, while at the same time remain fully compliant with the industry's leading standards.

Correct Procedures

Providing an information sharing infrastructure is only part of the solution. Worldwide organizations are constantly challenged to find ever more efficient ways of getting the job done. No matter what the department's function in an enterprise, that department will continually find more efficient ways of working. Moreover, the enterprise becomes more efficient as a whole only when the various departments function together as cohesive and well coordinated units. Until now, workflow software products have focused on single department applications. By using the technological infrastructure provided by Microsoft Exchange, these departments can automatically link each of their processes one to another.

Example in Action

Consider the impact of this approach on a manufacturing company where a customer has just written concerning a defective part. In the non-automated case, the letter is slowly shuffled from department to department, from one disorganized pile of paper to another while person after person plays "telephone tag" trying to figure out what's wrong with the part. If the customer were to call in to ask the status of the letter, chances are that the company would have a difficult time even locating the correspondence, let alone answering the customer's question accurately and promptly. The move toward Business Process Reengineering is greatly eased by having tools flexible enough for department personnel to use, yet powerful to span and control all of the enterprise activity.

In a company where Microsoft Exchange and Keyfile workflow technology are used, the customer letter is automatically routed from one responsible person to another. The system monitors the progress of the problem resolution and ensures that the customer is given a response quickly. In the case where an Engineering Change Order (ECO) needs to be initiated, the complete process—from initial Engineering Design, to Cost Accounting, Purchasing, Contracts, Receiving, Fabrication, and Quality Control—can be automatically initiated. Each of the discrete departmental processes become part of the coherent whole. While each department is still responsible for making its own processes as streamlined as possible, each process is automatically tied to the other. The completion of one department's tasks automatically triggers activity in the following department. And all the while, the image of the original customer letter is managed as part of the electronic case folder as easily as the engineering drawings, contract, cost models, bill of materials, or any other piece of relevant data.

An Enterprise is a collection of Departments. The "Reengineered Enterprise," is one where workflow automation software is used together with infrastructure technology to enable people to create ever more efficient processes joining every department of the company. The union of Microsoft Exchange and Keyfile workflow technology makes it all possible—today!

Roger K. Sullivan, Vice President, Marketing

Keyfile Corporation

"Microsoft has created a comprehensive development platform...."

The Microsoft Exchange development platform offers tools, templates, and sample applications that make it very simple for people with or without programming experience to create workgroup applications. Applications that ship with Exchange such as the Electronic Forms Template Wizard and the Electronic Forms Designer are tightly integrated with other development tools such as Microsoft Visual Basic 4.0 and Microsoft® Visual C++® 4.0, and components such as the messaging API (MAPI) and object linking and embedding (OLE) automation. This comprehensive development platform empowers all levels of user and developer to be Exchange developers.

The Electronic Forms Template Wizard and the Electronic Forms Designer enable the user to design and install a fully functional electronic form. Much like other wizards found in Microsoft products, the Electronic Forms Template Wizard steps the user through the various decisions necessary to determine the basic functionality of the form. To help get the creative juices flowing, several template forms ship with Exchange. From there, the Electronic Forms Designer can be used to further customize the form. The combination of these two components provide the developer with a great way to develop simple electronic forms and prototype more complex workgroup applications.

Using the Forms Designer, a complete Visual Basic project can be generated from the prototype. Then, using Visual Basic, the functionality of the form can be extended.

The power in the Exchange development platform really lies in its extensibility. And what better tools to take Exchange forms design to the next level than Visual Basic 4.0 and Visual C++ 4.0. The number of developers familiar with these two development tools is huge, and all their skills, such as GUI design and code writing are leveraged in the Exchange forms design environment. This is in contrast to the Lotus Notes developer, who must become familiar with the Notes development and database environment in addition to third party products such as the Hi-Test API for Notes to provide the link between Visual Basic developers and Notes. Several sample applications ship with Exchange which can help provide a base for developers to learn from and expand on in their messaging projects.

Although Visual Basic and Visual C++ are very powerful in their own right, they really provide the glue between the Exchange information store, the messaging API (MAPI), object linking and embedding (OLE) automation technology and the form with which the user interacts. The Exchange forms developer can use OLE automation to enable Exchange forms to interact with other Visual Basic applications. MAPI provides the developer with the necessary functions that allow Visual Basic applications to interact with the Exchange information store database. Although MAPI may not be as mature a technology as OLE, it is quickly emerging as an industry standard. It will eventually be the base of other messaging products such as Lotus Notes and Lotus cc:mail and is currently incorporated into operating systems such as Windows 95 and Windows NT. Developers who have been working with simple MAPI to create MS Mail based forms will have a decided advantage on the rest of us, however, everyone will encounter a learning curve when they tackle extended MAPI, which provides full access to Exchange.

By leveraging existing development tools, and providing new ones to bridge the gaps, Microsoft has created a comprehensive development platform for Exchange. The typical Exchange user can do simple forms design using the Electronic Forms Template Wizard component of the Exchange client application. More experienced developers can either extend existing forms using the tool of their choice (Electronic Forms Designer, Visual Basic 4.0 or Visual C++ 4.0), or create their own applications from scratch. Although some developers may encounter a learning curve with MAPI and OLE automation, the good news is that all other design and development skills are leveraged for Exchange development.

Loren Kaneshige, Consultant
Lante Corporation

"Microsoft Exchange addresses a number of problems...."

When LAN messaging systems were introduced in the mid-1980s, the prevailing paradigm was that of the file server and attached workstations. This led naturally to messaging products such as Microsoft Mail that made use of the shared file system of the file server to act as the medium of exchange for message files.

A shared file system model allowed vendors to take advantage of the file system as the "infrastructure" and concentrate on providing an elegant user interface. As post offices grew to hold more people than could readily use a single file server, the vendors invented protocols to move message files between file servers. This usually involved dedicated workstations acting as mail routers. This, in turn, led to the need to synchronize the messaging directories on each file server. Eventually, vendors implemented directory synchronization schemes so that the directory on each of the file servers would contain entries for users on other file servers, and that changes made to one directory would propagate to other directories in the messaging domain.

These file sharing environments have inherent limitations because the original design goal was to provide local e-mail capabilities for a limited number of participants. The architecture was stretched to meet the rapidly expanding reach, range and responsiveness requirements of the organization. As e-mail spread within and between companies, a more sophisticated system was required that would provide not only an easy to use human interface, but meet the widely extended management, administration, directory and scalability requirements.

Microsoft Exchange addresses a number of problems inherent in the shared file system model. The key benefits of Exchange to customers include:

1 Better scalability. Exchange can handle five to ten times as many users on a server, thanks to the transaction-oriented nature of the client-server protocols.

2 Central processing. Exchange server provides a new source of centralized processing power, making it possible to implement server-based rules processing and agents and to serve as a platform for workflow automation, collaboration and information sharing.

3 Integration. Exchange's SMTP and X.400 capabilities provide much better interoperability and management.

4 Directory services. Exchange directory is more flexible, robust and easier to manage.

5 Universal Inbox. The Exchange client offers a taste of the universal inbox by handling incoming email, Schedule + and fax messages but does not go so far yet as to provide voice integration.

6 Mobile Client. The Exchange mobile capabilities are much improved over Microsoft Mail. The offline mode gives users a much more efficient system and client replication of public folders improve the information sharing capabilities significantly.

7 Administration and management. Administration and management in Exchange is vastly improved over the file sharing environment, particularly the administrative interface, message management, tracking and reporting and directory administration.

Microsoft Exchange is an excellent messaging platform. The product's messaging features, basic information sharing (that is, shared folders) and backbone connectivity (SMTP and X.400) are excellent. Exchange also has good support for Internet messaging including client support for POP3.

There are three areas we expect improvement over time:

1 Integration outside the Exchange environment, particularly with legacy systems and non-Microsoft client-server systems such as Lotus Notes.

2 Information sharing and collaboration including workflow automation, agent technology and search and retrieval capabilities.

3 Integration with Windows NT particularly administration and management, security and directory services.

Microsoft Exchange - A Thumbnail Analysis
Nina Burns, President and CEO
Creative Networks, Inc.

"...Microsoft Exchange will... change the face of computing...."

I was first introduced to Microsoft Exchange in the fall of 1993 as part of a small, select group of customers. At that time, the product was in its formative stages. Just enough of the code was working to help set the vision of where the product would eventually be. At the time, it was incredible the amount of functionality that was planned for the product. It was clearly much more than just another E-mail product. The vision of an enterprise tool that connects all of the desktops into an integrated solution was clearly an attempt to formulate the future direction of desktop computing.

The importance of building an enterprise infrastructure, and eventually a global infrastructure, has been a dream that many companies have invested significant amounts of time and money. The OSI efforts in the 80's and 90's was a pursuit of building a computing infrastructure where information at your fingertips would become a reality. The Microsoft Exchange promise takes a significant step forward towards this global vision.

During the development of the product, the Microsoft Exchange team was continuously challenged with the issue of defining the line between a proprietary solution and a standards-based solution. At times, it was unclear which direction these design decisions would take. But every time doubt would set in, I was extremely pleased that the direction was toward interoperating with other messaging systems, including X.400 and SMTP.

During my own testing, I found that conformance to standards was well tested. Anytime a nonconformant error was found, it was quickly corrected, and the Microsoft Exchange team demonstrated a very good knowledge of the standards.

I believe that Microsoft Exchange will have a prominent role in the corporate world and will change the face of computing throughout the industry.

Alexis Bor, Directory Project Manager, Technology Services
Boeing Computer Services

"...the future brings these together with one infrastructure...."

The future for Microsoft Exchange really revolves around its inclusion with Microsoft BackOffice and the power of extension provided there. As a messaging system, Microsoft Exchange will first be employed to replace systems that are primarily handling electronic mail.

Moving forward, Microsoft Exchange will gain tighter hooks to the Internet, leveraging the Internet engine already present in the system to allow for more and varied connector technology.

Publishing to and from the World Wide Web will be transparent to the users and will allow corporations to include the Intranets as simply another connection to the infrastructure. This will serve a higher purpose of shielding business from the complexity of building yet another information delivery system and spare the expense of managing a separate collection of information.

Directories will merge across the board so that one account can register with any number of systems and an application can register itself as well. This will allow for the complete integration of database, messaging, network, security, management, and communication services. Today, these are different systems with differing levels of complexity and expense and the future brings these together with one infrastructure for distribution.

Bill Kilcullen
Microsoft Corporation

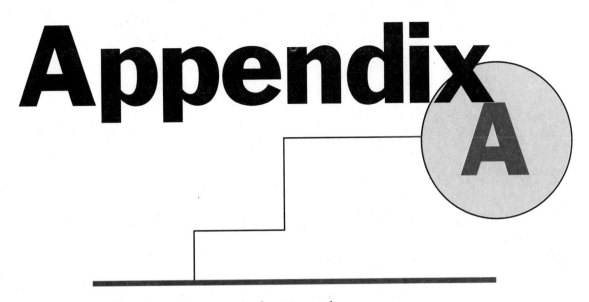

Appendix A

The Microsoft Exchange
Server Compact Disc

On the compact disc, you will find four directories.

1. Demos1
2. Demos2
3. Papers
4. Tools

Demos1

In Demos1, you will find a README.TXT file that will provide instructions for setting up a demonstration of how Microsoft Exchange and Keyflow workflow technology work together to provide workgroup and workflow solutions. You will also find a directory called Source that contains sample code to assist the developer in evaluating the process required in building this demonstration solution. Special thanks to Roger Sullivan and Ed Staub of Keyfile for this demonstration.

Demos2

In Demos2, you will find a file called SETUP.EXE, which will se tup up a series of Microsoft Exchange automatic demonstrations on your Windows system. There is a set of demonstrations for the Microsoft Exchange Client that will lead you through the features and functions as well as more advanced functionality such as the Inbox Assistant. There is also a demonstration of the Schedule+ 7.0 client software and a server setup demonstration to show the ease of installation.

Papers

In Papers, you will find a set of Microsoft Exchange White Papers covering a wide range of topics such as Migration, Administration, Planning, and the Development Environment. These papers were written by members of the Microsoft Exchange Team. You will also find a white paper covering Windows NT to assist you in your evaluation of Microsoft Exchange and the network operating system.

There is a complete copy of the Dunn and Bradstreet case study that is referred to in the book. There is also a tutorial covering the more popular messaging and transport standards in the industry today written by Daniel Chu, a senior consultant at Microsoft.

Tools

In Tools, you will find the following:

1 Windows NT Server Domain Planning Tool: A graphical modeling tool to assist the network administrator in planning for a Windows NT Server Domain security model that best suits the organizational model. Go to the Domplan directory and run SETUP.

2 Microsoft Exchange Site Modeling Tool: A graphical modeling tool that allows for establishing the best Microsoft Exchange Server site model based upon a complex set of metrics such as network links, number of locations, and bandwidth available. This serves as a planning tool as well as an educational experience by providing extensive information boxes at critical junctions in the model. After setting up the Windows NT Domain Planning Tool, run SETUP in the Tools directory to install this tool.

3 Microsoft Exchange Administration Visual Aid: A graphical help file to aid the reader in conceptualizing the unique administration world of Microsoft Exchange without having to install a server and setup Windows NT Servers. This can be run from the File Manager or Explorer. Found in the Admin subdirectory.

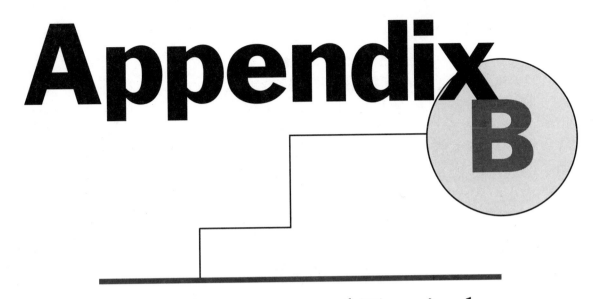

Appendix B

X.400 Concepts and Terminology

Introduction to the CCITT X.400 Standard

X.400 is a recommendation for computer-based message handling of electronic messages. The goal of the recommendation is to enable electronic mail users to exchange messages no matter which computer-based messaging system they may use. The foundation for this kind of global messaging requires the ability to transfer messages between different messaging environments that may be operated by different organizations.

X.400 is designed to be:

✗ **Hardware-independent**

✗ **Software-independent**

The X.400 recommendations were developed by a treaty organization maintained by the United Nations known as the Comité Consultatif International Télégraphique et Téléphonic (CCITT). This organization is known as the International Telegraph and Telephone Consultative Committee.

The X.400 recommendations are based on the Open Systems Interconnection (OSI) reference model and the protocols defined by ISO (in English, the International Organization for Standardization).

Microsoft Exchange is compliant with the 1984 and 1988 X.400 recommendations.

Publication Schedule

The first standards were published by CCITT at the end of a 1981-1984 study period. These standards appeared in 1984 as the "X.400 Red Book" series of recommendations. (The CCITT activities are organized into four year study periods and the publications of each is identified by a specific color.) These recommendations specify the aspects necessary for interconnection and operation of Message Handling Systems (MHS).

Publications to date are as follows:

✗ **1984: "Red Book"**

✗ **1988: "Blue Book"**

✗ **1992: "White Book"**

Frequent publications allow the committee to correct problems with the recommendation and include new functionality as technology advances.

OSI Concepts

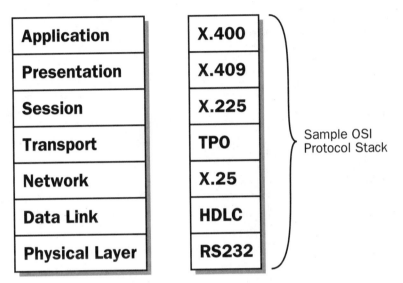

Application	**X.400**
Presentation	**X.409**
Session	**X.225**
Transport	**TP0**
Network	**X.25**
Data Link	**HDLC**
Physical Layer	**RS232**

Sample OSI Protocol Stack

The OSI reference model defines a standard set of communication layers between applications and the physical equipment they rely on to communicate with other applications. There are seven layers: application, presentation, session, transport, network, data link, and physical. The three "upper" layers generally involve the operating system and applications that run on it, while the remaining "lower" layers determine the way networks interconnect. This modular construction allows an administrator to choose the type of physical network to be used, the protocols and transports transmitted over that network, and even the host platform on each end of the connection. As long as each layer receives and transmits information properly to the layers above and below, it does not matter what combination of hardware and software is used in each layer.

X.400 is a specification for the application layer (layer 7) of the OSI reference model. The application layer allows applications processes to access network services. X.400 represents services that directly support user applications such as software for file transfers, database access, and electronic mail.

X.400 Message Handling Components Overview

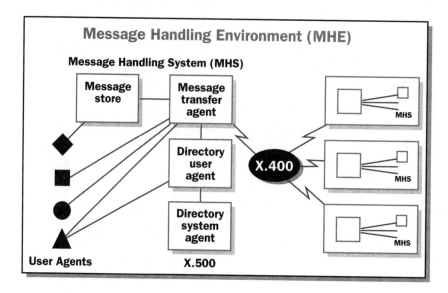

Message Handling System

An X.400 message handling system (MHS) is a collection of user agents, message transfer agents, and other components that work together to transfer messages from one point to another.

An X.400 messaging system typically consists of the following components:

✗ **User agents (UA)** that act on behalf of the user (a person or process sending or receiving mail).

✗ **Message transfer agents (MTA)** that move messages between users and exchange messages with other message transfer agents. A message transfer agent is analogous to a local post office.

✗ **Message transfer system (MTS)** which is a collection of message transfer agents.

✗ **Message stores (MS)** that send and receive messages from both user agents and message transfer agents.

The following components are typically a part of any message handling system; they are not specific to X.400. These components are specified in a separate specification known as X.500, which will be discussed later.

✗ **Directory user agents (DUA)** that represent a user in accessing the directory. Each DUA serves a single user so the directory can control access to directory information on the basis of the DUA name.

✗ **Directory system agents (DSA)** which are part of the directory, and whose role is to provide access to the directory information base to DUAs and other DSAs.

Message Handling Environment

The set of all message handling system components and users is called a message handling environment (MHE). A message handling environment can include several messaging systems connected through gateways or public services, or it can include just one message handling system that limits messaging to users within that system.

Other X.400 Components

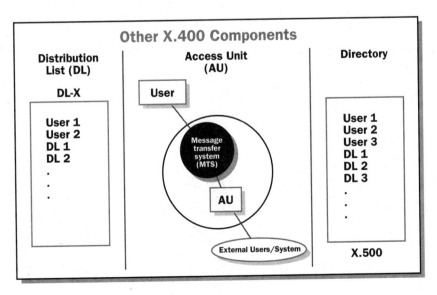

Other components of an X.400 system include:

✗ **Distribution lists (DL)** which identify zero or more members, each of which is either an MHS user or a DL.

✗ **Access units (AU)** link another separate communications system (for example, a postal system or a Telex network) to the message transfer system. In more common terms this would be known as a gateway.

✗ **The directory** which functions as a general purpose object and maintains information about other objects. This was implemented in 1988 as an optional feature and is not specific to X.400

Although the Microsoft Exchange directory uses a structure similar to X.500, it does not specifically follow the X.500 specification.

X.500

While the directory *object* is considered to be an X.400 object, most directories are governed internally by a different set of recommendations. There is a separate, published recommendation which covers how a directory works internally. This recommendation is known as X.500. While it is not specifically linked to X.400, the X.500 directory recommendation is an integral part for virtually all X.400 messaging systems.

Management Domains

The primary building blocks used in the organizational construction of the MHS are called management domains (MD). A management domain is a set of messaging systems, at least one of which is an MTA, managed by an organization.

The intent of the X.400 series of recommendations is to enable the construction of a global message handling system (MHS) that provides intra- and inter-organizational as well as national and international message handling worldwide. In order to facilitate this, the management domain concept has been broken down into two parts: administrative management domains (ADMD) and private management domains (PRMD).

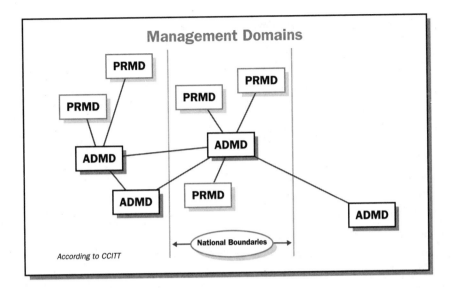

Administrative Management Domain (ADMD)

An administrative management domain, according to the CCITT, "comprises messaging systems managed by an administrator or registered private operating agency (RPOA)."

ADMDs are top-level management domains that handle third-party traffic. This is a service typically provided by a major telephone carrier such as Sprint or AT&T or a PTT.

When addressing an X.400 message, the ADMD will provide the highest-level identifier in an X.400 addressing field. This is similar to telephone service being provided by a telephone carrier.

Private Management Domain (PRMD)

Private management domains are unique subscriptions to an ADMD. This is similar to an individual telephone number subscription being received by a household (that is, the carrier would be the ADMD and the telephone number would be the PRMD). While there may be several telephone users in a household, the telephone number is the highest level of identification held in common with all of them.

A PRMD will send and receive messages to and from an ADMD but will not communicate directly with another PRMD under the CCITT recommendation. However in practice, it is not uncommon for a PRMD to directly connect to another PRMD.

Message Transfer System

The main purpose of the message transfer system (MTS) is to provide submission, transfer, and delivery of messages. It exists as a collection of one or more message transfer agents (MTA).

In a typical scenario, a message transfer system user submits a message to the MTS for eventual delivery to one or more MTS users. The MTS accepts the message and then attempts transfer of the message to the final destination. While in transit, the MTS provides any necessary store and forward features (for example, the splitting of multi-recipient messages), routes the message(s) within the MTS to the appropriate destination(s), and delivers the message(s) to the intended MTS user(s).

Message Transfer System (MTS) Protocols

There are two categories of protocols used by the message transfer system. The first category is concerned with access to the MTS and the second with the transfer of messages within the MTS. The access protocols allow MTS users to access (submit and delivery messages) the MTS by means of the MTS access protocols. The MTS itself is composed of a number of interconnected message transfer agents (MTAs). These MTAs cooperate by means of the message transfer protocol.

X.400 Interpersonal Messages (IPM)

X.400 Interpersonal Message Protocols

The purpose of the MTS is to support the submission, transfer, and delivery of messages between MTS users. An X.400 message consists of two basic components: an envelope and its content. The envelope functions just as the envelope for a postal letter; it identifies the addressing information necessary to route the enclosed message from the point of origin to the point of destination. The postal service does not need to know the contents of the message. One distinct difference from a postal service is the MTS has the capability to make multiple copies of the message when there are multiple recipients.

The envelope is used by the MTS for routing within the MTS. The MTS is not aware of any of the message contents. (Conversion on the content may take place if configured by the administrator at the destination system.)

The content includes an identification section that is similar or identical to the information that is part of the envelope. This is known as the header. Following the header is the actual content of the message. This content is known as the body part. The X.400 recommendations describe a number of body parts for the different types of content in a message. This division of message content into header and body parts used by electronic mail applications is called the interpersonal message (IPM) format.

Message Envelope

The envelope of a message is formatted using the X.400 P1 protocol. The P1 envelope contains the information required to deliver the message. This information includes the address of the originator and recipient, delivery priority, and the message trace information.

Delivery Priority

The delivery priority denotes the urgency of the message. A message and its contents may be designated as any one of three priorities:

Description	Priority
Normal	0
Non-urgent	1
Urgent	2

P1 Protocol and Trace Information

Trace information logs the time and location of a message as it passes through a series of message transfer agents to its destination. This trace information is added to the message's P1 envelope while in transit, resulting in a log of transactions that becomes a part of the message as a whole. This trace information allows each message transfer agent to determine whether a loop has occurred, requiring action such as returning or "bouncing" the message to the sender as undeliverable.

Messages that travel through many systems can develop a very large amount of trace information very quickly. Accordingly, trace information is divided into two categories: internal and external. When a message travels within the same country, private management domain

(PRMD), and administrative management domain (ADMD), internal trace information is added by each message transfer agent as the message travels through the message handling environment. If the message is passed to a message transfer agent that has a different country, PRMD, or ADMD, the internal trace information is stripped from the message, and external trace information is added to the P1 envelope. As a message nears its destination, it may again begin to be handled by message transfer agents that have identical country, PRMD, and ADMD information. The external trace information is never removed.

Trace information is usually only of concern to message transfer agents within and between X.400 messaging systems. You cannot view trace information in the normal course of messaging or administration, but message transfer agents, including X.400 service and error events can be logged.

Message Content

The content of the message is the actual information to be delivered: sender name and address, recipient name and address, and the message text. IPM format divides these contents into two parts: the header and the body.

The header contains the informal names and address information of the originator and the recipients, information on whether a reply is required, and so on. The body consists of body parts that contain the text of the message, an indicator of the text format, and any non-text attachments and their format. The header and each body part are encoded using P2/P22 protocol. P2 denotes the 1984 IPMS content while P22 denotes the 1988 content.

Originator/Recipient (O/R) Addresses

Message transfer system (MTS) users are identified by their originator/recipient names (O/R). These O/R names are carried in the message envelope and used the MTS to route and deliver the message to final destination(s).

The O/R name is made up of an O/R address (used by the MTS for routing and delivery), a directory name (a user-friendly identification that can be translated by the directory into the corresponding O/R address), or both.

To meet global messaging requirements, O/R addresses are divided into four address types:

✗ **Mnemonic address,** which identifies a user (or a distribution list) relative to the ADMD through which the user is accessed.

✗ **Numeric address,** which numerically identifies a user relative to an ADMD by means of a keypad.

✗ **Terminal address,** which identifies a user relative to an ADMD by means of the network address of a terminal.

✗ **Postal address,** which identifies the physical delivery system though which the user can be reached.

When addressing a message to a recipient, only the highest level of information that qualifies a user uniquely is needed for delivery. All field names, which comprise a full X.400 address, are not necessarily required for successful delivery. The required fields can vary from system to system. All required fields by the receiving system must be used and correctly formatted for the address to be valid.

O/R Address Fields

Above are listed the full set of attributes related to the four O/R address forms. An M indicates a mandatory or required field while O indicates an optional field. Most commonly used fields are displayed in reverse.

O/R attributes are abbreviated when composing an X.400 address.

Attribute Type	Abbreviation	Label	Length
Given Name	Given name	G	16
Initials	Initials	I	5
Surname	Surname	S	40
Generation Qualifier	Generation	Q	3
Common Name	Common Name	CN	32
X.121 Address	X.121	X.121	15

(continues)

Attribute Type	Abbreviation	Label	Length
User Agent Numeric ID	N-ID	N-ID	32
Terminal Type	T-TY	T-TY	3
Terminal Identifier	T-ID	T-ID	24
Organization	Organization	O	64
Organizational Unit 1	Org.Unit.1	OU1	32
Organizational Unit 2	Org.Unit.2	OU2	32
Organizational Unit 3	Org.Unit.3	OU3	32
Organizational Unit 4	Org.Unit.4	OU4	32
Private Management Domain	PRMD	P	16
Administration Management Domain	ADMD	A	16
Country	Country	C	2
Domain Defined Attribute	DDA	DDA	8,128

Allowable abbreviations for attributes are as follows:

With the exception of "DDA," the format for all the above fields is *Label=Value;* like "g=Paul;". The "DDA" uses the format "DDA:type=value" for example "DDA:SMTP=PaulJones@Microsoft.COM". There may be up to four DDAs in a single X.400 address and because there is nothing that indicates order in the label (like DDA1 or DDA2...), they are order dependent. That means that when the address is parsed from left to right, the first DDA will be encoded first, the second DDA will be encoded second, and so on. The DDA field is case sensitive; other attributes are not.

This textual representation of the X.400 addresses is actually itself a standard and can be found in the Annex to CCITT Rec. F.401 and ISO/IEC 10021-2/Am.1.

Address Composition

An X.400 address is composed by providing data for all mandatory and any optional fields until a unique address exists.

An O/R address must be unique to ensure delivery to the recipient. This may require many of the optional fields to have data entered and continued levels of detail in order to reach a level where the address is completely unique.

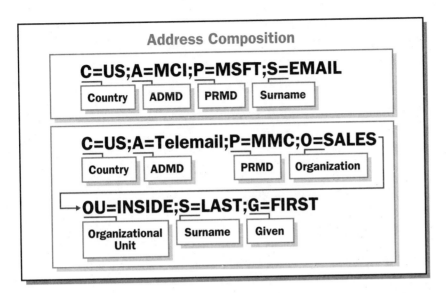

Address Composition

C=US;A=MCI;P=MSFT;S=EMAIL

| Country | ADMD | PRMD | Surname |

C=US;A=Telemail;P=MMC;O=SALES

| Country | ADMD | PRMD | Organization |

OU=INSIDE;S=LAST;G=FIRST

| Organizational Unit | Surname | Given |

Because of this, an X.400 address can differ greatly from user to user. Most users at a company will have a similar level of detail based on how the administrator has set the message-handling system.

An X.400 address is composed by specifying a value for an attribute. The attributes necessary for a valid address vary between recipient systems. Once the correct attributes are identified, the attribute and its value are strung together in an address format with an equal sign (=) separating the two. A delimiter is added between attributes for parsing reasons.

When specifying the individual attributes, either the abbreviation or the label may be used to identify the specific attribute. Please refer to the previous table for valid abbreviations and labels.

Following are some examples of valid X.400 addresses:

X.400 fields can be separated by a semicolon (;) or a slash mark (/). Different systems may require different delimiters.

C=US;A=MCI;P=MSFT;S=EMAIL

C=US;ADMD=MCI;PRMD=MSFT;S=EMAIL

C=US/ADMD=MCI/PRMD=MSFT/S=EMAIL

C=US;A=TELEMAIL;P=MMC;O=SALES;OU=INSIDE;S=LAST;G=FIRST

C=US;ADMD=TELEMAIL;PRMD=MMC;O=SALES;OU=INSIDE;S=LAST;G=FIRST

C=US/A=TELEMAIL/P=MMC/O=SALES/OU=INSIDE/S=LAST/G=FIRST

C=US/ADMD=TELEMAIL/PRMD=MMC/O=SALES/OU=INSIDE/S=LAST/G=FIRST

Legal X.400 Addresses

There are four possible X.400 address formats shown below (excluding postal). The attributes surrounded with square brackets "[]" are optional in the given X.400 address format, and the rest are mandatory:

Mnemonic: (most common)

- ✗ [Personal Name] ([Given Name], [Initials], Surname and [Generation])
- ✗ [Common Name]
- ✗ [Organization]
- ✗ [Organizational Units]
- ✗ [PRMD]
- ✗ ADMD
- ✗ Country
- ✗ [DDAs]

Numeric:

- ✗ User Agent Numeric ID
- ✗ [PRMD] (for 1988 X.400 compatibility)
- ✗ ADMD
- ✗ Country
- ✗ [DDAs]

X.121:

- ✗ X.121 Address
- ✗ [PRMD] (for 1988 X.400 compatibility)
- ✗ ADMD
- ✗ Country
- ✗ [DDAs]

Terminal:

✗ **[Terminal Type] (for 1988 X.400 compatibility)**

✗ **[Terminal Identifier]**

✗ **X.121 Address**

Interpersonal Messaging System (IPMS)

If the *Personal Name* attributes are used, the *Surname* is mandatory.

One of the most important applications of the message transfer system is the support of interpersonal messaging (the exchange of messages among people). This is provided by the interpersonal messaging system (IPMS).

A single blank character may be used in the *ADMD* field to indicate that no ADMD is specified.

IPMS users interact with the IPMS for the purpose of originating and receiving IPMS messages. A message origination is started by

In the first format, at least one of *Personal Name, Common Name, Organization, Organizational Units* or *PRMD* must be used in addition to *ADMD* and *Country.* (This means that if a DDA is used, you still must specify one of the other optional fields.)

the passing of an IPMS message by the user to the IPMS. The IPMS invokes the services of the underlying MTS to submit and deliver the message to its intended destinations. Message reception is the passing of the delivered message from the IPMS to the IPMS users.

IPMS Message Types

There are two distinct types of information objects provided by IPMS:

1 Interpersonal message (IPM): Conveys the end-user information such as message text or graphic between the IPMS-users. An IPM will also convey a read receipt as well.

2 Interpersonal notification (IPN): Conveys information on the fate of IPMs (that is, receipt or non-receipt)

Each IPMS message is carried through the MTS with the content type of "interpersonal-messaging."

IPM Structure

The design of the interpersonal message (IPM) was heavily influenced by standard business messaging practices. The IPM resembles a business message or memo. Each IPM has a header and a body.

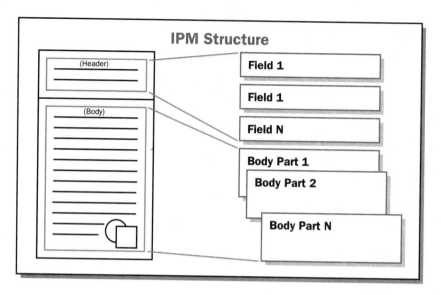

Header

The header carries information on the recipients of the message and additional instructions about how the message will be handled during transport.

This information is stored in a sequence of header fields, each an information item that describes an action to be taken on the message. These fields describe such information as the originator of a message, recipients of a message, and expiration time of the message.

Body

The body contains the actual information (text, graphic, and so on) of the IPM. It is composed of a sequence of body parts, each an information object (for example, a document) intended to convey information between users.

There are different types of body parts defined, each designed to standardize on the transmission of different types of information.

Category	Field	Underlying Type
Identification of users involved	Originator	O/R Descriptor
	authorizing-users	list of O/R Descriptors (send on behalf of)
	primary-recipients	list of Recipient specifiers (To:)
	copy-recipients	list of Recipient specifiers (CC:)
	blind-copy-recipients	list of Recipient specifiers (BCC:)
	reply-recipients	list of O/R Descriptors
Relationships among IPMS	this-IPM	IPM identifier
	replied-to-IPM	IPM identifier
	obsoleted-IPM	list of IPM identifiers
	related-IPMs	list of IPM identifiers
Times relevant to the IPM	expiration-time	Time
	reply-time	Time
Information describing the IPM	subject	(128 characters max)
	importance	
	sensitivity	
	language	(P22)
	incomplete-copy	(P22) conversion couldn't be completed
	autoforwarded	

Body Part	Body Part Number
IA5 Text	0
Telex (ITA2 5-bit)	1
Voice	2
G3 Facsimilie	3
Text Interchange Format (TIFO)	4
Telex (T.61)	5
Videotex	6
Nationally Defined	7
Encrypted	8

Body Part	Body Part Number
Forwarded IPMessage	9
Simple Formatable Document (SFD)	10
Text Interchange Format 1 (TIF1)	11
Octet String	12
ISO6937 Text	13
Bilaterally-defined (Binary)	14
Binary File Transfer	15

Interpersonal Notification (IPN)

An interpersonal notification (IPN) is a secondary class of information object conveyed between IPMS users. The IPN may take either one of two forms:

1 Receipt notification (RN) which reports the originator's reading of an IPM.

2 Non-receipt notification(NR) which reports the originator's failure to read an IPM.

An IPN is an indication returned to the originator of a subject IPM, reporting the status (read/not read) from the final recipient(s). The IPMS-user (receiving) will originate (if requested by the message originator) a receipt notification (RN) message to the IPMS.

X.400 Protocol Number Assignments

The X.400 recommendation assigns protocol numbers when referring to communications between two X.400 objects or specifying the content of an object. These protocol numbers are referred to when specific message components are discussed. The most common protocols are listed here:

Protocol	Reference
P1	Envelope
P2	Message Content (1984)
P3	Client-MTA Communications
P7	Client-Message Store (MS)
P22	Message Content (1988)

Appendix C

Advanced Security

What is Advanced Security?

Microsoft Exchange Server provides users with the ability to protect and verify messages as they are transferred through a Microsoft Exchange organization by using message encryption and certification features. These combined features are known within Microsoft Exchange Server as *Advanced Security*.

Advanced Security is available within Microsoft Exchange Server on the following client platforms:

✗ **Windows 3.x**

✗ **Windows NT Workstation**

✗ **Windows 95**

✗ **Macintosh**

The MS-DOS and UNIX clients do not support Advanced Security.

Advanced Security appears to the user as two separate features: one allows the user to place a 'signature' on a message, or in other words, certify a message's origin; the other feature allows the user to encrypt or scramble a message. These features are known as *signing* and *sealing*. They may be used individually or simultaneously on any message generated by the Microsoft Exchange Client.

Signing

Signing allows a recipient to be certain of the identity of the sender and also verifies the content has not been modified during transit. This is to prevent situations in which the originator of a message may attempt to send a message under the premise of another identity.

When a sending user 'signs' a message, the Microsoft Exchange Client stamps a special value on it. This value is generated by sending the body part of a message through a complex series of computations. The end result is a unique number that is transmitted with the message.

This unique number also verifies that the message is not changed in any way during transit. This ensures the message is indeed the original message.

When a recipient receives a signed message, they can authenticate this special value or *verify* the message by recalculating the number.

Sealing

Sealing allows the sender to encrypt the body part and any attachments of a message. (P1 header information is not encrypted when sealing a message.) Sealing provides for confidentiality of messages as they transfer through a Microsoft Exchange system.

In order to send a sealed message, both the sender and the recipient must have Advanced Security enabled.

When a user sends a sealed message, the Microsoft Exchange Client scrambles or encrypts the message using a complex algorithm. This ensures the message cannot be read until the message is unscrambled.

When a recipient receives a sealed message, the message is decrypted or *unsealed*. The recipient can be assured the message has not been read during its transfer because of the complex security algorithms.

Keys

The signing and sealing of messages is provided within Microsoft Exchange Server under the X.509 recommendation. *X.509* is a CCITT (ITU) recommendation that relates to the storage of authentication information.

In order to facilitate the signing and sealing of messages Microsoft Exchange Server utilizes an industry encryption standard known as *public/private key technology*. Using this technology, each mailbox is given a key pair. One of these keys is publicly known and the other is kept private to the user.

Public Key

A *public key* is implemented as a fixed-length security string. This key is "publicly" known, in other words, available to all users.

There are two public keys utilized by Microsoft Exchange: one is used for sealing messages and the other is used for verifying messages.

When a user sends a message they wish to seal, a public key created for sealing messages is used to complete the encryption process. When a user receives a message that has been signed, a public key used for verifying messages is used to verify the sender.

Private Key

A *private key* is implemented as a fixed-length security string stored in a local, encrypted security file on each user's computer. The private key is known only by the sending user.

There are two private keys utilized by Microsoft Exchange Server: one is used for unsealing messages and the other is used for signing messages. When a user receives a message that has been sealed, a private key created for unsealing is used to unseal the message. When a user sends a message they want to sign, a private key created for signing is used to secure the message.

Key Types and Uses

There are four separate keys:

- ✗ **Public Sealing Key**
- ✗ **Private Sealing Key**
- ✗ **Public Signing Key**
- ✗ **Private Signing Key**

In review, they are used at the following times:

	Seal	**Sign**
Sending	Public Sealing Key	Private Signing Key
Receiving	Private Sealing Key	Public Signing Key

Certificates

Key pairs are managed through the use of special certificates within a Microsoft Exchange organization. In turn, these certificates are created by a central authority.

Certification Authority

Public and private key pairs are generated by a central process known as a *certification authority (CA)*. The CA is responsible for creating and maintaining the security key pairs and special certificates. Within the encryption industry, the CA is generally a central process that manages these certificates.

Certificates

A *certificate* is an authentication method used within security. It can be considered similar to a notary public's seal on a document in that it actually authenticates a signed or sealed message. Certificates are compliant with the X.509 security recommendation. They are generated by the certification authority by compiling various security information from the system. A certificate is created by the CA for each user who has Advanced Security enabled. A user who does not have Advanced Security enabled will not have a certificate. This certificate primarily houses a user's public key and is transported through the Microsoft Exchange network via the directory service.

Specifically the certificate contents comprise:

✗ **A unique serial number** generated by the CA for each certificate

✗ **The encrypted password** of the CA. This is known as the CA's *signature*

✗ **The CA's directory name (DN)**

✗ **The user's directory name (DN)**

✗ **The user's public** key (sealing or signing)

✗ **The expire date** of Advanced Security for the user

There are two primary X.509 certificates created for each user who has Advanced Security enabled. One certificate is utilized for storage of the public sealing key information and the other is used for storage of the public signing key information.

CA's Certificate

Just as certificates are created for each user, there is also a certificate created for the certification authority. This certificate is used to validate information that identifies each user as being part of the Microsoft Exchange Server system. A copy of the CA's certificate is kept in a file by every Advanced Security user.

Encryption Types

Encryption or the scrambling of data, in general, is an industry standard utilized in Microsoft Exchange. There are many different methods of encryption and certification. Microsoft Exchange utilizes the RSA security system while specifically using DES or CAST for actual encryption.

RSA

RSA refers to a public-key encryption system that is used for both encryption and certification. It can be considered as a security "framework." It was developed in 1977 by Ron Rivest, Adi Shamir, and Leonard Adleman (RSA is formed from the initials of their last names) at the Massachusetts Institute of Technology. RSA is the most widely used public-key encryption system in use today and is often called a de-facto standard.

The RSA method utilizes a data encryption standard to encrypt information and decrypt or unscramble it at the receiving end. RSA provides the definitions and usage of public and private key pairs.

DES

DES or *Data Encryption Standard* is an algorithm for the encryption or coding of data designed by the National Bureau of Standards that is so efficient it is nearly impossible for anyone without the decryption key to get the data back in unscrambled form. The DES standard encrypts and decrypts data using a 56-bit key specified in the Federal Information Processing Standard Publication 46, dated January 15, 1977. It uses a binary number as an encryption key with 72 quadrillion possible combinations. The key, randomly chosen for each session, is used to create the encryption pattern for transmission.

CAST

CAST is a proprietary encryption method created by Northern Telecom for data encryption. Originally it was developed by Carlisle Adams and Stafford Tavares (CAST is formed from the initials of their first and last names) as a "drop-in" replacement for DES. CAST provides more flexible encryption standards by allowing a 40- to 128bit variable input key. The *input key* is a number specified in bit length that is utilized to encrypt data. Longer input keys are more secure than shorter ones.

Microsoft Exchange Server uses two variations of CAST:

✗ **CAST 40**

✗ **CAST 64**

CAST 40 utilizes a 40-bit input key and CAST 64 utilizes a 64-bit input key.

International Considerations

The utilization of the two variations of CAST is due to import/export laws. Any product shipped from the United States that incorporates cryptographic functions requires an export license. The license and approval process can vary depending on the product, the relative strength of the cryptographic mechanisms, its end use, and the destination country.

Currently it is not possible to obtain an export license to any country for the CAST 64 or DES algorithm. Because of this Microsoft will ship the 40-bit version of CAST to each country as permitted by export laws.

France does not allow the import of any type of data encryption. Therefore any Microsoft Exchange software destined for France may not contain Advanced Security. It may not be possible to install Advanced Security on a French server.

Architecture

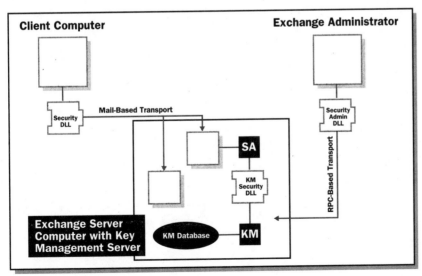

There are multiple components and processes involved with Microsoft Exchange Advanced Security. They reside on both the client's computer and a Microsoft Exchange Server computer.

The server-based components may reside on any Microsoft Exchange Server computer within the organization. These components are integrated with Microsoft Exchange Server software. They are implemented as a Windows NT service, a DLL, and a storage database. Together these items are known as the *Key Management Server* or *KM server*. The KM server can be identified as the Certification Authority within Microsoft Exchange Server.

There can only be one key management server per Microsoft Exchange organization.

The person who manages the KM server is known as the *KM administrator*. This is usually the same person who administers Microsoft Exchange Server. The KM administrator must have access to the Microsoft Exchange Administrator program, but access to the Administrator program does not automatically grant the ability to manage the KM server.

The following information details each component of Advanced Security and the function it provides:

Security DLL

The Security DLL resides on the client computer. It is used to sign/verify and seal/unseal Advanced Security messages. It interacts with the System Attendant of the key management server via mail during the process of enabling Advanced Security for the user. It also interacts with the directory service of the local server when signing or sealing messages.

There are two DLLs involved in the Windows operating systems:

Platform	Security filename
Windows 16-bit Operating Systems	ETEXCH.DLL
Windows 32-bit Operating Systems	ETEXCH32.DLL

From here on, we will refer to the security DLL as ETEXCH.DLL, not ETEXCH32.DLL.

Security Administration DLL

The Security Administration DLL resides on any Administrator's console. It is used by the Microsoft Exchange Administrator program whenever Advanced Security is being configured for a user account. This component is used to initiate any requests regarding Advanced Security to the KM server. These requests may relate to the creation, revocation, and recovery of keys and certificates. Each of these actions will be discussed later.

The filename of the Security Administration DLL is **SECADMIN.DLL**.

Microsoft Exchange Server Computer

Key Management Service

The key management service is a Windows NT service that accepts requests from the Administrator program (security administration DLL) and the KM Security DLL. It performs any actions and maintains its information in a database.

KM Database

The KM Database is a file database that manages Advanced Security information for the Microsoft Exchange organization. It is managed by the key management service.

KM Security DLL

The KM Security DLL resides on the Microsoft Exchange Server computer running the KM server. It responds to any Advanced Security configuration requests from the user. The KM Security DLL extracts message-based requests and submits them to the key management service.

The filename of the KM Security DLL is **SECKM.DLL**.

Microsoft Exchange System Attendant

The System Attendant of the Microsoft Exchange Server computer running KM server service retrieves requests from the user for initialization of Advanced Security. The System Attendant then interacts with the KM Security DLL to store and manage key pairs as required by the system.

Enabling Advanced Security

To allow a user to sign or seal messages, both the administrator and the user must perform actions to enable Advanced Security for a particular mailbox.

The process of enabling Advanced Security for a mailbox involves the creation of:

✗ **Public** and private signing keys.

✗ **Public** and private sealing keys.

✗ **A random** eight-character string used during the setup of Advanced Security known as a *security token*.

✗ **Signing** and sealing certificates.

✗ **A user** access password.

The creation and management of these items can be viewed as a two-stage process.

In stage one, the KM administrator utilizes the Microsoft Exchange Administrator program to enable a mailbox for Advanced Security. This involves:

✗ **Generating** a public and private sealing key and storing them in a database maintained by the KM server.

✗ **Generating** a security token to be used later by a mailbox user.

In stage two of the process, the user must utilize the security token provided by the KM administrator to:

✗ **Create** the public and private signing key pair.

✗ **Send** the public signing key to the KM server.

✗ **Retrieve** the sealing key pair created by, and stored within, the KM Database.

✗ **Retrieve** the X.509 certificates from the KM server.

✗ **Store** and distribute the X.509 certificate generated by the KM server.

✗ **Identify** a user-defined access password that is used to encrypt a security file.

Enabling Advanced Security—Stage One

Overview

Stage one is completed entirely by the Microsoft Exchange administrator and assumes prior installation of the KM server.

In this stage, the KM administrator utilizes the Administrator program to generate a security token for every user wishing to utilize Advanced Security. The administrator uses RPC to send needed information to the KM server, which then generates sealing key pairs and returns the security token.

Process

The process the administrator performs is as follows:

1 The KM administrator initiates the enabling of Advanced Security for a specified user. This is accomplished by selecting the user's mailbox from within the Microsoft Exchange Administrator program and obtaining properties on the mailbox.

The administrator selects the security property tab and is prompted by Microsoft Exchange for the KM server administrator's password. This is a separate password provided by the Microsoft Exchange administrator at KM server setup time.

After the password is provided, the Advanced Security property page is displayed. The administrator will then choose the Enable Advanced Security button.

2 The Security Administration DLL (SECADMIN.DLL) retrieves the location of the KM server. The location is stored within an attribute value for a site object. This value is automatically created and inserted into the site object at KM server setup time and can be viewed by displaying the Encryption property page of the site. It can also be displayed using the administrator's raw mode functionality if needed.

The SECADMIN.DLL uses this information to pass the directory name (DN) of the selected user, and the KM server administrator's encrypted password or *signature* via RPC calls to the Windows NT KM server service. Because this operation is accomplished via RPC, the administrator must be enabling Advanced Security from a Microsoft Exchange administrator's console that has network access to the KM server.

3 The KM service creates a sealing key pair. The key pair is written into the KM Database.

4 The KM service generates a random eight-character security token. It encrypts that token with the security administrator's signature and returns it to SECADMIN.DLL on the administrator's machine using RPC. The sealing key pair is not passed back to the administrator; rather it is simply written into the KM Database.

5 The SECADMIN.DLL decrypts the eight-character security token. This token is then displayed in a modal dialog box on the screen of the KM administrator. This token will be passed later to the end user for the completion of stage two.

It is important to create the tokens used by Advanced Security in a secure manner. Without using an elaborate technique to generate and store the sealing key pairs, the process could be "eavesdropped" upon and vital information discovered about the encryption of future messages.

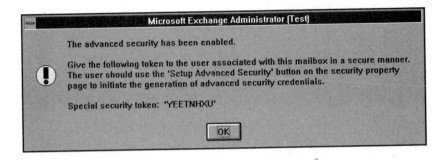

Enabling Advanced Security—Stage Two

The stage two process is performed entirely by the user and utilizes mail-based transport provided by Microsoft Exchange Server to accomplish the required tasks.

Overview

In this stage, the user submits the security token to the KM server. The KM server returns the sealing keys as generated in stage one and several X.509 certificates. Because this exchange of information is performed utilizing mail-based transport, there are no site boundary considerations. As long as there is mail transport configured between the client computer and the KM server, Advanced Security can be enabled.

Process

That process as the user performs tasks and as they occur internally to Microsoft Exchange Server are as follows:

1. The user is provided with the security token created in stage one by the KM administrator. The passing of this token should be accomplished only via a secure method. At this point, a mail message is not considered completely secure. Therefore, the administrator should use a more conventional method such as telephone or paper-based distribution.

2. The user begins enabling Advanced Security by accessing the Security property page. This property page is located under the Tools/Options menu. The user selects the Setup Advanced Security button.

At this time the user will provide the security token provided by the KM administrator. Additionally they will identify a location for a file for the storage of private security information. This file will be discussed later.

Finally, the user provides a password only they know. This password will be used later to sign/verify and seal/unseal messages. This password is completely separate from any other logon or access password maintained by the user.

Setup Advanced Security

Your TOKEN must be obtained from your exchange administrator to enable advanced security for this user.

OK

Cancel

One time token   YEETNHXU

Security file   c:\markadco.epf

The following password will be used to secure your digital keys. It is very important that this password remain absolutely private as your "signature" can be forged if this password is compromised.

Password: ******

Confirm Password: ******

---

3 The ETEXCH.DLL generates the user's public and private signing key pair. The public signing key is encrypted and placed into a mail message using the security token provided by the KM administrator. This message is automatically addressed to the System Attendant's hidden mailbox on the KM server. The address information is again provided by the KM server attribute obtained from the value on the site object. Once the message has been transferred to the user's Microsoft Exchange server, the user is notified of the successful submission.

4 If the KM server is not resident on the client's Microsoft Exchange server, the message is transferred to the Microsoft Exchange Server computer running the KM server.

5 The message is extracted from the System Attendant's mailbox by the Windows NT Service Attendant service and passed to the Windows NT KM server service via SECKM.DLL.

Originally this message was encrypted using the security token provided by the KM administrator. Since the KM server knows the security token, it is able to decrypt the user's message.

6 Once the KM service accesses the contents of the message it retrieves the enclosed public signing key and writes it to the KM Database.

7 The KM service now generates two certificates, one for sealing messages and one for signing messages. These certificates are generated utilizing various information from the Advanced Security System. They are generated using:

✗ **The user's** public sealing or signing key

✗ **The certification** authority's private key

✗ **The user's** directory name (DN)

✗ **The CA's** directory name

✗ **The expiration** date of the certificate

✗ **A unique** serial number which identifies the certificate

The KM service generates a mail message addressed to the user and encloses items to complete stage two. These items are:

✗ **X.509** sealing certificate

✗ **X.509** signing certificate

✗ **CA's** certificate

✗ **User's** private sealing key (from stage one)

8 Upon arrival of the message at the user's mailbox, a dialog box is presented that requests the user's unique password as defined in step two. This password is used to verify that the receiving user is the same person as the originating user. Since the KM server generated the return message containing the X.509 certificates and the private sealing key based on the user's token, the password must be re-entered to verify the recipient of the certificates as the original sender of the request.

9 ETEXCH.DLL extracts the public sealing certificate and submits it to the local Directory Service for storage and replication. This certificate will be used later to seal messages being addressed to this user.

There can only be one .EPF file for each user. If a user requires Advanced Security to be enabled on multiple computers, the user must have access to the .EPF file from each computer.

Additionally, the private signing key, the certification authorities certificate, and the signing and sealing certificates are written into a separate security file. This file is named by the user and utilizes an extension of .EPF. By default the Microsoft Exchange Client will attempt to name the file with the mailbox name.

The .EPF file is written to disk using a CAST 64 encryption algorithm. This prevents the EPF file from being accessed by unauthorized users. It is possible to store this file in any location. For maximum security it is possible to keep the file on a PC (PCMCIA) card or even a floppy disk. The PC card or disk can then be inserted when signed or sealed messages must be accessed and always assures the file cannot be accessed by anybody except for the owner.

Where Are Items Stored?

The process of enabling Advanced Security is very complex. There are many components that reside in different places throughout the Microsoft Exchange organization. In review, there are four main storage locations of security information throughout Microsoft Exchange Server.

	Directory Store	Security File .EPF	KM Database	X.509 Certificate
CA's certificate		✗		
CA's directory name				✗
CA's signature				✗
Certificate expiration date				✗
Certificate serial number				✗
Private sealing key		✗	✗	
Private signing key		✗		
Public sealing key				✗
Public signing key			✗	✗
Sealing certificate	✗	✗		
Signing certificate		✗		
User's directory name				✗

Sending a Sealed Message

Overview

When a user has indicated a message should be sealed, the Microsoft Exchange Client initiates an elaborate sealing process. This process occurs entirely at send time (rather than creation or composition).

The process as the user views it is to simply indicate the preference using a property sheet or a toolbar button and provide their security password. The Microsoft Exchange Client software completes the process by generating an encryption key which it utilizes to encrypt the message. It then retrieves the recipient's public sealing key from the Microsoft Exchange directory and utilizes that key to encrypt the first encryption key. That information is then sent to the Information Store for delivery.

Process

The process as the user and Microsoft Exchange system performs tasks internally occurs as follows:

1 After the user has completed composing the message and initiates the send procedure, the client initiates a single RPC call to the directory service. During that RPC call it retrieves the DS attribute User-Cert. This attribute simply defines if Advanced Security is enabled for each of the recipients and, if so, at what level (CAST 40, CAST 64, or DES).

Since a sealed message can only be sent from a user who has Advanced Security enabled to another user who also has Advanced Security enabled, the Microsoft Exchange Client must know which of the recipients are capable of receiving a sealed message. If a recipient does not have Advanced Security enabled, the sender is warned.

For each recipient who has Advanced Security enabled, the Microsoft Exchange Client retrieves a copy of their sealing certificate.

Since each user's sealing certificate contains their public sealing key, the Microsoft Exchange Client extracts the public key for each recipient from each certificate retrieved from the directory store.

2 The user is prompted for their security password. Once provided, the Microsoft Exchange Client decrypts the .EPF file and extracts the stored sealing certificate. The certificate will be sent later with the encrypted message. The certificate is enclosed only so the sender themself can decrypt the message if they need to access it again.

3 The Microsoft Exchange Client then generates a bulk encryption key for each recipient. This is a key similar to the public and private keys except it is generated on demand for each message which is marked as sealed. The type of key generated is based on the type of Advanced Security each recipient has enabled. (CAST 40, CAST 64, or DES).

The message is then encrypted with the bulk encryption key.

4 After the encryption of the message is complete, the Microsoft Exchange Client then encrypts or "locks" the bulk encryption key with each recipient's public sealing key. The result of this encryption is known as a lock box.

If the message is addressed to multiple recipients, there is a lockbox created for each recipient. The message is only encrypted and sent once, but multiple lock boxes will be created and sent with the message.

5 The encrypted message, the lock box(es), and the sender's sealing certificate are then submitted to the information store for delivery.

Unsealing a Sealed Message

Overview

The process of unsealing a message utilizes similar concepts to those of sealing a message; only in reverse. To unseal a message so the recipient may display requires the recipient to decrypt the lock box with their own private sealing key. By decrypting the lock box, the original bulk encryption key can be accessed which is then used to decrypt the message.

Process

That process as the user and Microsoft Exchange system performs tasks internally occurs as follows:

1 The user attempts to read the message.

2 Since the message is secure, the user will be prompted by Microsoft Exchange for the user's security profile password.

The private sealing key is extracted and used by Microsoft Exchange to decrypt the lock box which was created at the time of sending.

3 Microsoft Exchange Client then utilizes the decrypted bulk encryption key to decrypt the original message. The message can now be displayed on the screen.

Sending a Signed Message

Overview

When a user has indicated a message should be signed, the Microsoft Exchange Client generates security information that, when utilized by the receiving user, guarantees the message was indeed sent by the sender and that the message was not tampered with or read during transit. This process utilizes the sender's private signing key and a technique called hashing.

Hashing, or the creation of a *hash,* is a complex one-way mathematical function that reduces a message of any length to a unique 128-bit result. The result of a hash is referred to as a *messaging digest.* The same message will always hash to the same message digest value, but even if one bit in the message is changed, the message digest will change dramatically. The sender and the recipient each perform the same hash computation on the message. If the hash produces the same value for both parties, it proves the message has not been altered along the way.

Signing a Microsoft Exchange message involves hashing the message, which results in a unique message digest. That digest is then encrypted with the user's private signing key before it is sent to the recipient. The encrypted digest is known as a *digital signature.*

Process

That process is as follows:

1. The original un-encrypted message is hashed to obtain a unique message digest.

2. The user is prompted to enter their security profile password. Once the correct password is entered, the .EPF file is decrypted and the private signing key is extracted.

   The messaging digest is then encrypted with the sender's private sealing key creating a digital signature.

3. Microsoft Exchange Client transmits the copy of the signing certificate, the digital signature, and the message to the information store for delivery.

Verifying a Signed Message

Overview

Verifying a message which has been sealed is a simple process of recalculating the messaging digest on the original message and verifying the hash is the same as the one contained in the messaging digest included in the message. If the messaging digests do not match, the message has been tampered with.

The encrypted hash is decrypted using the sender's public signing key (which is retrieved from the enclosed certificate). The receiving client computer generates its own hash based on the message and compares that hash against the decrypted hash transmitted within the message.

If the result is the same, the user can be assured the message has not been altered during transport, if they are not, the message is not valid.

Process

That process as the user and Microsoft Exchange system performs tasks internally occurs as follows:

1. The user attempts to read the message.

2. Since the message is secure, the user will be prompted by Microsoft Exchange for the user's security profile password.

    With the security profile password, Microsoft Exchange can decrypt the local .EPF file, which contains the CA's certificate. The local CA's certificate contains the CA's signature, which is verified against the signature contained in the sender's signing certificate.

3. The enclosed certificate—the sender's public signing key—is extracted and used to decrypt the digital signature. After the signature has been decrypted the original message digest should remain.

4. Microsoft Exchange Client performs a hash on the original message. Since hashing produces the same outcome every time, the resulting message digest should match the decrypted one.

5. Digests are compared. If they are identical, then the message is guaranteed to be from the sender and is guaranteed to be unopened.

Key and Certificate Management

In general, the keys and certificates maintained by the KM server require no management. Occasionally however, it may be necessary to perform some management-related duties.

The administrator may perform two of these duties:

✗ **Rescinding** or revoking a user's ability to send signed and sealed messages.

✗ **Recovering** a forgotten or corrupt key pair and certificate.

A final management task is the updating of security information which is about to expire. This is referred to as *updating*.

Revocation

At times it may be necessary for a user's Advanced Security to be revoked. This usually occurs if the user is considered untrustworthy.

If this occurs, the KM administrator must disable or revoke the right for the user to send signed and/or sealed messages. This is accomplished by marking the user's keys as invalid and revoking the right to use the sealing certificate stored in the directory service database.

That process is as follows:

1 The KM administrator initiates the revocation of Advanced Security for a specified user. This is accomplished by selecting the user's mailbox from within the Microsoft Exchange Administrator program and obtaining properties on the mailbox.

Once the administrator has the property sheets available for the user, they then select the Disable Advanced Security button. The SECADMIN.DLL prompts the administrator for the KM administrator's password and requests verification of the revocation.

2 The Security Administration DLL (SECADMIN.DLL) retrieves the location of the KM server. The location is stored within an attribute value for a site object. These attributes are automatically set at KM server setup time. It can be viewed by displaying the Encryption property page of the site. It can also be displayed using the administrator's raw mode functionality if needed.

The SECADMIN.DLL then passes the display name of the user to be revoked to the KM server via RPC calls.

3 The KM server then adds the user's signing and sealing keys to its internal revocation list and authorizes it with the KM administrator's account.

4 The KM service instructs the directory to revoke the user's sealing certificate as well. This is actually accomplished by adding the unique serial number of the certificate to a revocation attribute that is stored on the CA's configuration object.

5 The user's ability to sign and seal messages has now been revoked. A message is displayed on the administrator's console reflecting the revocation.

The KM Database does not delete the keys, but rather maintains a copy of the user's keys in order to decrypt or verify any signed and/or sealed messages still maintained in the messaging network.

Once a user has had their key certificates revoked and serial number of the sealing certificate has been placed on the revocation list, no other user may encrypt a message for that user.

Recovery

If a user forgets or deletes his or her advanced security password or the .EPF file becomes corrupt, the security keys must be recovered.

The process of recovering keys is similar to enabling advanced security for a mailbox as described earlier except that the administrator must perform Recover Advanced Security instead of Setup Advanced Security. From a user perspective, recovering advanced security is the same as enabling advanced security because after the user receives the token from the administrator the user will have to set up security again. The main difference is the KM server does not create a new encrypting key pair, but rather retrieves the original key pair stored within the KM Database. The current key information is returned to the ETEXCH.DLL so the .EPF file can be recreated.

There is no mechanism to change the default validation period.

Update

User key certificates by default are valid for a period of one year from validation. At the end of this validation period, the certificate must be "rolled over" or updated. This update is not the responsibility of the administrator; rather it is the responsibility of the Microsoft Exchange Client software. When certificates near expiration, the Microsoft Exchange Client will send a request to update the validity of the certificates for an additional year.

Managing the KM Database

Backup

The KM Database contains the public and private encryption keys and public signing keys of every Advanced Security-enabled mailbox. A history of these keys associated with a mailbox is sent to the user every time a key recovery operation is performed. If the history of these keys is lost for a user and a recover operation is performed, the user will not be able to read mail that was previously encrypted for that user.

Because of the importance of the information in the KM Database, it is essential that regular backups of the KM Database are made. The KM Database comprises all the files and directories under the SECURITY\MGRENT directory. The Windows NT Backup and Restore utility should be used for this purpose.

Each user's security file is accessed only by the KM administrator, so it is possible to back up the security database while the server is online. There is a remote chance that a file will be busy during backup, but regularly scheduled backups will ensure all files are safe. To avoid the chance of a busy file, the KM server service may be stopped during the backup.

Restore

If the KM server database is damaged or needs to be restored, the KM Database can simply be replaced from a copy. In order to do this, the KM server process should be disabled and the KM Database file location restored.

After the database has been restored, the KM server process can then again be started.

Moving the KM Server

Because there can be only one KM server within a Microsoft organization, it is likely that an administrator will want or need to move the KM server from one Microsoft Exchange server to another.

The KM server can only be moved to a different server in the same site; it cannot be moved to a server in a different site.

Moving the KM server is a simple process of transferring the database, service, and DLL to a new location.

Changing the KM Administrator Password

During installation of the KM server, the administrator is prompted for a password that is used to authenticate the administrator when KM-related operations are performed. The password can be changed using the administrator's console.

Refer to the documentation for specific instructions on changing the password.

Security Import

The Security Import, or SIMPORT.EXE utility, allows the KM administrator to create security tokens for a set of mailboxes in bulk. It supports the same file format as the Directory Export, which is available through the Tools/Options menu option in the Administrator program. The output of the Security Import utility is a file called SRESULTS.TXT, which contains a list of all mailboxes in the input file together with the token associated with that mailbox.

The SIMPORT.EXE utility is run from the command line as follows:

```
SIMPORT /o=organization name /ou=sitename /f=filename.csv
```

For example:

```
simport /o=Microsoft /ou=wga /file=RECIPS.CSV
```

The Security Import utility then creates sealing key pairs in the KM Database for every mailbox that was in the RECIPS.CSV file and generates a file called SRESULTS.TXT, which contains the directory names of all users in the file together with the token associated with each entry.

Appendix D

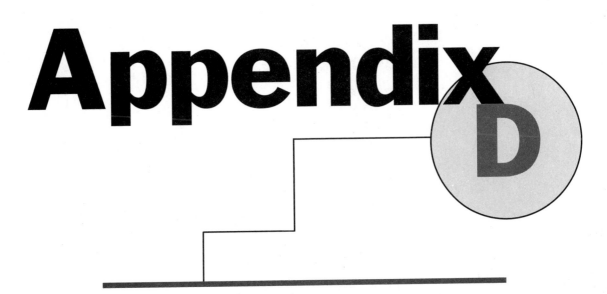

Use of Remote Procedure Calls in Microsoft Exchange Server and Clients

Description of RPC

RPC stands for Remote Procedure Call. RPC is a service that allows a programmer to create an application consisting of any number of procedures, some that run locally and others that run on remote computers via a network. It provides a procedural view of the networked operations rather than a transport-centered view, thus simplifying the development of distributed or client-server applications.

An application that has other libraries of functions linked statically to it will resemble the architecture shown here.

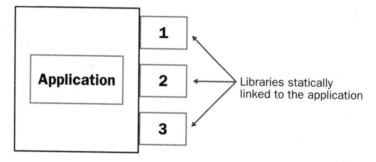

Here, the application will call a procedure in one of the libraries. That procedure will be run and the results will be given to the application. The application and the library both reside on the same computer and run in the same physical memory space.

In the case of RPC, the architecture of the application is similar to the one shown below. Here, some of the procedure libraries run on a remote computer, whereas others run locally. To the RPC application, all procedures appear to run locally. In other words, instead of the programmer actively writing code to transmit computational or I/O related requests across the network, RPC software handles these tasks automatically.

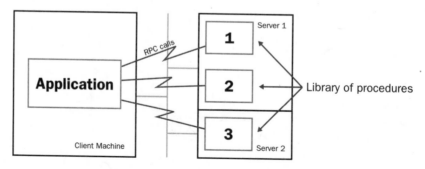

The Compute Server Model

Networking software for personal computers has been built on the model of a powerful computer, the server, that provides the specialized services to the workstations, or client computers. In this model, servers are designed as file servers, print servers, or communication (modem) servers, depending on whether they are assigned to file sharing or are connected to printers or modems.

RPC represents an evolutionary step in this model. In addition to its traditional roles, a server shares its own computational power with other computers on the network. A workstation can ask the compute server to perform computations and return the results. Using RPC, the client not only uses files and printers, it also uses the central processing units of other computers.

How RPC Works

The RPC architecture makes it seem as if a client can directly call a procedure located in a remote server program. The client and the server have their own address spaces; that is, each has its own memory resource that is allocated to data used by the procedure. This is what the RPC architecture looks like:

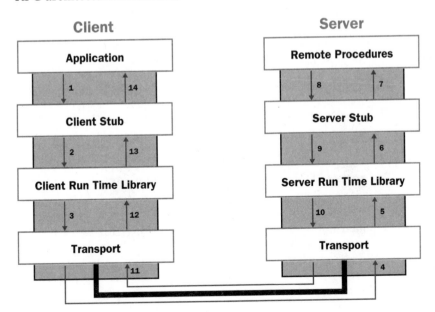

The client application calls a local stub procedure instead of the actual code implementing the procedure. Stubs are compiled and linked with the client application. Instead of containing the actual code that implements the remote procedure, the client stub code performs the following functions:

- ✗ **It retrieves** the required parameters from the address space.

- ✗ **It translates** the parameters as needed into a standard network data representation format for transmission over the network.

- ✗ **It calls** API functions in the RPC client run-time library to send the request and its parameters to the server.

The server performs the following steps to call the remote procedure:

- ✗ **The server** RPC run-time library API functions accept the request and call the server stub procedure.

- ✗ **The server** stub retrieves the parameters from the network buffer and converts them from the network transmission format to the format the server needs.

- ✗ **The server** stub calls the actual procedure on the server.

The remote procedure runs, perhaps generating output parameters and a return value. When the remote procedure is complete, a similar sequence of steps returns the data to the client:

- ✗ **The remote** procedure returns its data to the server stub.

- ✗ **The server** stub converts output parameters to the format required for transmission over the network and returns them to the RPC run-time library functions.

- ✗ **The server** RPC run-time library API functions transmit the data on the network to the client computer.

The client completes the process by accepting the data over the network and returning it to the calling function:

- ✗ **The client** RPC run-time library receives the remote procedure return values and returns them to the client stub.

✗ **The client** stub converts the data from this network data representation to the format used by the client computer. The stub writes the data into the client memory and returns to the calling program on the client.

✗ **The calling** procedure continues as if the procedure had been called on the same computer.

How Clients Identify Remote Procedures

The client application must have a method of identifying the correct remote procedure to bind to or client applications may end up calling some other remote procedures that happen to have the same name but not the same functionality. To ensure that the remote procedures have unique names, universally unique identifiers (UUIDs) are used. When a programmer creates a client-server application on RPC, it is the responsibility of the programmer to select a UUID for the application and then insert it into the client side and the server side code of the application. When the client side tries to connect to the server side, it compares its UUID with the server side's UUID and will only connect if the UUIDs match. UUIDs can be generated by utilities provided in the Microsoft Win32 Software Development Kit.

How RPC Is Implemented in Microsoft Windows NT Server

The main RPC functionality of Windows NT Server resides in the RPCRT4.DLL. This is the RPC run-time library of Windows NT Server. This component sits between the RPC stubs and the RPC transports on both the client and the server and performs several tasks:

✗ **It loads** and initializes the RPC transport and the application specifics for use. Depending upon whether the RPC transport being loaded is the client version or the server version, the RPC run time will retrieve either client transport information or server transport information.

✗ **It passes** data between the RPC stubs and the RPC transport, and vice versa.

✗ **It exports** a large number of RPC APIs, such as RpcBindingxxxx, RpcMgmtxxxx, and RpcServerxxxx APIs.

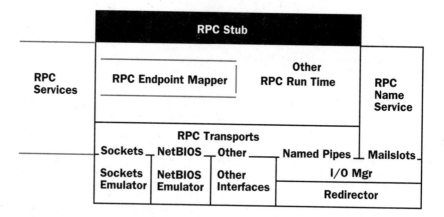

RPC Endpoint Mapper Service

The RPC endpoint mapper allows the RPC run time to dynamically resolve and assign endpoints to applications. An endpoint specifies the communications port the client application will use to make the remote procedure calls to the server application. The RPC server application registers its endpoints with the RPC endpoint mapping service. The RPC client applications can then make a remote procedure call with a partially bound handle and the RPC Endpoint Mapper will be queried to find the appropriate endpoint (for instance, the named pipe). The server side of the endpoint mapping service is RPCSS.EXE and the client side of the mapping service is implemented in the RPCRT4.DLL.

RPC Name Service Database

The RPC name service database maps a name to a binding handle and maintains "entry name to binding handle" mappings. This makes it easier to install, configure, and use RPC applications because the RPC client application can find the location of the RPC server application through the RPC name service database.

On startup, an RPC server application that uses the RPC name service database must register the entry names for its procedures in the name service database so that those procedures can be used by the RPC client application. Because each system's RPC name service manages the entry names that are available on the system on which it is running, the name service database is distributed across multiple machines. When the name service is queried for the location of an entry name, the name service first checks the cache it maintains. If the specified entry name is not in the cache, the name service then tries the primary domain controller, tries all backup domain controllers, and finally, broadcasts (via mailslots, to \Mailslot\RPCLoc_s) to its workgroup or domain, looking for the specified entry name. When the name service receives a response, once again via broadcast (to \Mailslot\RPCLoc_c), from another name service database that has a match, it adds the response to a cache it maintains. Entries remain in the name service database cache for two hours.

Universally Unique Identifier (UUID)

A UUID is used to uniquely identify objects such as interfaces, RPC client stubs, and RPC server stubs. The RPC run time compares the UUID of an RPC client application with the UUID of an RPC server application to check for compatibility between the applications and to select among multiple implementations of a procedure. If the UUIDs of the RPC client and the RPC server application do not match, the RPC run time will not establish a session between the two applications. A UUID consists of a string of five groups of hexadecimal digits, separated by hyphens, that contain 8, 4, 4, 4, and 12 digits, respectively. For example, the following is a valid UUID: 5DEF7892-0ABC-1234-4556-123456789ABC.

RPC Client Application Binding

In order to actually make a remote procedure call, the RPC client application must first obtain a binding handle to the RPC server application. Binding is the term used to describe the logical connection made between a client and a server. The binding handle represents this connection in a value that is opaque to the application using it. The binding handle can be obtained by either the RPC client stub or the RPC client application, which leads to two types of binding:

1 Auto binding

2 RPC client application-managed binding

Auto Binding

The RPC stub automatically calls the correct RPC run-time API functions in order to obtain a valid binding handle for the client. Auto binding is most useful when the RPC client does not require a specific server for its server side component. The server side of an application that uses auto binding must call the appropriate APIs to set up its endpoints. In addition, a name service provider, such as the Windows NT RPC locator service, must be running on a client accessible server.

RPC Client Application-Managed Binding

There are two methods an RPC client application can use to obtain a binding handle:

1 Construct a string that is then used to create the binding handle. This process requires the client applications to supply the UUIDs for the connection, the transport to use, the network address, and the endpoint. This method is most useful if the RPC client application allows the user to specify the transport, endpoint, or server name on which the RPC server application is running.

2 Import from the name service database. This method will only work if the RPC server application has registered itself with the RPC name service database. The client application will use APIs to get the binding information from the name service provider and then it will perform the binding.

How Microsoft Exchange Server Uses RPC

Microsoft Exchange Server uses RPC built into Windows NT Server for establishing connections among the Microsoft Exchange Server processes (such as connections between Microsoft Exchange Server message transfer agents) and for connecting clients and servers in the network. Microsoft Exchange Server can use RPC over named pipes, TCP/IP, NetBIOS, and IPX/SPX. When it tries to use RPC, Microsoft Exchange Server first tries to establish a drive connection to the \\ServerName\IPC$ share. If it is successful, Microsoft Exchange Server tries to establish a named pipe connection over that drive connection, and then tries to start RPC over the named pipe. If, for some reason, the named pipe connections are not supported on that network, Microsoft Exchange Server then proceeds through the list of the protocols given above and tries to establish RPC binding to the server.

Microsoft Exchange Binding Mechanism

All the Microsoft Exchange clients use the RPC client application-managed method of binding to the Microsoft Exchange server. This means that the clients have to know the server to connect to, hence the need to specify the server name in the profile creation dialog box. The Microsoft Exchange servers within a site communicate over RPC and also use the application-managed method to bind to the other servers.

NetWare Clients Connecting to Microsoft Exchange Server via RPC

In a NetWare network, the Windows NT Server that runs Microsoft Exchange Server will register its name with a NetWare server via service advertising protocol (SAP). This registration will occur if the Gateway Services for NetWare are running on the Windows NT Server. SAP is used by file servers, print servers, and gateway servers on a NetWare network to advertise their services and addresses. Using SAP, clients on the network can determine what services are available on the network and can obtain the address of the node where the services are available. SAP is important because a client cannot initiate a session with a server without first having that server's address. Because the Windows NT Server is visible to the NetWare clients via SAP, it will be able to initialize a session for RPC connection to the Microsoft Exchange Server.

If, for some reason, no NetWare server is available on the network, the Windows NT Server must be running the SAP service to ensure that it is advertising its services and is visible to the NetWare workstations.

Key Considerations for Ensuring that RPC Works on Your Network

Because RPC over named pipes is the preferred method of connectivity in Microsoft Exchange Server environments, the network redirector should be capable of supporting named pipes. Only MS-NET compatible networks with enhanced redirectors have this capability. If you have an MS-NET compatible network, make sure all the redirectors are Enhanced and not Basic. Also, check that as a user you can do a net use of the IPC$ share on the server. In NetWare environments, RPC will be established on IPX.

In NetWare environments, make sure that the Windows NT Server that runs Microsoft Exchange Server is running the Gateway to NetWare Service and is able to connect to the NetWare servers. If all workstations are using IPX/SPX as the protocol and no NetWare server is available, the SAP service must be running on the Windows NT Server.

The RPC name service database of Windows NT Server is updated by the use of broadcasts to the mailslots on the Windows NT servers. If the servers are connected via routers, make sure that these broadcasts are passed through the routers so that the RPC name service database/RPC locator service can work reliably.

References:

Custer, H.: *Inside Windows NT,* Microsoft Press, 1992, pp. 315-319.

RPC Programmer's Guide and Reference, Microsoft Win32 Software Development Kit, Microsoft Corporation, 1992-1993.

Finnegan, J.: "Building Windows NT-Based Client/Server Applications Using Remote Procedure Calls," *Microsoft Systems Journal,* vol. 9, pp. 65-79, October 1994.

RPC Module, Microsoft Network Architecture — Windows NT, Microsoft Corporation.

Microsoft Exchange Server Specifications, Microsoft Corporation.

"NetWare Communications Processes," NetWare Application Notes, Novell, September 1990.

Appendix E

Acronyms and Abbreviations

ADDMD   Administrative Directory Management Domain. A directory management domain run by a PTT authority.

ADMD   Administrative Management Domain. An MHS management domain run by a PTT authority. Each ADMD must contain MHS routing information to all other ADMDs.

ANSI   American National Standards Institute. An organization made up of members from government and industry and formed to develop standards.

ANSI X12   US standard for the structuring of EDI data.

API   Application Program Interface. A standardized set of procedure calls that can be used to interface applications with telecommunications protocols.

APIA   API Association. A consortium of corporations that develop API specifications for X.400 protocols.

APPC   Advanced Program-to-Program Communications. A subset of SNA functions and protocols used specifically to allow programs on one site to communicate with programs at another using LU 6.2. APPC is designed to make SNA more usable in a distributed application.

ARP   Address Resolution Protocol in the DOD protocol suite (TCP/IP)

ARPA   Advanced Research Project Agency. See DARPA.

ASCII   American Standard Code for Information Interchange

BSC   Binary Synchronous Protocol. An IBM protocol that defines a handshaking technique used between terminal controllers or remote communications processors and the host computer or front-end processor.

BSI   British Standards Institute. The UK national standardization body. BSI is a member of ISO.

CCITT   International Telephone and Telegraph Consultative Committee. International organization that creates and publishes telecommunications standards, including X.400.

CICS   Customer Information Control System. An IBM communications monitor.

CIV   Conversation Verb Interface. IBM's structured application program interface for distributed LU 6.2 application programs.

CLNS   Connectionless-mode network service.

CONS   Connection-oriented network service.

CRC   Cyclical redundancy checking. A procedure performed on transmitted data at the data link level and used for detecting errors.

CSU   Channel Service Unit. A device designed to function in the same manner as a modem except that it works with digital signals rather than analog signaling.

DAD   Draft addendum to an international standard. If ratified, the draft addendum advances to addendum (AD) status.

DAP   Directory Access Protocol. The protocol used between a directory user agent (DUA) and a directory system agent (DSA).

DARPA   Defense Advanced Research Projects Agency. An agency of the US Department of Defense that sponsors high-risk, high-payoff research. The Internet suite of protocols was developed under DARPA auspices. DARPA was previously known as ARPA, the Advanced Research Project Agency, when ARPANET was built.

DCE   Data Communications Equipment. Equipment such as a modem used to establish, maintain, and terminate a connection.

DIA   Document Interchange Architecture. An application-level architecture that defines protocols and data structures for the consistent exchange of documents and files among distributed office applications such as DISOSS and Personal Service products. DIA supports such functions as distribution, application services, and document library.

DIS   Draft International Standard. If ratified, the draft advances to international standard (IS) status.

DISOSS   Distributed Office Support System. An application subsystem that provides a variety of office automation functions, including document distribution services and library services. Allows users to send, receive, distribute, and file documents. Utilizes various IBM protocols, such as DIA and SNADS.

DIT   Directory Information Tree. The global tree of entries corresponding to information objects in the Directory.

DMD   Directory Management Domain. A collection of DSAs that holds a portion of the DIT. For political reasons, there are two kinds of DMDs: ADDMDs and PRDMDs. This distinction is largely artificial.

DN   Distinguished Name. The global, authoritative name of an entry in the OSI Directory.

DP   Draft Proposal. If ratified, the draft proposal advances to draft international standard (DIS) status.

DSA   Directory System Agent. An application entity that offers the directory service.

DSP   Directory System Protocol. The protocol used between two DSAs.

DSU   Digital Service Unit. The DSU operates in tandem with the CSU (incorporated into the same component) and supports digital transmission over the telephone company's digital network.

DTE Data Terminal Equipment. The source or destination of the signals to or from DCE. Usually a terminal or computer system.

DUA Directory User Agent. An application entity that makes the directory service available to the user.

DUNS Number An EDI name issued by the Dun and Bradstreet company.

ECMA European Computer Manufacturer Association. A group of computer vendors that have performed substantive pre-standardization work for ISO.

EDI Electronic Data Interchange. Computer-to-computer exchange of data related to commercial transactions using agreed upon formats and networks.

EDI Name An alpha-numeric string which identifies a particular EDI application.

EDIFACT Electronic data interchange for administration, commerce, and transport. International standard for the structure of EDI data (ISO 9735).

EDIMS EDI Messaging System: Pedi

EDIN An X.400 message sent to the originator to inform him of the disposition of his EDIM (forwarded, responsibility accepted, or responsibility refused).

Encapsulation A mechanism within a gateway that supports using the foreign mail system as a bridge between Microsoft Mail for PC Networks LANs. You can think of this as double-enveloping.

FEP Front-end Processor. A communications computer associated with a host computer whose specialized function is to handle communications to and from terminals and nodes in the network.

FTAM File Transfer, Access, and Management. OSI file service.

FTP File Transfer Protocol. The application protocol offering file service in the Internet suite of protocols.

F.435 CCITT Recommendation that specifies the EDI Messaging Service, that is, the service requirements that Pedi is expected to meet.

GAL   Global Address List. A new address list introduced as part of the Microsoft Mail 3.0 server that lists all user names accessible by given post office in a single list.

IAB   Internet Activities Board. The technical body overseeing the development of the Internet suite of protocols. The IAB consists of several task forces, each charged with investigating a particular area.

IETF   Internet Engineering Task Force. A task force of the Internet Activities Board (IAB) charged with solving the short-term needs of the Internet.

IFIP   International Federation of Information Processing. A research organization that performs substantive pre-standardization work for OSI. IFIP is noted for having formalized the original MHS model.

Internet   A large collection of connected networks, primarily in the US, running the Internet suite of protocols. Sometimes referred to as the DARPA Internet, NSF/DARPA Internet, or the Federal Research Internet.

IP   Internet Protocol. The network protocol offering a connectionless-mode network service in the Internet suite of protocols.

IPM   Interpersonal Message. A structured message exchanged between two MHS user agents, consisting of a well-defined heading and one or more arbitrary body parts.

IS   Either Intermediate-system or International Standard, depending on context. Intermediate system is a real system performing functions from the three lower-layers of the OSI model. Intermediate-systems are commonly thought of as routing data for end-systems. International standard is what ISO consider as published standard.

ISO   International Organization for Standardization. The organization that produces much of the world's standards. OSI is only one of many areas standardized by the ISO/IEC.

ISODE   ISO Development Environment. A research tool developed to study the upper-layer of OSI. Some commercial ISO products are based on this framework.

LU 6.2   Logical Unit 6.2. Part of IBM's Advanced Program-to-Program Communications that provides a standard communications protocol for distributed application programs.

MHS Message Handling System. A store-and-forward mail system for delivering arbitrarily structured messages. X.400 term.

MMDF Multi-Channel Memorandum Distribution Facility. A software package developed for memo-based message handling under the Internet suite of protocols.

MOTIS Message-Oriented Text Interchange Systems. ISO term for MHS. The ISO MOTIS standards are essentially identical to the CCITT MHS Recommendations.

MS Message Store. An entity acting as an intermediary between an MHS user agent and its local message transfer agent.

MTA Message Transfer Agent. An application entity that offers the message transfer serve. Perform P1 protocols.

MTS Message Transfer System. A collection of connected Message Transfer Agent.

NBS National Bureau of Standards. See NIST.

NFS Network File System. A file service defined by Sun Microsystems, Inc.

NIST National Institute for Standards and Technology (formerly National Bureau of Standards). The branch of the US Department of Commerce charged with keeping track of standardization. NIST is member of ISO.

OSI Open Systems Interconnections. An international effort to facilitate communications among computers of different manufacture and technology.

OSI RM OSI Reference Model. A seven-layer model developed by the ISO for creating data communications networks.

PDAD Proposed Draft Addendum to an International Standard. If ratified, the proposed draft addendum advances to draft addendum (DAD) status.

Pedi Protocol designed for structuring and transmitting EDI Interchanges. Specified in CCITT Recommendation F.435 and X.435.

PRDMD Private Directory Management Domain. A directory domain not run by a PTT authority.

PRMD Private Management Domain. A MHS management domain run by a private organization. Each PRMD must contain MHS routing information to its parent ADMD. In addition, by bilateral agreement, a PRMD may have MHS routing information to other ADMDs and PRMDs.

RDN Relative Distinguished Name. A component of an entry's distinguished name, usually consisting of an attribute/value pair.

RFC Request for Comments. The document series describing the Internet suite of protocols and related experiments.

RTSE Reliable Transfer Service Element. Sometimes called RTS. The application service element responsible for transfer of bulk-mode objects. X.400 usually uses this service to transfer messages. Practically non-existent in 1984 standard. 1988 standard started to define this service better.

SAP Service Access Point. A way for OSI layers to keep track which protocol machine (of lower layer) it is using.

SDLC Synchronous Data Link Control. A communications protocol like BSC, normally used in SNA networks.

SMTP Simple Mail Transfer Protocol. The application protocol offering message handling service in the Internet suite of protocols.

SNA Systems Network Architecture. A seven-level architecture that supports the IBM data processing/data communications environment.

SNADS SNA Distribution Services. An application-level architecture that provides asynchronous (delayed delivery) distribution of documents and files between users. SNADS implements a store-and-forward mechanism that allows information to be stored until the path to the receiver is available.

TCP Transmission Control Protocol. The transport protocol offering a connection-oriented transport service in the Internet suite of protocols.

TCP/IP Internet suite of protocols. see TCP, IP, UDP.

TEDIS Program to promote EDI within the European Economic Community. Funded and managed by Directorate General XIII of the Commission of the European Community.

TELNET The application protocol offering virtual terminal service in the Internet suite of protocols.

TRADACOMS Version of the UN/TDI syntax for EDI Interchanges. Commonly used in the United Kingdom.

TWA Two-way alternate.

UA User Agent. An application entity that makes the message transfer service available to the user.

UDP User Datagram Protocol. The transport protocol offering a connectionless-mode transport service in the Internet suite of protocols.

UN/TDI United Nations standard for the structuring of EDI data. Widely used in the United Kingdom in the TRADACOMS version.

VTAM Virtual Telecommunications Access Method.

X.25 A connection-oriented network facility.

X.121 The addressing format used by X.25 base networks.

X.435 CCITT recommendation that specifies the EDI Messaging System, that is, the Pedi protocol that meets the service requirements of F.435.

Index

F

facsimile, 7, 53
fast bus architecture, 215
fax machines, 7, 53
fiber optics, 6, 154
field events, customizing, 242
fields
    adding custom, 242
    basic properties of, 239
    calculation or derived, 242
    preprogrammed message, 239
file transfer, network, 12
File Transfer Body Part (FTBP),
        97, 129
filtering tasks, 45, 81
Finder, The, 61
folder applications, 47
folders, 37, 38–39, 47
    creating, 48
    custom views, 39
    designing, 238–39
    filters to, 63
    hierarchy of, 38, 61
        conversation threading, 70
    offline, 60, 65
    as part of application, 231
    personal, 39, 59–60
        Registry, 240
    public, 26, 29, 39, 40, 60
        for bulletin boards, 69
        group needs for, 200–203
        on Microsoft Exchange
            Server, 124, 125
        naming, 178
        for OLE 2.0-compatible
            documents, 64
        Registry, 240
    replication, 100–101, 183
        for bulletin boards, 69–70
        conflict resolution of, 70
        control of, 101, 131
    searching, 40
    storage options for, 99–100
    types of, 59–61
    views, 62
font, 41, 55
font size, 55
font style, 55

formats
    configuration of default, 31
    per-domain basis, 31
    rich-text, 41, 54–55
forms, 47, 132
    access control for, 132–33
    creating, 48
    designing. *See* Microsoft
        Exchange Forms
        Designer
    for discussion topics, 242
    extending, 241–42
    for folder applications, 47
    managing, 240–41
    as part of application, 231
    routing, 235
    survey and answer, 243, 244
Forms Manager, 133
Forms Registry, 132, 240

G

gateways
    disk space needed for, 215
    Microsoft Mail, 88
    planning, 185
    in Telex system, 8
    third-party, 22
geographic profile, identification
        of, 149, 170
Getting Started application, 243
Global Address List, 56
graphical controls, 239
graphical interface, 137
graphical user client (GUI), 11
Group by Conversation, 70
group computing, 16, 26, 230. *See
        also* sharing
    as Microsoft Exchange Server
        function, 20
group discussions. *See* bulletin
        boards
groups
    public folder needs, 200–203
    schedules for, 42, 43
    of users, defining, 197–98
groupware applications, replica-
        tion of, 29
GUI, 11

H

hand-held devices, 82
hard drives, adding, 218
hardware, estimating server
        requirements, 214–22
Help Desk application, 243
hierarchy
    of Administrator Program, 107
    of folders, 38, 61
    of Microsoft Exchange Server,
        102–4
    of system organization, 33
host-based systems, 88
hotlinks, 30
Hot Topics, 242
HTML format, 29
hunt system, 207

I

implementation of new messaging
        system
    co-existence approach, 145
    network concerns. *See* network
    roll-out plan, 188–91
    shotgun strategy, 144–45
    12 steps to, 148–91
Inbox Assistant, 40, 62, 63
inboxes, 40, 51–53, 62, 63
industry messaging standards, 17, 22
information, sharing, 4, 50, 64,
        71. *See also* group
        computing
information management, 21, 58–
        64
    personal, 42, 43
information overload, 13
Information Store, 99–100, 112, 135
    definition, 35
    private, 114, 115
    public, 115–16
input/output system, 215, 219
installation, cost of, 144
integrated interface, 16, 24–25
Integrated Services Digital
        Network (ISDN), 66, 154,
        206

(T)

IMPORTANT—READ CAREFULLY BEFORE OPENING SOFTWARE PACKET(S). By opening the sealed packet(s) containing the software, you indicate your acceptance of the following Microsoft License Agreement.

MICROSOFT LICENSE AGREEMENT
(Book Companion Disks)

This is a legal agreement between you (either an individual or an entity) and Microsoft Corporation. By opening the sealed software packet(s) you are agreeing to be bound by the terms of this agreement. If you do not agree to the terms of this agreement, promptly return the unopened software packet(s) and any accompanying written materials to the place you obtained them for a full refund.

MICROSOFT SOFTWARE LICENSE

1. GRANT OF LICENSE. Microsoft grants to you the right to use one copy of the Microsoft software program included with this book (the "SOFTWARE") on a single terminal connected to a single computer. The SOFTWARE is in "use" on a computer when it is loaded into the temporary memory (i.e., RAM) or installed into the permanent memory (e.g., hard disk, CD-ROM, or other storage device) of that computer. You may not network the SOFTWARE or otherwise use it on more than one computer or computer terminal at the same time.

2. COPYRIGHT. The SOFTWARE is owned by Microsoft or its suppliers and is protected by United States copyright laws and international treaty provisions. Therefore, you must treat the SOFTWARE like any other copyrighted material (e.g., a book or musical recording) except that you may either (a) make one copy of the SOFTWARE solely for backup or archival purposes, or (b) transfer the SOFTWARE to a single hard disk provided you keep the original solely for backup or archival purposes. You may not copy the written materials accompanying the SOFTWARE.

3. OTHER RESTRICTIONS. You may not rent or lease the SOFTWARE, but you may transfer the SOFTWARE and accompanying written materials on a permanent basis provided you retain no copies and the recipient agrees to the terms of this Agreement. You may not reverse engineer, decompile, or disassemble the SOFTWARE. If the SOFTWARE is an update or has been updated, any transfer must include the most recent update and all prior versions.

4. DUAL MEDIA SOFTWARE. If the SOFTWARE package contains both 3.5" and 5.25" disks, then you may use only the disks appropriate for your single-user computer. You may not use the other disks on another computer or loan, rent, lease, or transfer them to another user except as part of the permanent transfer (as provided above) of all SOFTWARE and written materials.

5. SAMPLE CODE. If the SOFTWARE includes Sample Code, then Microsoft grants you a royalty-free right to reproduce and distribute the sample code of the SOFTWARE provided that you: (a) distribute the sample code only in conjunction with and as a part of your software product; (b) do not use Microsoft's or its authors' names, logos, or trademarks to market your software product; (c) include the copyright notice that appears on the SOFTWARE on your product label and as a part of the sign-on message for your software product; and (d) agree to indemnify, hold harmless, and defend Microsoft and its authors from and against any claims or lawsuits, including attorneys' fees, that arise or result from the use or distribution of your software product.

DISCLAIMER OF WARRANTY

The SOFTWARE (including instructions for its use) is provided "AS IS" WITHOUT WARRANTY OF ANY KIND. MICROSOFT FURTHER DISCLAIMS ALL IMPLIED WARRANTIES INCLUDING WITHOUT LIMITATION ANY IMPLIED WARRANTIES OF MERCHANTABILITY OR OF FITNESS FOR A PARTICULAR PURPOSE. THE ENTIRE RISK ARISING OUT OF THE USE OR PERFORMANCE OF THE SOFTWARE AND DOCUMENTATION REMAINS WITH YOU.

IN NO EVENT SHALL MICROSOFT, ITS AUTHORS, OR ANYONE ELSE INVOLVED IN THE CREATION, PRODUCTION, OR DELIVERY OF THE SOFTWARE BE LIABLE FOR ANY DAMAGES WHATSOEVER (INCLUDING, WITHOUT LIMITATION, DAMAGES FOR LOSS OF BUSINESS PROFITS, BUSINESS INTERRUPTION, LOSS OF BUSINESS INFORMATION, OR OTHER PECUNIARY LOSS) ARISING OUT OF THE USE OF OR INABILITY TO USE THE SOFTWARE OR DOCUMENTATION, EVEN IF MICROSOFT HAS BEEN ADVISED OF THE POSSIBILITY OF SUCH DAMAGES. BECAUSE SOME STATES/COUNTRIES DO NOT ALLOW THE EXCLUSION OR LIMITATION OF LIABILITY FOR CONSEQUENTIAL OR INCIDENTAL DAMAGES, THE ABOVE LIMITATION MAY NOT APPLY TO YOU.

U.S. GOVERNMENT RESTRICTED RIGHTS

The SOFTWARE and documentation are provided with RESTRICTED RIGHTS. Use, duplication, or disclosure by the Government is subject to restrictions as set forth in subparagraph (c)(1)(ii) of The Rights in Technical Data and Computer Software clause at DFARS 252.227-7013 or subparagraphs (c)(1) and (2) of the Commercial Computer Software — Restricted Rights 48 CFR 52.227-19, as applicable. Manufacturer is Microsoft Corporation, One Microsoft Way, Redmond, WA 98052-6399.

If you acquired this product in the United States, this Agreement is governed by the laws of the State of Washington.

Should you have any questions concerning this Agreement, or if you desire to contact Microsoft Press for any reason, please write: Microsoft Press, One Microsoft Way, Redmond, WA 98052-6399.

Register Today!

Return this
Introducing Microsoft® Exchange
registration card for a Microsoft Press® catalog

U.S. and Canada addresses only. Fill in information below and mail postage-free. Please mail only the bottom half of this page.

1-55615-941-2A   *INTRODUCING MICROSOFT® EXCHANGE*   *Owner Registration Card*

_____

NAME

_____

INSTITUTION OR COMPANY NAME

_____

ADDRESS

_____

CITY   STATE   ZIP

Microsoft Press
Quality Computer Books

For a free catalog of
Microsoft Press® products, call
1-800-MSPRESS

BUSINESS REPLY MAIL
FIRST-CLASS MAIL   PERMIT NO. 108   REDMOND, WA

POSTAGE WILL BE PAID BY ADDRESSEE

MICROSOFT PRESS REGISTRATION
INTRODUCING MICROSOFT® EXCHANGE
PO BOX 3019
BOTHELL WA 98041-9946